A COMMON SKY
Philosophy and the Literary Imagination

A COMMON SKY

Philosophy and
the Literary Imagination

By

A. D. NUTTALL

Professor of English, University of Sussex

UNIVERSITY OF CALIFORNIA PRESS

Berkeley and Los Angeles 1974

University of California Press
Berkeley and Los Angeles, California

ISBN: 0-520-02581-4
Library of Congress Catalog Card Number: 73-85372

22 0 8 7

AUG 1 4 1974

Printed in Great Britain

BD
201
.N87

To
STEPHEN MEDCALF

Contents

Preface

I have been greatly helped in the writing of this book by Terry Diffey, Bernard Harrison, Beynon John, Laurence Lerner, Stephen Medcalf and Christopher Taylor. Each has saved me from some absurdity, none would agree with everything in the book. I am very grateful to them all. As for the published works which have helped me, these are, I hope, acknowledged in due place in the text. There is one exception: Kristian Smidt's *Poetry and Belief in the Work of T. S. Eliot* was of far more crucial assistance to me than appears from the notes to my fifth chapter.

A. D. NUTTALL
The University of Sussex

Introduction

This book is about solipsistic fear; that is, the fear that the external world of trees, tables, bricks and mortar may not exist at all. Solipsism as a settled system of belief is quite properly regarded as something absurd, or even comic; no one but a philosopher—no, a *lunatic* philosopher—could believe *that*. But it sometimes happens that an idea which is in the strictest sense of the word incredible can prove a fertile source of disquiet (indeed, one of the ways of dealing with solipsistic fear is to stop flinching from the thought and try believing it instead). Thus, although there have been few doctrinaire solipsists, the number of those touched by an intermittent solipsism has, since the eighteenth century, been very great. The possibility that the very principles of British empiricism imply a solipsistic conclusion has occurred, at one time or another, to most philosophers, and has called forth some remarkable displays of circumventive guile. Among the philosophers we find an *argument*, with a life of its own, making persistent head against natural belief and intuition. But meanwhile among the novelists and poets, something very strange is happening: natural belief and intuition have quietly crossed over to the other side. *Feelings* of unreality, *intuitions* of solipsism become more frequent, and the deepest scepticism of Hume or Bradley finds a distorted echo in the poetry of Wordsworth or Eliot. I have tried to tell the story of the rise, obvious in philosophy, less obvious perhaps in literature, of solipsistic unease, and at the end of my book I have presumed to judge it.

CHAPTER 1

The Sealing of the Doors

I

The boy is there, in a tiny room. We can see, for we are looking at a cross-section, that the room is set high in a curious sort of house, close to the roof, but well away from any outside wall. There is something obscurely alarming about the house – perhaps it is the suggestion of disproportionately huge cellars, of dark regions below ground, to which ladders and brick shafts descend. But there are plenty of windows, and a stout front door, opening on a landscape of English innocence. The boy's room, however, has neither door nor window. It is indeed a sort of cell. The light which shines in at the windows does not reach this part of the house. Instead it is transmuted into something called nerve-wires, and the boy, it seems, picks up all the information he needs about what is going on outside by using his private telephone exchange to tap the wires. He has never been out of his cell. All he knows of that distant, grey spire, those feathery trees has been mediated to him through this bizarre apparatus. He has never seen them.

This is a picture of the mechanics of knowledge. It comes from an undated edition of Arthur Mee's *The Children's Encyclopaedia*,[1] published some time in the 1930s. It tells us that there is an 'external world', and, irretrievably cut off from it, there is the interior consciousness.

And now another picture: two knights are being conducted through a castle by a lady. She leads them up a staircase of wrought alabaster into a turret. They find themselves in a vaulted chamber, filled with flowers and greenery –

That Turrets frame most admirable was,
    Like highest heaven compassed around,

[1] p. 2799.

And lifted high above this earthly masse,
Which it survew'd as hils doen lower ground[1]

This too is a picture of the mind. We are in Spenser's allegorical
House of Alma. Thus the Elizabethan poet, towards the end
of the sixteenth century, uses the same architectural metaphor
that Arthur Mee used in the twentieth: the soul dwells in the
body as a man dwells in a house. But though they have this
much in common, they have nothing else. Spenser's knights,
unlike the boy, move freely, discourse gaily. Most important of
all, *they can look out of the windows.* By the time of Arthur Mee
the palace has become a prison.

Between the two lies the scientific revolution of the seventeenth century. To be sure, the image of the body as the prison
house of the soul antedates the scientific revolution. But
whereas in our illustration the mechanism of perception underlines the fact of isolation, in Elizabethan literature it is normal
to view the senses as mitigating the soul's confinement. When
Sir John Davies, writing at the end of the sixteenth century,
uses the image of the prison, the place he describes remains
obstinately pleasant:

Thus by the organs of the Eye and Ear
The Soul with knowledge doth herself endue:
Thus she her prison may with pleasure bear,
Having such prospects, all the world to view.[2]

This is more like Spenser's high turret than the telephone
exchange. Moreover, when the image of the soul's confinement
occurs in Donne, it is as a grim hypothesis, as what *would be*
our plight, were it not for the senses:

So must pure lovers soules descend
T'affections, and to faculties,
That sense may reach and apprehend,[3]
Else a great Prince in prison lies.

[1] *Faerie Queene* II.ix.45, in Edwin Greenlaw's Variorum edn., *The Works
of Edmund Spenser*, vol. II, 1933, p. 121.

[2] 'Nosce Teipsum' in *Silver Poets of the Sixteenth Century*, ed. Gerald
Bullett, the 1962 reprint of the 1947 edn., p. 375.

[3] 'The Extasie', 65-68, in *The Elegies and The Songs and Sonnets*, ed.
Helen Gardner, 1965, p. 61.

For the historian of ideas these lines carry a special pathos. Donne's lovers are supremely aware of one another. The poet weaves a fantastical design, exploring the rich intricacy of their intellectual union. The mere thought of isolation occurs only as a passing shadow. It is ironic that in another hundred years the pedestrian figure of Locke will have arisen to involve these vigilant and beautiful lovers each in a separate web of epistemological circumstance.

Of course it is unfair to blame everything on Locke. He merely said at greater length and with more authority what many others had said before him. Yet if a representative name is needed, his is the obvious choice. Locke's *Essay* on the Human Understanding (1690) is a huge, rambling work which codified the prejudices and dogmas of the century. It is, as everyone knows, the cornerstone of English empiricism. What concerns us here is the account it gives of how we know the world. In spite of the difficulties it has generated, the doctrine can be stated very simply: we have no direct knowledge of anything in the external world, all that we know directly are ideas, that is, tiny representative pictures of the world, relayed to the mind by eye, ear, *etc.* These and these only are the immediate objects of knowledge. In Locke's own words: 'Since the mind, in all its thoughts and reasonings, hath no other immediate object but its own ideas, which it alone does or can contemplate, it is evident that our knowledge is only conversant about them.'[1] This is the bed-rock of Locke's epistemology. It is very doubtful whether the philosopher himself ever saw the full extent of its implications. Earlier in the *Essay*, he had asserted that every man's thoughts were private: 'Man, though he have great variety of thoughts, and such from which others as well as himself might receive profit and delight; yet they are all within his own breast, invisible and hidden from others, nor can of themselves be made to appear.'[2] But that is a mild and un-disturbing thesis compared with the claim that the whole range of knowledge is private to the knower. The earlier passage merely suggests what can be contemplated with a certain quiet pleasure—that we all retain an inviolable area of

[1] *An Essay Concerning Human Understanding*, Book IV, Chapter 1, §1, in A. C. Fraser's edn., Oxford, 1894, vol. II, p. 167.

[2] *Ibid.*, III.ii.1, vol. II, p. 8.

privacy, of thoughts and images which no-one can get at. It implies indeed a strong distinction between my ability to know that Peter's tie is green and my complete inability to know what Peter's thoughts are *really* like. But the later passage has deprived me even of the modest sort of 'direct' knowledge allowed by the earlier. Peter's tie—in itself—has become as mysterious and inaccessible a thing as Peter's thoughts. Thus for Locke, no less than Plato, ultimate reality is elusive, transcendent, unperceivable. There is a delicious irony here, for Locke has found his way to this deeply counter-intuitive doctrine by the most innocent of paths—that of the plain, scientific Englishman. He undoubtedly believed himself to be cutting through the baseless metaphysics of the Schoolmen in order to clarify the simple facts. In him, as in virtually every major thinker of the seventeenth century, contempt for the scholastic tradition is automatic. Equally automatic is his reverence for the contemporary scientist. There is no reason to believe that the modesty with which he described his philosophic task is disingenuous:

> . . . in an age that produces such masters as the great Huygenius and the incomparable Mr Newton, with some others of that strain, it is ambition enough to be employed as an under-labourer in clearing the ground a little, and removing some of the rubbish that lies in way to knowledge . . .[1]

The scientists had investigated the mechanics of perception, and it was only natural that Locke, never strong on the distinction between physiology and epistemology (still less on that between philosophy and psychology) should be strongly influenced by their findings. The physiological fact that there really is an image on the retina has proved singularly unfortunate for the progress of philosophy. Thinkers anxious to answer the question 'what is knowledge?' could scarcely avoid the inference that knowledge, scientifically speaking, is direct acquaintance with an image, offered up, so to speak, to the eye of the soul, a mysterious being which lives in the skull and alone truly knows.

[1] 'The Epistle to the Reader', prefixed to the *Essay*, in Fraser's edn., vol. I, p. 14.

Of course, the philosophers soon took the minor step of changing the physiological image on the retina into a non-physical mental image, or idea, but they did not draw the inference that if they were to make *that* change, they might just as well reject the whole model of the mind as contemplating a picture of external reality. The notion has only to be stated in bald terms by someone like Professor Ayer for its absurdity to be manifest: '. . . it is maintained that we have no access to physical objects otherwise than through the contents of our sense-experience, which themselves are not physical.'[1] The result is the subversion of common sense. The ordinary man knows that Peter's tie is green, but has not the faintest notion what the image on his own retina is like. Yet Locke felt that his masters had shown that strictly speaking the ordinary man knew nothing *but* the inner image (or 'idea' as he would call it). We have only to ask a few childish questions to realise that something has gone badly wrong: is the idea before my mind the same colour as Peter's tie? Is it like Peter's tie at all? How does the mind become 'acquainted with' the ideas presented to it? Does it touch them? But contact is not the same thing as knowledge. Does it look at them? Has it, too, got eyes, then? The creaking of concepts is easily audible.

That Locke's epistemological doctrine implicitly outrages his moderate, open-minded, common-sensical temperament is a view which, though substantially right, requires a certain qualification. Not that the theory of knowledge is less bizarre than it seems; rather, it is the picture of Locke as by nature a plain man that requires revision. There are signs that Locke had more of the Platonist in his temperament than is usually recognised. This appears most strongly in his strange distinction between real and nominal essences. According to this distinction the way in which we normally name and classify a thing has little or nothing to do with the real essence of the thing itself; the 'essence' which we trap in our definition is nominal only. It seems that Locke means several things at once by this doctrine. First is the notion that the properties we can talk about are really the product of an inner material constitution itself inaccessible to observation. I can *say* that I know that the ring

[1] A. J. Ayer, *The Problem of Knowledge*, Penguin: Harmondsworth, 1956, p. 76.

on my finger is gold because of its 'colour, weight, fusibility, fixedness, &c.'[1] if I wish. But all these qualities depend on 'the real constitution of its insensible parts',[2] and this we cannot perceive. Whether the internal 'constitution' is *in principle* unobservable, or whether the investigations of the scientist, armed with his instruments, can show it to us is unclear. We may feel, as often in Locke, that a scientific and a philosophical theory are both trying to squeeze into the same seat. By the philosophical theory the scientist gazing into a microscope, no less than the ordinary man who is just gazing, is contemplating an *idea*. By the scientific theory, what is seen through the microscope is shown to undercut—and explain—what we see with our eyes, and hence to be the more authentic source of knowledge. Locke likens the real essence to the internal mechanism of the 'famous clock at Strasburg'.[3] As the yokel gapes at the clock, so man (instructed by Locke in the limitations of his knowledge) gapes at the physical mystery of the ring on his finger. The degree to which the 'clock at Strasburg' provides an analogy and the degree to which it might count as an *instance* of Locke's theory is—again—not explained.

But in pursuing subsidiary equivocations we must not lose track of the principal ambiguity. The second sense in which the theory of real and nominal essence is to be understood turns on the uneasy relation between universal and particular. Locke is wrestling with an ancient difficulty: while on the one hand every individual thing is unique, our language is a system of generalities. We may plot the position of a given individual on our conceptual map, but we never exhaust its real identity; perhaps we never even touch it. Locke, in a passage that looks forward to Sartre, complains of the irremediable abstractness of all language (he is speaking of nominal essence):

> That is properly the essence to *us*, which determines every particular to this or that *classis*; or, which is the same thing, to this or that general name: and what can that be else, but that abstract idea to which that name is annexed; and so has, in truth, a reference, not so much to the being of particular things, as to their general denominations?[4]

[1] *Essay*, III.iii.18, vol. II, p. 29.   [2] *Ibid.*
[3] *Ibid.*, III.vi.9, vol. II, p. 64.   [4] *Ibid.*, III.vi.8, vol. II, p. 64.

Note that neither form of the distinction between real and nominal essence involves the radical view from which we began. The possibility of ordinary perception is indulgently allowed to pass, if not presupposed. Yet, although the whole argument is separable from that other great distinction between the outer world and the inner world of ideas, once again we find reality slipping through our fingers, escaping our direct observation. One begins to feel that Lockian analysis is little more than a technique of losing the world. Who but a philosopher could lose so large a thing? Who so good at it, as an empiricist?

For even in the distinction between real and nominal essence, there is as much of the *Zeitgeist* as of personal temperament at work. I have called Locke a covert Platonist and the point of comparison was the tendency of both philosophers to make reality into something not readily accessible, something ulterior. Yet in a way Locke out-Plato's Plato; for although Plato's forms inhabit their proper heaven they are less completely inaccessible than Locke's reality. In the Republic (490b4) Plato tells us that the soul is 'akin' to the Forms, and in the *Phaedo* (79d3) we find the same thesis in a slightly more mystical form. The truth is that Locke did not only echo Plato in making reality transcendent; he also made our isolation doubly complete by inverting the Platonic ascription of reality. That is to say, while Plato ascribed reality to the stable objects of knowledge, and denied it to the fluctuating objects of sense, Locke denied reality to ideas and reserved it for a physical world which could never be observed. In the words of Leslie Stephen, Locke's ideas were the sole 'unreal representatives of unknowable objects'.[1]

But the altered ascription of reality is not the work of Locke only, but of the age. It shows itself in dozens of forms. One has only to open a good dictionary and look up the word 'substance' to observe the change. 'Substance', as its etymology implies, means 'underlying reality'. So far the phrase is philosophically colourless; you may paint it blue or red as your fancy takes you. In the middle ages the word was frequently used to denote spirit, especially God himself as the supreme substance. After the sixteenth century it came to be reserved, almost exclusively, for material substance. That is because the scientists of the

[1] *History of English Thought in the Eighteenth Century* (first published 1876), 3rd edn., 1902, vol. I, p. 40.

seventeenth century became much less interested in questions like 'What is that object for?' and asked instead the old question of the pre-Socratics: 'What is it made of?' And with the change of interest comes an altered account of what is real. If one showed a plastic ashtray to a mediaeval man and asked him what it was, he might reply, 'Well, its form is concave; from the form we learn the function; I suppose it is really a receptacle for some small object or objects.' If one showed the same ashtray to a seventeenth century man he would probably measure it, weigh it, and finally try to melt it. 'You who are not a natural philosopher,' he might say, 'are content to think of this as a hard smooth box or whatever. Really it is an aggregate of minute particles disposed in such a fashion as to provoke the ordinary man's unconsidered definition.' The honorific use of 'real' is always revealing.

Of course this is a simplified account of the semantic history of *substance*. The sense 'material' can be found in late Middle English sources. But there is a perceptible drift away from the notion that reality inheres in the formal (which is, in Platonic or Aristotelian terms, the intelligible) aspects of things, and towards the notion that the reality of things consists in their being material objects. For Aristotle, things attain 'thinghood', become real, in so far as they are intelligibly formed; the form declares the function, the function determines the definition and so reality is firmly integrated with the knower. For the hardheaded seventeenth century man all this has been lost.

The seventeenth century tendency to restrict 'the real' to 'the material' does not necessarily exalt the authority of experience. And indeed this is in a way the opposite of what happened. For the seventeenth century thinker, 'matter' is not tangible, or smellable, or tasteable. The senses merely provide us with subjective ideas of a material reality itself colourless, scentless, tasteless, inaudible. 'Empiricism' is derived from the Greek word for 'experience'. It is the great irony of English empiricism that, through reverence for a scientific metaphysic, it soon proved hostile to experience.

Indeed, it was long before any distinction was perceived between the claims of science and the claims of experience. Yet the crudest examples were readily available. It was not experience that led Copernicus to postulate the revolution of the earth about the sun. On the contrary, experience daily teaches us the opposite.[1] Francis Bacon, a true empiricist in the etymological sense,[2] could never advance an inch in scientific research[3] because of his refusal to allow ideas to run before experience. Useful as he was to the real scientists of his day as a public relations man, he was forever obstructing their research with demands that they abstain from such viciously aprioristic activities as setting up controlled experiments. Gilbert (who was working on magnetism) was repeatedly attacked by Bacon on this ground.[4] As Sir Herbert Butterfield has observed, Bacon was opposed to Galileo's essentially mathematical treatment of the problem of motion; so far from wishing to cut out 'accidental' features of the experimental situation, such as air resistance, he wished rather 'to load all the concreteness back into the problem, to see a picture which included air-resistance and gravity and the internal texture of the body itself'.[5]

Naturally, the real scientists could do nothing by such methods. The ordinary man's uncontrolled experience is, from the scientist's point of view, an *embarras de richesse*. The smells, sounds, sights and tastes which crowd in upon, say, a man eating an ice-cream at London Airport on a hot Tuesday morning are possible material for a novelist, but hardly for the physicist. The scientist's first enemy is the fecundity of experience, and his first task is to sterilise it.

[1] As Hume noticed; see *Hume's Dialogues concerning Natural Religion*, ed. Norman Kemp Smith, 2nd edn., 1947, p. 138.

[2] The fact that Bacon uses 'empirical' to mean almost exactly the opposite, viz. 'those who restrict their awareness of the world to "the narrowness and darkness of a few experiments" ', though it may momentarily daze us, need not divert us. It is in fact interesting evidence of the degree to which the term 'empiricism' had become attached to the artificially restricted experiences of the scientist as early as 1620. See Bacon's *Novum Organon*, I.lxiv, in *The Philosophical Works of Francis Bacon*, 'reprinted from the texts and translations, with the notes and prefaces, of Ellis and Spedding', ed. J. M. Robertson, 1905, p. 271.

[3] See E. J. Dijksterhuis, *The Mechanisation of the World Picture*, trans. C. Dikshoorn, 1961, pp. 399–400.

[4] *Novum Organon*, I.liv, lxiv, lxx, in Robertson's edn., pp. 59, 268, 271, 275. I am aware that not all Bacon's criticism of Gilbert is at this level. See for example the interesting discussion of magnetic theory at *Novum Organum*, II.xxxvi, pp. 346 f.

[5] H. Butterfield, *The Origins of Modern Science, 1300–1800*, the 1962 reprint of the edition of 1957 (first published 1949), p. 106. See also Paolo Rossi, *Francis Bacon: from Magic to Science*, trans. Sacha Rabinovitch, 1968, esp. p. 220.

Thus while Bacon kept his eyes and ears wide open, Galileo was hard at work distinguishing the material of science from the world we all observe:

> Hence I think that tastes, odours, colours, and so on are no more than mere names so far as the object in which we place them is concerned, and that they reside only in the consciousness. Hence if the living creature were removed, all these qualities would be wiped away and annihilated.[1]

This is an early instance of the distinction between mathematically measurable qualities on the one hand, and merely sensed qualities on the other. Real objects have length, breadth, weight and so on, but colour, taste, sound and smell are mere interpretation. The distinction was, in a slightly different form, known to the ancient world. Democritus advocated it, and Aristotle reviled it. But in the seventeenth century it rose again with renewed force. It appears fully formed in Locke as the distinction between primary and secondary qualities. It is no accident that the century of its revival was also the century of scientific revolution. As A. N. Whitehead wrote,[2] Aristotle had said to the natural philosopher 'classify' when he should have said 'measure'. The scientists of the seventeenth century were beginning implicitly to recognise this. And it is clear that one motive behind the distinction (for to be sure, it has other philosophical credentials) is the scientist's concern with what he can and cannot handle. I have already used the phrase 'the honorific use of "real"'. It has a certain relevance here. 'Properties A, B and C are amenable to scientific analysis; properties D, E, F, G and H are not; so properties A, B and C are the real ones.' This represents one, sublogical strand which was present. The distinction survived intelligent criticism from such great men as Boyle,[3] Berkeley,[4] and Hume,[5] and, when

---

[1] Galileo, *The Assayer* (first published 1623), in *Discoveries and Opinions of Galileo*, trans. Stillman Drake, New York, 1957, p. 274.

[2] *Science and the Modern World*, 1927, p. 57.

[3] See his 'An Excursion about the Relative Nature of Physical Qualities', in *The Works of the Honourable Robert Boyle*, Birch edn., 1772, III.22 f, 36.

[4] In *The Principles of Human Knowledge* (1710) and *Three Dialogues of Hylas and Philonous* (1713), *passim*.

[5] *A Treatise of Human Nature* (1739–40), I.lv.4 f., in the edn. of L. A. Selby-Bigge, 1888, pp. 227–8.

the scientific world picture had been consolidated by Newton, in the eighteenth century it reigned supreme. E. A. Burtt has written:

> . . . it was of the greatest consequence for succeeding thought that now the great Newton's authority was squarely behind that view of the cosmos which saw in man a puny, irrelevant spectator (so far as a being wholly imprisoned in a dark room can be called such) of the vast mathematical system whose regular motions according to mechanical principles constituted the world of nature. The gloriously romantic universe of Dante and Milton, that set no bounds to the imagination of man as it played over space and time, had now been swept away. Space was identified with the realm of geometry, time with the continuity of number. The world that people had thought themselves living in–a world rich with colour and sound, redolent with fragrance, filled with gladness, love and beauty, speaking everywhere of purposive harmony and creative ideals–was crowded now into minute corners in the brains of scattered organic beings. The really important world outside was a world hard, cold, colourless, silent, and dead; a world of quantity, a world of mathematically computable motions in mechanical regularity. The world of qualities as immediately perceived by man became just a curious and quite minor effect of that infinite machine beyond.[1]

II

Thus the grand paradox of English empiricism lies in its hostility to experience. Even in the twentieth century, though no living philosopher would subscribe to the full Lockian view, its effects can still be felt. English logical positivism is one of the children of English empiricism, and, though positivists are happy to accept the testimony of the senses, that 'testimony' is only admitted in a somewhat constricted form. The fuzzy edges of experience, the things that happen to us when we fall in love, enter a monastery, listen to music are trimmed away. This in

[1] *The Metaphysical Foundations of Modern Physical Science* (first published 1924), the 1959 reprint of the 2nd edn. of 1932, pp. 236–7.

itself is relatively innocuous since the effects are easily recognised. What is perhaps more dangerous is that the same harsh exclusiveness is, inevitably, applied in more unexpected places. Not only will, say, an experience of conversion be ruthlessly rejected but the experience of an ordinary country walk might well survive a positivist recension only in a curiously gutless condition. But this by illustration only.

The truth is we are none of us free from the effects of the revolution I have described. The present writer, a few lines back, used the phrase 'testimony of the senses'. It will have caused few readers to pause, for it has passed into the language. Yet it is really exactly on a par with the children's illustration from which we began. Both are model descriptions deriving from the epistemological belief that our observation of the world is indirect. Given this, whether we regard the senses as voices chirping on the telephone or witnesses undergoing interrogation is immaterial. In fact it is nonsense to suggest that the senses provide us with testimony which we subsequently peruse in the secret chamber of the soul. A moment's thought will show how the notion, so far from explaining perception, merely generates an infinite regress. As soon as we ask how the mind 'peruses', or merely takes in the testimony, we realise that the true epistemological problem has not been resolved but merely postponed.

The moral of this is that we should not be too quick to condemn the crude allegory of the frontispiece. In fact its very crudeness is in a manner salutary. For example, it shows with an admirable candour the implicit regress I have just been trying to uncover. At the centre of the system, where the incoming information is actually being reviewed—that is, at the point where the actual *knowing* or *perception* is going on—*the artist has drawn a small boy*. Inside the huge architectural head is just another head, whose 'ear window' is presumably at this moment admitting the sounds from the telephone exchange. And so the whole drawing is to be done again; in the head of the small boy. And then again. And so on *ad infinitum*.

The problems inherited by twentieth century epistemology have often been blamed upon the 'ghost in the machine' theory, that is to say, the Cartesian view that there are in the world two sorts of substance, on the one hand mathematically measurable, extended matter, and on the other mind, itself unextended. Yet, as we have seen, this phrase alone does not carry us to the root of the problem. It is quite easy to imagine a philosophy in which the ghosts are allowed directly to inspect their environment. The crucial factor is the indirectness of our relation with the world. After all, although the notion of a ghost inhabiting a *machine* may be essentially post-Cartesian, the rough idea that the soul is something spiritual inhabiting something (merely) physical is immemorial. An age betrays itself in its imagery. Spenser's knights looked out on distant prospects. But Bishop Butler, writing in the 1730s, gives a different picture:

> . . . if we consider our body somewhat more distinctly, as made up of organs and instruments of perception and of motion, it will bring us to the same conclusions. Thus the common optical experiments show, and even the observation how sight is assisted by glasses shows, that we see with our eyes in the same sense as we see with glasses . . .
>
> Thus a man determines that he will look at such an object through a microscope; or being lame supposes that he will walk to such a place with a staff a week hence . . . Nor is there any ground to think . . . that his eyes are the seers or his feet the movers in any other sense than as the microscope and the staff are . . . Nor consequently is there any probability, that the alienation or dissolution of these instruments is the destruction of the perceiving and moving agent.[1]

This passage (which I have abridged within an inch of its life) is an argument for the immortality of the soul proceeding from stock Cartesian principles. It turns on the complete separation of the true mystery of perception from its physical instrument. The seeing eye is turned into cold glass. The difference between windows and microscopes is merely a form of the difference between immediate and mediated perception.

The fact that the eye was traditionally described as glass must not be allowed to obscure the contrast between Spenser and Butler. Spenser does not tell us whether the windows in his high tower were glazed or not. If he had chosen to describe the

[1] *The Analogy of Religion* (first published 1736), Ch. I, 17–19, ed. W. E. Gladstone, 1896, vol. I, pp. 33–6.

glass of the windows we may be sure that the characteristic he would dwell on would be translucency. Such was the usual practice:

> His eyes are crystall *windows*, cleare and bright;
> Let in the object, and let out the sight.[1]

These lines of Francis Quarles are nothing if not typical. To the older poets the hard, mechanistic implications of 'glass' are, if anything, an embarrassment. But for Butler they constitute the chief attraction of the image–the more mechanical the eye, the more purely immaterial the soul. Phineas Fletcher illustrates the older feeling very clearly:

> That *Thracian* shepherd call'd them Natures glasse;
> Yet then a glasse in this much worthier being:
> Blinde glasses represent some neare-set face;
> But this a living glasse, both seen and seeing.[2]

For Fletcher, as for Quarles, glass is useful as an image because of its translucency; but Butler chose to think in terms of *lenses*, which modify the object they present, while Fletcher feels he must explain that, although the eye resembles glass in its transparency, yet, strictly, the eye is the more translucent of the two:

> Here *Visus* keeps, whose Court then crystall smoother
> And clearer seems . . .[3]

Fletcher is in fact an interesting specimen of the transition from the older view to the scientific. *The Purple Island* is a long allegorical poem on the human body. It is on so ambitious a scale that its author is forced to enter very fully into the available physiological evidence. He thus encounters the image on the retina, and like many a better man he falls:

> The forms caught in this net are brought to sight
> And to his eye are lively pourtrayed.[4]

---

[1] Francis Quarles, 'Mans Bodie's like a house'; a commendatory poem prefixed to Phineas Fletcher's *The Purple Island* (1633). The poem is printed in *Giles and Phineas Fletcher: Poetical Works*, ed. F. S. Boas, Cambridge, 1908–9, vol. II, p. 11.

[2] *The Purple Island*, Canto V.24, in Boas's edition, p. 58.

[3] *Ibid.*, Canto V.25 p. 58.   [4] *Ibid.*, Canto V.34, p. 60.

The notion of the image on show inside the skull proved too tempting. This, then, is the true object of sight. As we have seen. It is a 'solution' which darkens more than it clarifies. The usual regress is laid before us. Within his explanation of what it is to see, Fletcher has used the term to be defined. If sight has 'eyes' which enable him to see the retinal image, are these too to be subjected to an allegorical anatomy? In such passages Fletcher looks forward to the eighteenth century. But in him the consequences are merely latent. All his overt instincts are according to the older model, and, when his attention strays from his medical crib, his imagery is thoroughly Elizabethan. For example, he like Spenser instinctively locates the eyes in a watchtower.[1] It is no accident that Spenser gave us freely moving figures, while Butler gave us a myopic cripple.

The powerlessness of the ordinarily intelligent eighteenth century man caught in this net is clearly shown by the intellectual tergiversations of Thomas Reid, Adam Smith's successor as Professor of Moral Philosophy in the University of Glasgow. Reid felt the impossibility of the situation keenly enough and in the second essay of his *On the Intellectual Powers* (1785) even succeeded in carrying out a perfectly sound preliminary diagnosis:

> The ideas, of whose existence I require the proof, are not the operations of any mind, but supposed objects of those operations. They are not perception, remembrance, or conception, but things that are said to be perceived, or remembered, or imagined.
>
> Nor do I dispute the existence of what the vulgar call the objects of perception. These, by all who acknowledge their existence, are called real things, not ideas.[2]

The true source of the philosophical difficulties lay, he perceived, in the belief that we cannot know reality except by way of ideas. When the moment comes, however, for Reid to say how we *do* know the world, he blunders back into the very Cartesian models from which he is striving to escape. Thus, later in the same essay, his language strongly suggests that what we sense

---

[1] *Ibid.*, Canto V.22, p. 57.
[2] *The Works of Thomas Reid, D.D.*, ed. Sir William Hamilton, 8th edn., Edinburgh, 1895, vol. I, p. 298B.

is not identical with what we perceive but is rather a means to perception: 'Nature has connected our perception of external objects with certain sensations. If the sensation is produced, the corresponding perception follows even when there is no object, and in that case is apt to deceive us.'[1] From this it is only a short step back to the original notion that we are directly aware only of a sensory idea, and from that idea infer an object. The truth is that the Lockian (or Cartesian) model of the mind as located beside some important nerve centre in the body could not easily be extirpated from eighteenth century thought. The great error—that of repeating the term 'perceive' *within* a description of the mechanics of perception—this error is quashed at one point only to reappear at another. Thus, as we have seen, it is a fact of optics that when I look at something a corresponding image appears on the retina. But obviously this does not mean that really I was looking not at the thing but at the retina. The infinite regress implicit in any such description is evident. The degree to which epistemology was perverted by this misalliance of physiology and philosophy is shown by the prolonged ponderings throughout the seventeenth and eighteenth centuries on the fact (in the circumstances delicious) that the image on the retina is upside down. Here once more we find Reid, the old lag of eighteenth century philosophy, breaking out of gaol only to re-enter it forthwith. Thus at one point he argues[2] that the communication of impressions to internal organs and nerves, though it certainly seems to be the condition of any successful perception, is not *per se* the cause of perception. At last, we feel, the argument is beginning to move, though we may feel some disquiet when we discover that only a few lines on he employs the stock Butlerian imagery of the telescope. Sixty pages later we find him speculating on the phenomenon of pain felt in the toe and anxious to assert that the pain is really felt, not in the toe but in the brain.[3] It is clear that there can be only one motive for this anxiety. It is Reid's involuntary allegiance to the picture of the soul as isolated deep within the body.

Reid's ambition was to cure mankind of the paralysing

---

[1] *The Works of Thomas Reid, D.D.*, p. 320B.

[2] *Ibid.*, p. 257B.

[3] *Ibid.*, p. 320A. See also Sir William Hamilton's Note C, *ibid.*, vol. II, pp. 816–24.

scepticism by which it was assailed. That the theory of indirect perception implies scepticism is easily shown. If we never look directly at things but instead merely receive accounts of those things, how are we to know that the accounts are correct? I may check a glimpse of a white shape in the darkness by stretching out my hand; I grasp a sheet, which, it seems, has been left hanging in the garden. This will do well enough for the unphilosophical man. But if the senses are regarded as messengers only it is clear that we have here, not a check in the fundamental sense but merely agreement on the part of the messengers. Now although it may seem improbable that *five* messengers should have conspired to deceive their master, it is by no means impossible (particularly when they arrived at their place of employment without references or testimonials). The truth is that we cannot so much as imagine (given the Lockian scheme) how such messages could ever be subjected to a decisive check. We may suppose, if we like, the existence of a sixth sense, posted to inform on the other five, but we could never know whether it had not at once joined the conspiracy. Talk of the 'testimony' of the senses suggests that the mind is like a judge, presiding in authority. But a judge is not confined to the accounts of the witnesses; he can examine photographs, the murder weapon, and can even, in special circumstances, witness actual events himself. The mind, it would seem, is really more like a blind man, led along roads he cannot see by guides he cannot choose but trust.

III

One really brilliant assault was made in the eighteenth century upon this problem. Bishop Berkeley came within an ace of resolving the entire difficulty. Indeed there are moments when the reader may well feel that Berkeley has succeeded, that man has been released from his prison. It is useful to reflect at such times that Thomas Reid was driven to begin his work by the sceptical despair he had fallen into as a result of reading Berkeley and Hume.[1] Indeed Reid began as a disciple of Berkeley.[2] And what happened to Reid we have seen.

*   *   *   *

[1] See Hamilton's 8th edn. (1895) of the *Works*, vol. I, pp. 103, 131-2, 273-4.   [2] *Ibid.*, p. 283.

It is well to begin any reading of Berkeley, therefore, with a *caveat*: do not allow yourself to be elated by the dexterous, liberating thought you are about to watch; only remember that you will end exactly where you began.

Berkeley is commonly supposed to have denied the reality of sensible things. This is an error. What Berkeley denied was the reality of material substance. If the difference between these two theses appears negligible, that is only because the full rigour of the seventeenth-century postponement of material reality has declined. The 'material substance' which Berkeley wished to remove from our conceptual scheme was the ulterior matter postulated by scientists and fashionable thinkers as an underlying 'support' for the various qualities read off by each mind according to its subjective capacity for interpetation. As for sensible things, for the tangible, the visible, the audible, and so on, these he very nearly saved. Berkeley's philosophy cannot be understood (any more than a boot-scraper can be understood) until we know what it is *for*; that is, in the present case, to whom and against what it is addressed. Berkeley gives a clear account of the view to which he is opposed in the preface which he wrote for the 1713 edition of *Three Dialogues of Hylas and Philonous* (it was omitted in the 1734 edition):

> Upon the common principles of philosophers, we are not assured of the existence of things from their being perceived. And we are taught to distinguish their real nature from that which falls under our senses. Hence arise *scepticism* and *paradoxes*. It is not enough, that we see and feel, that we taste and smell a thing; its true nature, its absolute external entity, is still concealed. For, though it be a fiction of our own brain, we have made it inaccessible to all our faculties.[1]

The scorn which lies behind this cool, expository prose, is the scorn of eighteenth century common sense which feels that it has been taken for a ride. The philosopher who later came to be regarded as the *ne plus ultra* of metaphysical extravagance was himself actuated by a hostility to speculative and unverifiable metaphysics. In a surviving notebook Berkeley wrote: 'Mem:

[1] In *The Works of George Berkeley, Bishop of Cloyne*, ed. A. A. Luce and T. E. Jessup, vol. II, 1949, p. 167.

To be eternally banishing Metaphisics, &c & recalling Men to Common Sense.'[1] The same note is struck repeatedly in the Preface to *Three Dialogues*. Near the beginning of the work itself Philonous, who is the spokesman for Berkeley, confesses that he has more in common with butchers than with high-flown technical philosophers: '. . . I have quitted several of the sublime notions I had got in their schools for vulgar opinions.'[2] In fact Berkeley wrote the *Three Dialogues* to make it clear to those who had been alienated by the seemingly wild notions of *The Principles of Human Knowledge* (1710) that he had common sense on his side.

The *Three Dialogues* is a work of consummate literary art. Its argument is conducted by two philosophers walking in a garden early in the morning. The garden in which they talk remains almost invisible to the reader's imagination – the lightly pencilled background to the principal subject which is the skirmishing philosophical notions themselves – save for one electrifying moment, when it bursts into the argument and into the foreground, as manifesting the sensible glory of the created world. Then we become aware that throughout the conversation the light has been growing, unnoticed. The participants of the dialogues are named Hylas (from Greek, 'matter') and Philonous (again from the Greek, and meaning 'Lover of mind', or 'Lover of spirit'). The materialist doctrine of the enemy is set forth by Hylas with admirable clarity:

> It is supposed the soul makes her residence in some part of the brain, from which the nerves take their rise, and are thence extended to all parts of the body: and that outward objects by the different impressions they make on the organs of sense, communicate certain vibrative motions to the nerves; and these being filled with spirit, propagate them to the brain or seat of the soul, which according to the various impressions or traces thereby made in the brain, is variously affected with ideas.[3]

That Philonous failed to scotch this view is made only too clear by our frontispiece which is substantially the same picture. And,

[1] *Philosophical Commentaries*, in Luce and Jessup's edn. of the *Works* vol. I, 1948, p. 91.
[2] Three Dialogues, I, *Works*, vol. II p. 172.
[3] *Three Dialogues*, II, *Works*, vol. II, pp. 208–9.

once more, the literal minded drawing exposes the difficult connections so smoothly glossed over by Hylas's 'scientific' terminology. The mind encounters the statement that 'outward objects' make 'impressions' on the 'organs of sense' and does not pause to ask whether 'impression' is here intended as a physical term (as in the 'impression' made by a seal on wax) or, if not that, then what? But in the drawing the way the light streaming in at the windows is twisted into ropes of nerves and subsequently 'converted' (here I am using 'scientific' language as Hylas does) into telephone messages—all this is shown with magnificently palpable improbability.

But Philonous has little difficulty in winning the first round. He shows clearly that Hylas can have no notion whether the information presented by his senses is correct or not; or even if the object it purports to describe is really there. He also shows that it is not even a case of 'might or might not'. It is hard to see how the theory as stated *could* be true. For when Hylas tries to say that our ideas resemble real objects and are thereby able to act as trustworthy representatives Philonous, instead of asking 'How do you know?' crushes his opponent with the question: 'Can a real thing in itself *invisible* be like a *colour* or a real thing which is not audible be like a sound?'[1] Of course if this is written specifically against Locke it is not fair. Locke had a causal theory (whereby things cause our perceptions) as well as the resemblance theory (according to which the perception is like the reality) and of course he knew that colours, above all, must be accounted for in terms of the causal theory. But Berkeley is addressing not Locke but the age. Whatever form the theory assumes, the Bishop falls joyously upon it. Here it is the resemblance theory which suffers; the causal theory will have its turn. Moreover it is at this point that the debate becomes philosophically radical. Philonous almost turns into a twentieth-century philosopher, as he undercuts Hylas with the remark that his notion of substance is not so much false as meaningless:

> I will not indeed thence conclude against the reality of any notion or existence of anything: but my inference shall be that you mean nothing at all, that you employ words to no

---

[1] *Three Dialogues*, I, *Works*, vol. II, p. 206.

manner of purpose, without any design of signification whatsoever.[1]

It becomes steadily clearer that the ulterior matter postulated by the scientists is a strong competitor for the airy fictions of the Schoolmen; that is, it involves exactly the sort of speculation which the age delighted to vilify in its predecessors. And the thing has appeared from the most unexpected quarter of all—metaphysics from the physicist! The clever reader could smell this in the wind as he read Hylas's strange speech expounding his notion of matter:

> I find myself affected with various ideas whereof I know I am not the cause; neither are they the cause of themselves or of one another, or capable of subsisting by themselves as being altogether inactive, fleeting, dependent beings. They have therefore some cause distinct from me and them of which I pretend to know no more than that it is *the cause of my ideas*. And this thing, whatever it be, I call matter.[2]

I do not know how much of Thomas Aquinas Berkeley might be presumed to have read at Trinity College, Dublin, at the turn of the century and therefore hesitate to describe this passage as an intentionally ironic echo of the great scholastic. If it *is* intentional (and it could well be) it must rank as one of the pinnacles of Berkeley's achievement as a literary artist. The objective fact —that the language of the materialist resembles the language of the Angelic Doctor—can scarcely be disputed. A string of quotations from Aquinas will show it at once:

> . . . and this is what everybody understands by God.
> *Summa Theologiae*, 1a.ii.3

> There is something therefore which causes in all other things their being, their goodness, and whatever other perfection they have. And this we call 'God'.
> *Ibid.*, 1a.ii.3

> Whatever this superior being may be, all know it by the name 'God'.
> *Ibid.*, 2a–2ae.lxxxv.1

---

[1] *Ibid.*, II, *Works*, vol. II, p. 223.
[2] *Ibid.*, II, *Works*, vol. II, p. 216.

B

. . . we may further infer that there is something that is supremely being. This we call God.

Summa Contra Gentiles, 1.xiii.34[1]

Anyone accustomed to reading Thomistic arguments for the existence of God would recognise in Hylas's words the usual concluding formula. There is of course an interesting difference between Hylas and Aquinas. The confident first person plural of the mediaeval philosopher has vanished, and we have instead only a cautious first person singular. But the similarity remains more important than the difference.

Berkeley, even had he wished to, could never have made this precise point explicitly. There was one 'airy fiction' of the Schoolmen which it was wise to leave unassailed. Even in the century of Hume and Gibbon it was unwise openly to attack the concept of God. Indeed the more one learns of the ordinary climate of opinion the clearer it is that the celebrated irony of Hume and Gibbon, though rightly praised for its literary merits, was in fact a thoroughly practical device. Their fine feathers were reversible; if necessary they could be used as camouflage. The modern reader of eighteenth century authors does well to remember Toland's maxim, namely, that when a man professes orthodox opinions he may or may not be sincere, but when he attacks orthodoxy, there is a distinct presumption in favour of his sincerity.[2] But to be sure, all this is scarcely applicable to Bishop Berkeley, who is safer than most men from the charge of religious hypocrisy. Nevertheless he doubtless knew very well which sort of religious argument would draw the fire of the *Zeitgeist,* and might very well have deliberately placed it in the mouth of *Hylas.* It is set far enough away from the strong light of consciousness to discharge its proper function without provoking irrelevant reactions: that is to say, it will insensibly invest Hylas with the character of an unrealistic metaphysician.

Hylas, until he is educated by Philonous, is a partly unconscious exponent of his own philosophy; in particular he does not see the full extent of the division between experience and matter

[1] *Seriatim;* in the Blackfriars edn. of 1964, vol. II, ed. T. McDermott, pp. 15, 17; vol. XXXIX, ed. Kevin D. O'Rourke, p. 115; *The Truth of the Catholic Faith* (translation of the *Summa Contra Gentiles* by Anton C. Pegis) New York 1955, vol. I, p. 96.

[2] *Tetradymus,* 1720, p. 96.

as he defines them. Like any twentieth century man he mistakenly assumes that when Philonous is drawing the conception of matter from under him, he is at the same time removing the world of experience. Berkeley, with great art, makes Hylas, chastened by long refutation, fall into a mood of repentance which proves quite as misplaced as his earlier confidence: 'I now clearly see it was a mere dream. There is nothing in it.'[1] Philonous is not above teasing his victim for a moment. After all he is on the point of giving him the whole world back again. 'Are you at length satisfied,' he asks, 'that no sensible things have a real existence; and that you are in truth an arrant skeptic?'[2] Hylas submissively agrees. But now Philonous has played with his opponent long enough. It is as if he takes him by the shoulder and shakes him awake:

> Look! are not the fields covered with a delightful verdure? Is there not something in the woods and groves, in the rivers and clear springs that soothes, that delights, that transports the soul? At the prospect of the wide and deep ocean, or some huge mountain whose top is lost in the clouds, or of an old gloomy forest, are not our minds filled with a pleasing horror? Even in rocks and deserts, is there not an agreeable wildness? How sincere a pleasure is it to behold the natural beauties of the earth! To preserve and renew our relish for them, is not the veil of night alternately drawn over her face, and doth she not change her dress with the seasons? . . . Raise now your thoughts from this ball of earth, to all those glorious luminaries that adorn the high arch of heaven. The motion and situation of the planets, are they not admirable for use and order? Were those (miscalled erratic) globes ever known to stray, in their repeated journeys through the pathless void? Do they not measure areas round the sun ever proportioned to the times? So fixed, so immutable are the laws by which the unseen Author of Nature actuates the universe. How vivid and radiant is the luster of the fixed stars? How magnificent and rich that negligent profusion, with which they appear to be scattered throughout the whole azure vault! Yet if you take

[1] *Three Dialogues* II, *Works*, vol. II, p. 210.
[2] *Ibid.*, II, Luce and Jessop, II. p. 210.

the telescope, it brings into your sight a new host of stars that escape the naked eye. Here they seem contiguous and minute, but to a nearer view immense orbs of light of various distances, far sunk in the abyss of space . . . How should those principles be entertained, that lead us to think all the visible beauty of the creation a false imaginary glare?[1]

At the lowest level, this is a superb gambit, an admirable specimen of Lifemanship. But of course the speech is very much more. Philonous' celebration of the sensible world is in fact a locus classicus for eighteenth-century sensibility, cosmological assumptions and the like. It may be thought more personal than such a description suggests in that parts of it seem to contain exactly the oscillation between conventional admiration of mechanical regularity on the one hand and some wilder source of wonder on the other that we should expect from a philosopher who had subverted the whole conceptual structure of contemporary science and was as yet not clearly aware how it was to be replaced.[2] Certainly Berkeley in this passage seems almost to have a double identity. From the contemplation of a peaceful English meadow (which tells us nothing, since the members of either party can admire *that*) we are swept away to an unambiguously Gothick landscape, to that which gives pleasure not because it is regular and intelligible, but precisely because it is not–'some huge mountain whose top is lost in the clouds'. But as we pass from this to the meditation on the heavens, we may feel that the Gothick element in Berkeley's sensibility is merely superficial, and the older taste for ordered beauty fundamental. After all, he raises the notion of a wild and incomprehensible heaven only to reject it, and apparently rejoices in the rejection –'Were those (miscalled "erratic") globes ever known to stray . . .?' C. S. Lewis has argued[3] that a vivid awareness of the incomprehensibility of the physical universe is an essentially new development in the seventeenth century. Pascal, with his 'le

---

[1] *Three Dialogues*, II, *Works*, II. pp. 210–11.
[2] It was not until the publication in 1721 of his *De Motu* that Berkeley perfected his account of scientific references to the imperceivable as methodologically useful fictions. The solutions offered before that date are a mere stop-gap.
[3] See his *The Discarded Image*, Cambridge, 1964, pp. 99 f.

silence eternel de ces espaces infinis m'effraie', voices a sentiment
which could have found no echo in the breast of Dante. But
Milton when he described the moon as wandering

> Like one that hath bin led astray
> Through the Heav'ns wide pathless way
>
> (*Il Penseroso*, 69–70)

anticipated Pascal's reaction. Further, anyone who reflects on
Milton's etymological vigilance, and on the fact that the Greek
ancestor of our word *planet* meant, precisely, 'wanderer', may
feel that these lines are as much the recovery of something very
old as the discovery of a new sensibility. Something in Berkeley's
language suggests that he, too, thinks that to call the heavenly
bodies erratic is more conventional than revolutionary. Be that
as it may, one is tempted to say that it is the aesthetic of
regularity which is here prevailing over the aesthetic of irregularity. Yet look again at the complete sentence. The epithet
'pathless' has survived that victory of order. Indeed the more
one examines the paragraph the more sceptical one grows about
the extent of this victory. As one moves from the 'fixed immutable laws' to 'the luster of the fixed stars' the reader senses a
suppressed antithesis between the conceptual and the phenomenal which never arises in the poetry of Dante. And after a
phrase like 'negligent profusion' one can only treat that 'appear
to be' as an apologetic gesture towards a vanishing ideal. Thus
our initial sense that Berkeley was showing us the beauty of
irregularity gradually transcended by the beauty of regularity,
the minor key replaced by the major, was wrong. What we have
is really an uneasy truce between the two conceptions.

It is however quite unnecessary to ascribe the mental division
to Berkeley's peculiar philosophical situation. It is in fact the
common possession of the century. Even Pope's *Essay on Man*
contains, besides such famous passages in praise of system as that
beginning 'We are all parts of one stupendous whole' many
other lines which breathe a hardly dissembled exultation in
disorder – e.g.

> Let earth unbalanc'd from her orbit fly,
> Planets and suns run lawless thro' the sky,
> Let ruling angels from their spheres be hurl'd,
> Being on being wrecked and world on world;

Heav'ns whole foundations to their centre nod,
And Nature tremble to the throne of God

(Epistle I, 251–6)

The tone of this is very different from Claudio's speech in
Measure for Measure (II.i.122–30) 'To be imprison'd in the
viewless winds' *etc.*, which is filled with real terror. Pope, placed
as he is at the beginning of the eighteenth century, is like a child
who finds he is beginning to enjoy riding on the Big Dipper.

It may be that with Berkeley some of the unease results from
the dual character of the regularity he is striving to praise. We
are uncertain whether we are called upon to admire the organic
order of the mediaeval universe or the mechanical order of the
new. Of course, as soon as he consciously considered the matter,
Berkeley discovered that he was implacably (and rationally)
opposed to the second of these.[1] Yet the 'immutable laws' of
planetary motion suggest Kepler and Newton rather than Dante.

Berkeley's great paragraph is an unusually rich specimen for
the literary critic, who finds himself fascinated by a retreating
series of questions: why does the style, apart from a few
astounding phrases like 'false imaginary glare' remain so
abstract? Is this merely because Berkeley was an eighteenth-
century man, and knew no other way of writing? Or does it
rather suggest that at some deeper level of his personality he
mistrusts his own restoration of reality? And so on. Yet when
all our reservations and doubts have spent their force, it remains
great writing. The irony is not merely tactical, but profound.
Locke, as Berkeley loved to point out, had duplicated the world.
A cold and colourless reality was somehow reproduced by a
second cosmos of magically various and colourful ideas. The
ideas were all we were ever permitted to see, but they, alas, were
unreal. Berkeley has shown that Locke's ulterior reality is
redundant, and that therefore the cosmos of ideas is autonomous
and fully deserves to be called real.

IV

So it seems that the crazy Bishop of Cloyne is the only man with
enough wit to beat the sceptics. And he has won because he was

[1] Berkeley was not, of course, an opponent of science itself. He willingly
applauded purely operational physics. It was really mechanistic metaphysics rather than mechanistic physics which aroused his anger.

willing to gamble. The reluctant sceptics had worn themselves out looking for reality where Locke had told them to look, that is, in the exterior source of our ideas. Naturally enough, having defined their substantial reality in such a way that it was in principle unobservable, they were unable to find it when they looked. Berkeley had the effect, so to speak, of a sudden cry heard over one's shoulder–'Don't look there; look over here!' That is, stop looking for an inaccessible material 'support' and try the hazard of ascribing reality to the ideas themselves; at least they are tangible.[1] Doubtless, Berkeley himself would have been delighted by this interpretation, at least initially. It makes his claim to be on the side of common sense a good deal more plausible.

But there is one snag. The Lockian reality has been overthrown, but the Lockian term, *idea*, has been retained. Thus the phrase 'Our "ideas" *are* reality' can be reworded as 'Our ideas are all that reality is' or 'reality is a tissue of ideas'. We wonder whether Berkeley's achievement is not more one of retrenchment than of conquest, whether he did not so much raise ideas to the status of reality as reduce reality to the status of ideas. Of course it may be thought that this sort of speculation is in the circumstances trivial. If Locke's 'reality' has been removed, the term *idea* must necessarily have lost its old function of distinguishing the unreal from the real: therefore 'the idea is real' and 'the real is ideal' become indifferent ways of expressing the same truth, and that a tautology. There are various signs that Berkeley saw this implication, and welcomed it. The strongest of these occurs in the third dialogue: 'I am not for changing things into ideas, but rather ideas into things'.[2] Here Berkeley, the champion of common sense, who put into the mouth of Philonous such imperiously modest gibes as 'What a jest is it for a philosopher to question the existence of sensible things . . .'[3] has achieved a fully philosophical formulation of his position. Yet, insidiously, it was the word *idea*, and not *thing*, which continued to be used. In fact the very thought of substituting *thing* for *idea* in Berkeley's subsequent writings is a curious one.[4] At most

[1] Such, in essence, is R. H. Popkin's view in his article, 'Berkeley and Pyrrhonism', *Review of Metaphysics*, vol. 2 (1951), pp. 223–46.

[2] *Three Dialogues*, III, *Works*, II, p. 244.

[3] *Ibid.*, III, *Works*, II, p. 230.

[4] This thought did not escape Berkeley himself: '. . . it sounds very

places it would simply result in meaninglessness. Elsewhere it would have the effect of transforming a metaphysical disquisition into a series of curiously platitudinous prosaic observations, at an intolerably general level—in fact into common sense. That is because common sense Berkeleianism has in these places achieved its object, and has nowhere else to go.

G. J. Warnock, considering the 'duplicated' Lockian world which Berkeley had before him, has asked a very simple question:[1] Why did not Berkeley eliminate the *other* half of this double universe? Why did he not throw away the intervening 'ideas' and retain the non-mental object as real? It is, of course, a good question, which by its very simplicity eluded the philosophers of the time. The immediate answer is obvious: Berkeley discarded the half he could not perceive. Warnock belongs to a philosophical age which has shaken itself free of the doctrine of primary and secondary qualities, but it was assumed by Berkeley as by everyone else that the redness of an object was a 'mental' characteristic of that object, entirely dependent on the perceiver. This view conditioned his entire philosophical outlook so that in the end Berkeley's austere rejection of everything he could not sense involved an assimilation of all primary qualities to the status of secondary.[2] Berkeleianism is in fact a resolution of the grand paradox of seventeenth century empiricism to which I have already referred more than once: the scientific empiricist gives us a world foreign to our experience. Berkeley's ambition was to reassert the claims of experience. But in 'correcting' the error of his predecessors he did not disdain to use their terms, and thus to use their thoughts. 'Experience',

---

harsh to say we eat and drink ideas, and are clothed with ideas' (*Principles*, I.38, *Works*, II, p. 56.)

[1] See his introduction to G. Berkeley's *The Principles of Human Knowledge* and *Three Dialogues of Hylas and Philonous*, Fontana Library. London, 1962, pp. 31–2.

[2] See for example *The Principles of Human Knowledge*, I.9–11, *Three Dialogues*, I, in *Works*, II, pp. 44–6 and 187. I have followed Berkeley in his modification of Locke's 'secondary quality'. Locke says (*Essay* II.viii.10, vol. I, p. 170) that secondary qualities are 'nothing in the objects themselves but powers to produce various sensations in us by their primary qualities'. Berkeley instead takes 'secondary qualities' to mean the qualities as subjectively perceived. This slight modification of the Lockian terminology happened very rapidly after the publication of the *Essay*. Berkeley would say, I suppose, that it was bound to happen.

for Berkeley, meant the way things taste, smell, *etc*. That is all experience is and (except for the thinking subject) there is nothing else. But tasting, smelling, *etc*., are things that go on in the mind. Berkeley is far too imbued with the spirit of his century to believe that the objects of mental tasting, *etc*., if immediate, could be other than in the mind themselves. Thus, for Berkeley, empiricism *is* idealism; or, to put it another way, *esse est aut percipere aut percipi*.

There is perhaps a further reason, of a less tangible kind, why Berkeley never asked Warnock's question. Despite his sincere preference for common sense over the metaphysical hypotheses of the scientist, Berkeley was temperamentally drawn to the immaterial. If a modern philosopher finds that an argument is tending to spiritualise phenomena he feels, before he knows, that something has gone wrong. Furthermore, we can probably say (the importance of the assertion is in inverse proportion to the disinterestedness of the philosopher) that he does not, in a general way, *want* his arguments to have that sort of effect. After all, we live in a period of reaction against post-Kantian idealism. But when Berkeley lived, Kant had not yet happened, still less Hegel or Bradley. We may suspect that when he saw all things turning into mind, Berkeley warmed to his task, and happily envisaged the rout of the scientist who had been eroding the Faith. We may as well quote his own words on the subject:

> If it be demanded why I make use of the word *idea*, and do not rather in compliance with custom call them *things*. I answer, I do it for two reasons: first, because the term *thing* in contradistinction to *idea*, is generally supposed to denote, somewhat existing without the mind: secondly, because *thing* hath a more comprehensive signification than *idea* including spirits or thinking things as well as ideas. Since therefore the objects of sense exist only in the mind and are withall thoughtless and inactive, I chose to mark them by the word *idea* which implies those properties.[1]

The first reason is the important one, and it is very simple. The word 'thing' smacks too much of the alien, of the independent,

---

[1] *Principles*, I.39, *Works*, II, p. 57.

of the *non-mental*. The wording suggests that the idealist
conclusion of Berkeley's argument, so far from being an embarrassment to him, was really a motive and a goal. He delights in
comparing the world to a dream:

> *Hylas:* Is it not certain I see things at a distance? Do we
> not perceive the stars and moon, for example, to be a
> great way off? Is not this, I say, manifest to the senses?
>
> *Philonous:* Do you not in a dream, too, perceive these or
> the like objects?
>
> *Hylas:* I do.
>
> *Philonous:* And have they not then the same appearance
> of being distant?
>
> *Hylas:* They have.
>
> *Philonous:* But do you not thence conclude the apparitions
> in a dream to be without the mind?
>
> *Hylas:* By no means.
>
> *Philonous:* You ought not therefore to conclude that
> sensible objects are without the mind, from their
> appearance or manner wherein they are perceived.[1]

Berkeley doubtless thought that his 'temperamental immaterialism' grew logically out of his philosophy. It seems rather
to have infected it. Certainly the point at which Berkeley
ascends to the theological plane is, from a strictly philosophical
point of view, the beginning of a pretty sharp descent. At
certain points one dimly discerns a kind of separation of the
two Berkeleys, the unswerving empiricist and the theologian.
One such point is his answer to the question 'If *esse* is *percipi*,
what happens to the objects when we are not perceiving them?'
Berkeley the empiricist offered an answer which startlingly
anticipates logical positivism:[2] to say 'There is a horse in that
stable' simply means 'If someone went into that stable he would
have a horse-perception'; this, though it may sound insubstantial
at first, will be found to yield just as vivid a reality as one has
been used to. Berkeley has virtually caught the notion that the
meaning of an empirical statement is its manner of verification.

---

[1] *Three Dialogues*, I, *Works*, II, p. 201.
[2] See F. Coplestone, *A History of Philosophy*, vol. V, the 1964 impression
of the edn. of 1959, p. 220.

But Berkeley the theologian gave the answer immortalised in Ronald Knox's limerick and its reply:

> There was a young man who said, 'God
> Must think it exceedingly odd
> If he finds that this tree
> Continues to be
> When there's no-one about in the Quad.'

Reply

> Dear Sir:
>   Your astonishment's odd:
> *I* am always about in the Quad.
> And that's why the tree
> Will continue to be,
> Since observed by
>   *Yours faithfully,*
>   GOD.

God enters the Berkeleian scheme in the following manner: taking it as proved that all reality, apart from perceiving subjects, is a tissue of mental ideas, we are forced to acknowledge that many of our ideas appear to be in one sense independent of us, distinguishable from the merely subjective. He gives two bases for the distinction; first the Humian contrast between the vividness of sense-perception as opposed to the relative faintness of mental imagery, and second the fact that our mental imagery is controllable while sensory imagery is manifestly recalcitrant. We thence conclude that the images we observe are not ours but another's and that the other is God. One itches to write a reply for Hylas:

> Hold Philonous, it were absurd to think that all ideas must be a kind of *fancy* or *chimera* or else belong to another. In like manner I am at a loss to understand why from the fact that an idea can only exist in a mind it should follow that an idea can only proceed from a mind, though this be true of the fancy; I freely grant that there may be something out of the way in the notion that I cannot manage my own ideas, but to resolve the matter as you have done makes many more difficulties which are yet harder of

solution. For, since a man cannot overlook the ideas of his neighbour, how shall he be admitted to those of the Deity? Moreover is there not an antecedent improbability in the hypothesis that the infinite Mind shall be immediately understood by every Tom, Dick or Harry? Is there not fully as much reason, Philonous, in saying that our ideas are manifestly of two kinds, those which are faint, and subject to our will, and those which are stronger than our will? Though the proposition may sound oddly, yet it includes nothing which is not seen and felt by every man. But to say more than this were to trespass beyond the limit of that we know.

But to attempt this is merely to discover that one cannot write like Berkeley. The truth is that our philosopher, as his contemporaries might have said, has turned Enthusiast and is soaring beyond the reach of argument. I must add that when I assert the philosophical superiority of the positivistic answer, I do not mean that I think it incontravertibly true.[1] I mean only that it is real philosophy and that it is no accident that the issues it raises are still being debated. It seems tolerably clear that the theological section of Berkeley's argument is eminently detachable from the main body of discourse. Philosophically, Berkeley is the father of Phenomenalism. But there is also a darker path, which leads, straight and level, towards solipsism. Turn again to the picture of the boy in the cell. Berkeley has emerged as merely the cruellest of his tormentors. He has asked him to put away his ear-phones, to leave the switchboard. He has made magical passes with his hands and has shown the boy for a moment trees, clouds and a church-tower. But the end of the performance was to reveal that all the boy saw was a cinematographic display. Everything was inside the architectural head – little more, indeed, than 'a false imaginary glare'.

[1] An important criticism of such positivistic phenomenalism was made by A. J. Ayer in his article 'Phenomenalism', *Proceedings of the Aristotelian Society*, 1947–8, and continued in his *The Problem of Knowledge*, 1956, pp. 123–9.

CHAPTER 2

Tristram Shandy

I

Laurence Sterne, the feline, satirical vicar of Sutton-in-the-Forest, was born in 1713, the year of Berkeley's *Three Dialogues*. No-one knew he was a literary genius until 1760 when he published the first two volumes of *Tristram Shandy*. In those forty-seven years English philosophy underwent a major transformation at the hands of David Hume, but Sterne, like most of his countrymen, seems not to have noticed the fact. Indeed, even Bishop Berkeley, whose mind innocently harboured such strange enthusiasms–for the medicinal properties of tarwater and the wilder shores of metaphysics–as to make him a natural inmate of Shandy Hall, escaped the sentimental mockery of Sterne. Locke was enough for Sterne. Where most readers are bored by the pedestrian prolixity of the *Essay Concerning Human Understanding*, Sterne was spellbound by its comic potentialities. At the same time, as we know from Suard[1] he was fascinated in a more serious manner. Tristram, the first person narrator of the book and very close to Sterne, speaks thus of Locke's great work:

> Pray, Sir, in all the reading which you have ever read, did you ever read such a book as *Locke's* Essay upon the Human Understanding?–Don't answer me rashly,–because many, I know, quote the book, who have not read it,–and many have read it who understand it not:–if either of these is your case, as I write to instruct, I will tell you in three words what the book is.–It is a history.–A history! of who? what? where? when? Don't hurry yourself.–It is a history-book, Sir, (which may possibly recommend it to the world) of what passes in a man's own mind . . .[2]

[1] See M. Garat, *Mémoires Historiques sur la Vie de M. Suard...et sur le XVIIIe Siècle*, Paris, 1820, p. 149.

[2] *The Life and Opinions of Tristram Shandy, Gentleman*, vol. II, Ch. ii, in the edn. of J. A. Work, New York, 1940, p. 85.

A real admiration can be detected here, beneath the devious irony. The description of the *Essay* as a history is shrewd. There is certainly something not quite philosophical in Locke's constant tendency to reduce epistemology to the piece-meal description of psychological contents. The unconscious comedy of the *Essay* was not its only attraction for Sterne. It is likely that at times he laughed aloud as he read, but his reading was not frivolous.

But to find a parodist half in love with the object of his satire is not unusual. If anything, a kind of affectionate vigilance seems to be an advantage, as anyone who looks through a good anthology of parody can see for himself. Was Housman contemptuous of Greek tragedy? Or Beerbohm of Henry James?

In any case much more went into the making of *Tristram Shandy* than a humorous admiration of Locke. Whatever the complexity of Sterne's view of the *Essay*, he had room for other interests. So complex an edifice naturally required more varied materials: *The Life and Opinions of Tristram Shandy, Gentleman*, to give it its full, solemn title, is a literary freak, or, in the language of the old biologists, a sport, a *lusus ingenii*. Purporting to chronicle the life of a small-time country gentleman, it in fact proceeds on the dangerous assumption that narrative is subordinate to digression. Aristotle, speaking of characters, recommended[1] that they should be consistent, but allowed that in certain circumstances an inconsistent character might be admitted—so long, that is, as it was consistently inconsistent. One surmises that the principle can be extended to cover plot. If so, we may say that Sterne's book is so consistently extravagant as almost to satisfy the philosopher's requirement (though one imagines that the experience of reading *Tristram Shandy* would have left him feeling shaken). It seems that this negative principle of coherence can still be invoked to comfort the classicist mind. With a truly Gallic instinct for order, Henri Fluchère announces[2] that it is the method of insistent digression which gives *Tristram Shandy* its organic unity.

Yet it is doubtful whether this recovery on the part of the formalist critic would have been pleasing to Sterne. One suspects

---

[1] *Poetics*, 1454a.

[2] *Laurence Sterne: from Tristram to Yorick*, trans. and abridged by Barbara Bray, 1965, p. 42.

that he wished to provoke first of all bewilderment and last, perhaps, a grateful submissiveness before the rich indefinability of a crowded universe. This, at least, is the simplest interpretation of his rhetorical strategy, which is to offer himself to the reader as a man ingenuously eager to pursue a linear narrative but endlessly seduced and frustrated by intractable material. Occasionally, it is true, Tristram grows sophisticated (almost becomes identified with Sterne) and allows that the habit of digression has its pleasures:

> Could a historiographer drive on his history, as a muleteer drives on his mule,–straight forward;–for instance, from *Rome* all the way to *Loretto*, without ever once turning his head aside either to the right hand or to the left,–he might venture to foretell you to an hour when he should get to his journey's end;–but the thing is, morally speaking, impossible:[1]

It is especially tempting to believe that Sterne himself is speaking here and thus to milk every possible meaning from the paragraph. We might argue, for example, that it anticipates existentialism, with its artistic commitment to the unmanageable real. To make it all a little more respectable historically, we might say that in this covert but very serious pledge to avoid any premature distortion of reality in the interests of formal coherence we have the faint echo of an earlier pledge, more solemnly delivered, to eschew apriorism: *naturae enim non imperatur, nisi parendo.*[2]

It has become commonplace to observe that Bacon was *too* open-minded to advance in the sciences; that the men who made the scientific revolution were men with bees in their bonnets or, at least, with profoundly imaginative hypotheses constructed as a basis for *subsequent* experiment. But–so the argument runs– what is unhealthy for a youthful science may be very salutary for the artist, who, if he has the strength, will achieve his highest results where his range is widest. A Conrad may proceed by a method analogous to the controlled experiment of the scientist. He will isolate his creations on, say, a ship, or in the jungle,

[1] *Tristram Shandy*, I. xiv, p. 36.

[2] Francis Bacon, *Novum Organum*, Book I, Aphorism cxxix, in *The Works of Francis Bacon*, ed. J. Spedding, R. L. Ellis and D. D. Heath, vol. I, 1858, p. 222.

in order to find out what they are made of. A George Eliot, on the other hand, will mistrust such specialised methods of trial; for her, to find out what a person really is, one must exclude nothing; one must watch him in his ordinary environment, trace the minutiae of his life through all the complex interstices of the social web; and that means, not the Belgian Congo but Middlemarch. One is at once reminded of Bacon's plea, noted by Butterfield,[1] that scientists should 'load all the concreteness back' into their experiments. Thus the artificial exclusiveness of Conrad achieves much, but the promiscuity of George Eliot achieves more. Further, it is not just the question of range which is before us; in the artist's attitude to the individual person a parallel distinction can be drawn, though in drawing it we must discard Conrad for, say, Jane Austen. On the one hand there is the writer who so lays down the terms of his book that he can transfix his creations with a conclusive moral judgment; on the other hand there is the writer who, like Shakespeare, leaves us with a sense that there will always be more to be said concerning any of his characters, or even, like Sterne, humorously underlines his and our utter inability to know anyone 'through and through'. On such a reading, this paragraph of Sterne's must assume great importance as defining his artistic stance. The lightly colloquial phrase, 'morally speaking', directs our attention to a genuinely moral relationship, that between the writer and reality. And Sterne is telling us that the pressure of this unmanageable world induces in him more zest than rage, and that his book will not subdue but will instead explore. The tracks of the Roman roads across England display one attitude, the track pursued by Tristram's narrative another.[2] Christopher Ricks writes,[3] 'These days, Sterne is often reproached for immorality, but he seems to me triumphant in this most basic morality of all.' The morality Ricks means is humility before the unknowability of our fellow creatures.

It might be objected that to extract all this from so light-hearted a passage is injudicious. Sterne continues, after all, not

[1] See above, p. 21.

[2] The reader may consult Tristram's own map of the plot of *Tristram Shandy*, volume by volume, in VI.xl, p. 473.

[3] The Penguin English Library edn. of *Tristram Shandy*, ed. G. Petrie with an introduction by Christopher Ricks, 1967, p. 14.

with any sort of sermon on truthfulness but with some observations on the pleasures of turning aside for a chat, or of being seduced by the aesthetic allurements of the landscape: 'For, if he is a man of the least spirit, he will have fifty deviations from a straight line to make with this or that party as he goes along, which he can no ways avoid. He will have views and prospects to himself perpetually solliciting his eye, which he can no more help standing still to look at than he can fly . . .'[1] But it would be unreasonable to expect Sterne, working as he is from behind so frivolous a *persona*, to give us the conception of artistic duty he really holds; we must be content with the mere hint.

In fact, Ricks's thesis embodies an important though partial truth. The indefinite humanity of the inhabitants of Shandy Hall makes Tom Jones and Pamela look like cardboard cut-outs. A few visual details are lightly pencilled in, with the swift grace of a Hogarth sketch–almost always in connexion with the same character: Uncle Toby's 'plump and muscular' game leg; Uncle Toby in his 'great ramallie-wig', his 'tarnish'd gold-laced hat and huge cockade of flimsy taffeta', blue and gold regimentals and tattered scarlet breeches, carrying his cane like a pike, followed by the loyal Trim as they set off in full military order to lay siege to the widow Wadman; Uncle Toby settling himself in 'an old set-stitch'd chair, valanced and fringed around with party-colour'd worsted bobs' to comfort his prostrate brother.[2] We have an occasional glimpse of Trim, an undefeated, immemorially servile, jauntily military figure in his Montero-cap, and, moving nearer to the idiom of Gilray, of Dr Slop: 'of about four feet and a half perpendicular height, with a breadth of back and a sesquipedality of belly, which might have done honour to a serjeant in the horseguards'.[3] But, as in a certain kind of portrait the unfathomable eyes of the subject draw us into a region of psychological and spiritual possibilities where we forget the features, so in Sterne the caricaturist's art is transcended by the novelist's. And this, as everyone knows, is the art of exploring reality.

Further, not only is the basic sequence of events in *Tristram Shandy* quite free from any imposed formal symmetry but the

---

[1] *Tristram Shandy*, I.xiv, pp. 36–7.
[2] *Ibid.*, VIII.vi, p. 545; IX.ii, p. 601; III.xxix, p. 216.
[3] *Ibid.*, II.ix, p. 104.

way in which it is gradually revealed to us is artfully informal. A chronicle shows us a military campaign in due chronological order, but had we been present ourselves, even at the general's side, we should have learned things in a much more piece-meal fashion, rejoicing in a sudden advance before we knew why it had occurred, and so on. This is the difference, after all, between a natural process of learning and learning artificially controlled by a teacher. Nature does not tell us her secrets; we overhear them. Similarly, in reading *Tristram Shandy* we are placed in the position of an invisible intruder in Shandy Hall, a baffled eavesdropper whose curiosity is for some time frustrated by unintelligible family jokes. This too is a kind of realism. As in life, we see before we understand.

In this Sterne is of course years before his time. Conrad's *Nostromo* applies a similar technique to events on a national scale, so that one can scarcely grasp the historical sequence at a first reading. But the mere mention of *Nostromo* should cause us to pause. It is, after all, so very different from *Tristram Shandy*. We are prompted to ask: what is it that distinguishes *Tristram Shandy* from the 'chunk-of-undifferentiated-real-life' novel it so brilliantly anticipates?

The answer is that although *Tristram Shandy* does not impose a formal order, it nevertheless presupposes one as the norm from which it departs. It is this that makes the book a classic of comic rhetoric. There is, after all, something in the negative formal principle which pleased Fluchère. The world of Sterne's book is too obtrusively eccentric to be real, and eccentricity is obtrusive only when we are aware of a contrasting norm.

Yet here we encounter a difficulty. Anyone who reads *Tristram Shandy* in isolation will feel that he is reading an anti-novel, a book designed to subvert literary convention. Yet ever since the publication of John Ferriar's *Illustrations of Sterne* the informed reader has known that Sterne is, if not actually a plagiarist, at least an ardent disciple. The fact that his sources were themselves frequently comic serves only to render his docility the more striking. D. W. Jefferson has traced[1] one line

[1] 'Tristram Shandy and the tradition of learned wit', *Essays in Criticism*, I (1951), pp. 225–48; adapted as 'Tristram Shandy and its Tradition', in *From Dryden to Johnson*, vol. IV of the *Pelican Guide to English Literature*, ed. Boris Ford, 1957, pp. 333–45.

of Tristram's genealogy descending from Burton (the author of the *Anatomy of Melancholy*) and from Rabelais. Sterne's frequent visual jokes with typography, black pages, reticent asterisks and the like, which look so revolutionary, have been related by Hugh Kenner[1] to a tradition whose greatest member is Jonathan Swift. A whole army of literary eccentrics can be mustered from the seventeenth and eighteenth centuries, with Cervantes at the head and the egregious Thomas Amory bringing up the rear. On the other hand, the straight novel is still in its infancy. Even Fielding, whom we might be tempted to cite as providing a contrastingly normal sort of story, uses almost all the narrative devices which later appear in Sterne.[2] It is almost as if the eccentrics outnumber the solid citizens. So what is to become of our concept of eccentricity? We begin to suspect that we, who live in an age when every local library is crammed with novels of the utmost chronological docility, may find *Tristram Shandy* more startling than anyone could in 1760.

Yet this difficulty need not detain us long. If the novel were in its infancy the arts of history and biography were not. As soon as we recognise that the convention disrupted by *Tristram Shandy* is not that of 'the novel' but simply that of the linear narrative, we shall find nothing wrong in calling it an extravaganza. And of course it took London by storm. It may be that Sterne did little that had never been done before, but he did it more ingeniously and more comprehensively, and succeeded in astounding his public.

Our formula, then, is that *Tristram Shandy* is an ingeniously sustained disruption of the norm of linear narrative. As long as we confine ourselves to a 'purely literary' point of view, this formula will work. But as soon as we grant that *Tristram Shandy*, like every great work of literature, demands more than a merely literary treatment, we shall find that we must extend our terms. For Sterne's book is intellectually as well as formally extravagant, and here the norm presupposed is the rock-hard scientific world-picture which Locke had codified.

It would, however, be a mistake to conclude that *Tristram Shandy* is an unequivocal satire on that world-picture. The

---

[1] In his *Flaubert, Joyce and Beckett: the Stoic Comedians*, 1964.
[2] See Wayne C. Booth, 'The Self-conscious Narrator in Comic Fiction before *Tristram Shandy*', *PMLA*, LXVII (1952) pp. 163–85.

relation between comic extravagance and its presupposed norm is not invariably hostile. I have already said that Sterne's attitude to Locke was ambivalent and have no wish to retract the suggestion.

The problem can be studied in a conveniently limited form if we consider the genre of mock-heroic. The very word 'mock-heroic' implies that in such literature the heroic is mocked by the trivial. Our earliest specimens confirm this impression. In the *Batrachomyomachia* (or *Battle of the Frogs and Mice*) small animals are described in the sonorous hexameters of Homer, and by this means it is certainly Homer who is mocked, and not the animals. But by the time of Pope the situation is more complex. In *The Rape of the Lock* epic diction is again applied to trivial material, but now we notice that the satire is flowing in the opposite direction; it is not Homer but Miss Arabella Fermor who is mocked. Yet the reversal is not complete. The eighteenth century reader who knew his classics might well have extracted from Pope's apparatus of Sylphs, Gnomes, Nymphs and Salamanders a pleasure essentially similar to that of *Batrachomyomachia*. In one and the same work, therefore, the epic style can be seen as once the object and the instrument of mockery.

In much the same way, it is not always easy to tell where Locke is being satirised. The reader may suspect that Locke's 'association of ideas' is ridiculed in the hobby-horsical obsession of Uncle Toby or the Pavlovian reactions of Mrs Shandy (it will be remembered that because Walter Shandy always wound the clock and attended to certain 'other little family concernments'[1] on the same night of each month, Mrs Shandy could not think of clocks without thinking of sexual intercourse, and *vice versa*). Locke's chapter on association of ideas (II.xxxiii) does not appear in the first edition of the *Essay*. It was in fact added in the fourth edition (1695) and never played more than an accidental part in the author's scheme of things. It is evident at once that we are in a pre-Humian world. The author of the *Treatise* has not yet reduced our mental lives to 'impressions and ideas' of greater or less vivacity, linked more by Locke, just as for Sterne, mere association is a by-play of the mind, and so far from constituting our mental lives, it produces eccentricity

---

[1] *Tristram Shandy*, I.iv, p. 8.

and folly. Sterne's comic psychology of hobby-horses is thus a simple application of Lockian principles.

II

But Shandy Hall is remarkable for not only obsessional but also intellectual eccentricity, and in this league it must be granted that neither Mrs Shandy nor Uncle Toby can ever hold first place. When it comes to real, insuperable waywardness of mind it is Walter Shandy who carries off the palm. And here we see Sterne sharply diverging from Locke. Indeed, it is the ratiocinative intelligence which, escaping from the control of instinct and sentiment, is the true principle of chaos in *Tristram Shandy*. Sterne has here triumphed over Locke merely by exaggerating an absurdity already latent in the *Essay*. Locke's 'plain man' prose seemed to promise the reader a speedy resolution of all 'sophistical' difficulties. There is real comic pathos in his account of how his work began: 'When I put pen to paper, I thought all I should have to say on this matter would have been contained in one sheet of paper.'[1] As it turned out, each simple clarification required a supplement, until the *Essay* became at last a kind of monster, in detail luminous but as a whole rambling and unintelligible. In structure the *Essay* is thus curiously like *Tristram Shandy*. Considered as comedy, it differs from the latter chiefly by having a more successfully dead-pan style (sufficiently so, indeed, to deceive its author).

However, some comic strokes were reserved for Sterne alone. Where Locke had argued philosophically that man is isolated from the world of material objects, Sterne, casually assuming the truth of common sense, has caused Walter Shandy to be isolated, *qua* philosopher. To begin with he borrows from Locke the notion that the thoughts of others are hidden from us (it is a passage I have already had occasion to quote): 'Man, though he have great variety of thoughts, and such from which others as well as himself might receive profit and delight; yet they are all within his own breast, invisible and hidden from others, nor can of themselves be made to appear.'[2] But Sterne has perceived that such a doctrine can be turned round and pointed at

---

[1] Epistle to the Reader, prefixed to the *Essay*, in Fraser's edn., vol. I, p. 10.
[2] *Essay*, III.ii.1, in Fraser's edn., vol. II, p. 8.

its author. If all our thoughts are private in this way, it can be argued (though Locke himself did not license the inference) that our thoughts are essentially incommunicable. There is no reason why this should not apply as much to a philosophical system as to, say, a twinge of repulsion. Sterne has remained a decent Lockian just long enough to transfix his master. The philosophical doctrine of privacy is accepted, but only in one single application—to the theorising philosopher himself. As Walter Shandy indefatigably assaults his complacent family with volleys of Lockian notions, one is reminded of the solipsistic philosopher who, according to current legend, wrote to an academic journal complaining that there were not more young solipsists about.

Of course such an account of Walter's function in the book is misleading. It makes *Tristram Shandy* sound far neater and more self-consciously critical than it really is. The notion of isolation is not applied to Walter with anything like full philosophical rigour. His separation from his fellow creatures is not an analytic consequence of his psycho-physical structure, but is rather a synthetic fact, which it would be quite possible to imagine reversed (possible, but not easy: try writing a paragraph in which Uncle Toby suddenly and perfectly follows his brother's reasoning—'Why, brother Shandy, I understand your drift *etc.*'—one cannot bring oneself to do it). Of course it is only the synthetic sort of isolation that can be presented imaginatively. Strictly speaking, therefore, Walter Shandy if he is an embodied mockery of Locke, is a highly figurative one. But as long as language is used in an unspecialised fashion, Sterne's gambit is effective. The intelligent eighteenth-century reader could certainly have said to himself 'Here Locke is overturned, for where he saw the exercise of philosophic reason as everywhere productive of light, toleration and amity, Sterne hath shown ratiocination—and not just the obsolete reasonings of the Schoolmen but of the moderns also—to lead a man to lose his fellow creatures in chasing moonbeams.'

Thus, while Locke retained his faith in the intellect and mistrusted the sub-rational part of the human mind, Sterne may be said to have presented the opposite view.

This suggestion that Sterne is a man who has intellectually lost his nerve may surprise some readers but really should not.

His attitude to the world of philosophy is very like his attitude to the world of theology–a sort of faintly hysterical flippancy. Christopher Ricks has brilliantly described *Tristram Shandy* as filled with a 'profane zest for theological speculation'.[1] The whole ethos of the book, the queer hilarity of intellect, the juggling with philosophical systems, presuppose an arid disbelief in the truth or usefulness of philosophy.

Of course there is one sense of the word 'philosopher' which wins from Sterne a very different response. The best definition is Sam Weller's:

> 'You are quite a philosopher, Sam', said Mr Pickwick. 'It runs in the family, I b'lieve, sir,' replied Mr Weller. 'My father's very much in that line, now. If my mother-in-law blows him up, he whistles. She flies in a passion, and breaks his pipe; he steps out and gets another. Then she screams wery loud, and falls into 'sterics and he smokes very comfortably 'till she comes to again. That's philosophy, sir, an't it?'[2]

Sam Weller, in describing his father, has described Tristram's Uncle Toby. To such philosophy as this, certainly, Sterne is willing to give ingenuous praise, as to true wisdom. It is, of course, philosophy entirely innocent of ratiocination. Philosophy in the more academic sense remains, in *Tristram Shandy*, a far less happy thing, having nothing to do with Toby's sociable stoicism. Walter typically expresses dissent from his brother with a regretful ' 'Tis a pious account, but not philosophical.'[3] The epigraph from Epictetus which appears on the title-page of the first volume is really very important (I have translated it): 'Men are harried, not so much by things, as by their notions of things.' Sterne does for the philosophico-scientific world-view of his contemporaries very much what Rabelais did for the Scholastic world-view of his predecessors; he celebrates its dissolution with a pyrotechnic display of impotent learning.

Thus, Henri Fluchère makes a serious mistake when he compares the mindless Mrs Shandy to Buridan's ass.[4] Buridan's

---

[1] Introduction to the Penguin *Tristram Shandy*, p. 11.
[2] *The Pickwick Papers*, Ch. xvi, the Oxford Illustrated Dickens, p. 209.
[3] *Tristram Shandy*, III.xli, p. 240.
[4] *Laurence Sterne*; *de l'homme à l'œuvre*, p. 500; in Barbara Bray's translation, p. 293.

ass is the beast who, when equally large bundles of hay were placed at an equal distance from him, having no preponderant reason to choose one rather than the other, starved to death.[1] Thus the whole point about Buridan's ass is that he was too rational. It is the sort of legend which naturally attaches itself to the excessively cerebral. Some years ago there was a story current about a distinguished lady philosopher who said to a pupil, 'One of those chairs is broken; I don't know which, so you'd better not sit down.' This sort of thing is scarcely applicable to poor Mrs Shandy, whose chief vice in her husband's eyes was that she would never ask the meaning of a word she did not know.[2] Fluchère's choice is the more perverse since there is already in the book a perfect candidate for the comparison. Walter Shandy could be confidently predicted to behave like Buridan's ass at every opportunity. Sterne in fact gives us a perfect example. When in volume IV Walter cannot decide whether to fence in and cultivate the Ox-moor or to send young Bobby abroad, he is, inevitably, paralysed. Tristram feelingly describes his father's condition: 'No body, but he who has felt it, can conceive what a plaguing thing it is to have a man's mind torn asunder by two projects of equal strength, both obstinately pulling in a contrary direction at the same time. . . .'[3] In Walter Shandy, as in no one else at Shandy Hall, action is conditional on reason, and it is almost too much for him.

In most respects (though not in all, as we shall see later) Sterne was in fact an outsider in the earnestly mechanist world of his time. We seem to catch the author's own words coming from the mouth of Tristram in Volume VII, chapter xxx (p. 519):

> Now, of all things in the world, I understand the least of mechanism—I have neither genius, or taste, or fancy—and have a brain so entirely unapt for every thing of that kind, that I solemnly declare I was never yet able to comprehend the principles of motion of a squirrel cage, or a common knife-grinder's wheel—

Parson Yorick, who is the other half of Sterne, betrays the same mental bias (but here the hostility is directed at the opposite

---

[1] The idea can be traced back to Aristotle (*De Caelo*, 295B32).
[2] *Tristram Shandy*, VI.xxxix, p. 472.
[3] *Ibid.*, IV.xxxi, pp. 335–6.

end of the rationalist spectrum); '. . . I wish there was not a polemic divine, said *Yorick*, in the kingdom;—one ounce of practical divinity—is worth a painted ship load of all their reverences have imported these fifty years.'[1] This has at once a bright and a dark side. Yorick clearly cares about the happiness of real human beings. Yet it is a sad state of affairs if charity must entail a complacent contempt for rational enterprise. It is, of course, very English. This is the authentic voice of that nation which, in opposition to the Europe of Descartes, Leibniz and Spinoza, produced John Locke, the genius of muddling through. But it also belongs to a narrower tradition, since it is essentially linked, as I have already suggested, to Sterne's comic method of learned wit. John Donne, who, like Sterne, tended to think of metaphysics primarily as the material of wit and epigram, expressed very similar views: 'Morall Divinity becomes us all; but Naturall Divinity and Metaphysick Divinity, almost all may spare.'[2] One begins to suspect that *Tristram Shandy* is at its deepest level more concerned with happiness than truth. The whole book seems to have been written as a sort of hedonistic device, an elaborate eighteenth century apparatus for combating melancholy. It is after all the beginning of the age in which hedonism was to be almost reduced to a science by the ingenious Utilitarians. We may think of Jeremy Bentham, who carried his technique successfully into the smallest details of everyday life:

> A serious joyless boy, he became a gay and whimsical old man . . . although he continued to wear black suits, he now added a broad-brimmed yellow straw hat and embroidered carpet slippers to his costume. He began to invent playful names for common objects. He never went anywhere without 'Dapple', his walking-stick, or 'Dick', his sacred tea-pot. Though he had always been fond of mice and cats and admitted that 'it was hard to reconcile the two affections', he now knighted his favourite cat 'Sir John Langborn'. As 'Sir John' grew older and more sedate, he became 'Reverend' and finally 'Reverend Doctor Sir John Langborn'. Bentham's dining-room was named 'the shop'; the table

---

[1] *Ibid.*, V.xxviii, p. 387.
[2] *Essays in Divinity* (1651), ed. E. M. Simpson, 1952, p. 88. See Helen Gardner's edn. of Donne's *Divine Poems*, 1952, p. xix.

was raised on a platform surrounded by a sunken walking passage named the 'vibrating ditch' or 'the well'. His work desk was 'the Caroccio'.

He often sang humorous little songs, composed on the spur of the moment, and he revelled in rituals. Daily he took a 'post-prandial circumgyration' and nightly he went to bed in a one-hour ceremony. After he had undressed and tied on a night-cap, his watch was delivered to a secretary, or 'reprobate', who then read aloud to him. Each of Bentham's amanuenses had to 'swear fealty to a *trinoda necessitas*—the asportation of the window—the transtration of the window—idem of the trap window'. Finally he climbed into a sleeping sack of his own design.[1]

Perhaps it was really from soil like this that *Tristram Shandy* grew. No-one who examines the circumstances of its composition will be able to blame Sterne for it. It is if anything an admirable memorial to his stoic fortitude. When philosophy means cheerfulness and courage, it is commended by Sterne, for it makes men happy. When philosophy means speculative ratiocination, it is satirised, for it makes men miserable. The two definitions of philosophy, Sam Weller's and Epictetus's, are placed for us in formal opposition by Sterne himself. Walter Shandy, exasperated beyond endurance by Toby's incapacity for abstract thought, bites Mrs Shandy's pin-cushion in two and fills his mouth with bran: 'By all that's good and great, Brother *Toby*, said my father, if it was not for the aids of philosophy, which befriend one so much as they do,—you would put a man beside all temper.'[2] Sterne artfully makes us feel that the true source of mental distress is not Uncle Toby but his own itch for rational speculation. And all the while that true philosopher (of the other stamp, of course) is smoking his pipe in complete equanimity.

In the practical art of living, then, a high I.Q. is no advantage. There is a memorable passage in Boswell's *Life of Johnson* in which the Doctor runs into a half-forgotten friend of his youth, a Mr Oliver Edwards. Edwards, manifestly unable to keep up with Johnson's intelligence, observes 'You are a philosopher,

[1] Mary Mack, *Jeremy Bentham: an Odyssey of Ideas*, 1748–92, London, 1962, pp. 6–7.
[2] *Tristram Shandy*, III.xli, p. 240.

Dr Johnson. I have tried too in my time to be a philosopher; but, I don't know how, cheerfulness was always breaking in.'[1] To anyone familiar with Shandy Hall the comedy of this is curiously poignant. For Dr Johnson's friend was *an Uncle Toby who would have liked to be a Walter Shandy.*

So far I have emphasised the satirical or hostile element in Sterne's use of the scientific world-view. It is time to redress the balance. One way of doing this (it may appear unnecessarily devious) is to tackle the question: 'Why is Sterne not a stream of consciousness writer?' Of course, according to the basic sense of the words, he very nearly is just this. In so far as we can claim that the second-by-second ticking over of the mind is as much a matter of ratiocinative windings, associative caprice, of flashback and prolepsis, as it is of imagery and impressions, so far might we extend the description 'stream of consciousness' to *Tristram Shandy.* The trouble is that the course of literary history has given the phrase a technical meaning, much as criticism of Donne and his followers gave the word 'metaphysical' a technical meaning. I believe my own mind rattles on in a manner more akin to *Tristram Shandy* than to *Ulysses.* But James Joyce and Virginia Woolf have been allowed to define the terms. They have achieved a more-than-Baconian receptivity to the flow of images and impressions only by the very un-Baconian exclusion of the ordering intellect. The result is a strangely luminous series of richly tinted 'experiences' suspended in a sort of vacuum. Mr Ramsay in *To the Lighthouse* is isolated not only from his family but from his creator also. For Mr Ramsay is a philosopher, a ratiocinative man, and yet, because of Virginia Woolf's fictional method, we can never know the real character of his thought. Instead, she is driven back upon diagram and allegory, so that in one place we are told that Mr Ramsay, having attained Q, is unable to proceed to R, and in another that he is on a journey in which at a certain point he must tether his horse and continue on foot.[2] The author can no more tell us what Q *is* than a Flatlander can describe a globe. Yet the third dimension of rational thought is the common possession of us all. The stream of consciousness novelist (in this

[1] April 17th, 1778, in the edn. of G. Birkbeck Hill, revised and enlarged by L. F. Powell, 1934, vol. III, p. 305.
[2] *Op. cit.*, 1927, pp. 56–9 and 71.

sense) must begin his quest for the truly open mind by locking up the intellect, much as the liberal must begin his abolition of authority by forcibly locking up the Fascist. But in literature the expense is heavy. There is a higher pathos in the would-be coherent incoherence of *Tristram Shandy* than in the licensed flux of *Ulysses*. Our question has now answered itself. Sterne is not a stream of consciousness novelist because he admits the stream of ratiocination.

It is true that the reasoning he shows us is a tissue of eccentric impotence; thus far we must admit that his attitude is implicitly destructive of scientific rationalism. But if we compare the view of the mind offered in *Tristram Shandy* with that bequeathed to us by Hume, we may well feel that it is Sterne's account which is friendlier to the great intellectual enterprise of the seventeenth century. Hume's philosophy fragmented the world into a series of discrete experiences, having no logical connexion but woven by the imagination into a web of fictitious causality. If Tristram's endless reasonings were represented as operating upon an utterly disconnected world, to which intelligence is inapplicable, then he might have ranked with Hume as a radical destroyer. But in fact the rationalist, subjective aspect of Tristram's world is answered by an objective universe of endlessly interlocking causes. Tristram is powerless to combat the malignant chains of circumstance which persecute him, but he understands them very well. I have said that Sterne had lost faith in the competence of reason. This assertion can now be made more precise. Sterne had lost faith in the *utility* of reason, but not in its power to apprehend. In the Humian world of ideas and impressions, distinguished merely by their greater or less vivacity, there is nothing to understand, just as, in a sense, the stream of consciousness novelist can describe, but cannot explain.

To be sure, it has been said that Tristram inhabits a world 'of contingency incarnate'.[1] But what is true of Sartre's Roquentin (or rather what Roquentin thinks is true of Roquentin) is not true of Tristram. In Sartre the will is supposed to be paramount in an arbitrary world; in *Tristram Shandy* human beings are comically paralysed by causes beyond their control.

---

[1] B. H. Lehman, 'Of Time, Personality and the Author, a Study of *Tristram Shandy*', *Studies in the Comic, University of California Studies in English*, VIII, no. 2 (Berkeley, 1941), pp. 233–50.

The famous opening of the book makes this clear. The gist of Tristram's complaint is that his mother's distracting remark at the moment of conception caused the animal spirits (whose hearty co-operation is essential in the production of a sound foetus) to disperse, so that Tristram sets out in life on half-rations, so to speak. We are moving into a universe in which genes, chromosomes, determinants and receptives are to become the disposers of human fate.

III

The inexorable character of causality in *Tristram Shandy* becomes still clearer if we look at Sterne's treatment of time. Just as the rhetoric of extravagance would be unintelligible without an understood norm, so the brilliant to-and-fro of Tristram's narrative would lose its comic force if there were not a hard chronological sequence plainly visible beneath it. Baird and Fluchère have shown[1] that Sterne (though he made a couple of mistakes) took great pains over this basic 'real' sequence. The narrative technique of hopping from one place to another makes chronological time appear, as Fluchère puts it, 'comme les morceaux d'un puzzle frappés de la même apparente immobilité'.[2] Perhaps the most vivid instance of this time-travelling is the Baroque vignette in volume VI[3] in which the funeral of Uncle Toby, years hence, is foreseen. It is one of the most brilliant things in the book. I have called it Baroque, and indeed its funerary imagery—the velvet pall, the military ensigns—are described with a certain zest which recalls the spirited collaboration of Vanbrugh and Grinling Gibbons at Blenheim Palace. Yet we are also shown what Vanbrugh would have excluded, Walter Shandy miserably wiping his spectacles. Sterne's sentiment has here had a genuinely humanising effect. And the result of it all is a special sort of vividness. We feel that we have glimpsed, in brilliantly illuminated detail, a scene at the far end of a long tunnel.

[1] 'The time scheme of Tristram Shandy and a Source', *PMLA*, LI (September 1936), pp. 803–20; Henri Fluchère, *Laurence Sterne: de l'homme a l'œuvre*, pp. 307 f., in Barbara Bray's translation, pp. 104 f.

[2] 'As odd pieces of a puzzle all frozen into the same immobility', *ibid.* p. 312.

[3] *Tristram Shandy*, VI.xxv, p. 452.

Thus we are presented with something very like scientific determinism. The universe is a huge, variegated block consisting of innumerable interlocking parts, extending into time and space. It is, so to speak, causally constipated. Like Laplace's omniscient observer[1] who could predict the state of the universe a thousand years hence merely by computing the direction and velocity of its constituent atoms, Tristram can spotlight any section he likes of his story. It is all there, and nothing can be done to make it otherwise than it is. Which is not what contingent means.

Of course such scientific determinism is very different from older forms of fatalism. Even astrological determinism, attacked by Christian orthodoxy at the Renascence for its erosion of free will, is almost amiable compared with this blind and faceless tyranny of causes. For the stars, though they might encroach on the intelligence of man, were themselves intelligences. This meant that they were actuated by motives, had good, intelligible reasons for the actions they instigated. Such a scheme naturally retains certain features comforting to human reason. The subjected mind can still make sense of things, can distinguish the important event from the trivial. But to the scientific determinist there is no such thing as a triviality. In the bleak democracy of physical causes the snapping of a needle is level with the execution of a Caesar. Sergeant Cuff, a fair specimen of the tradition, explained the point to Superintendent Seegrave.[2] Hume, with more sense of the implications of what he was doing, affirmed that there could be no distinction between important causes and trivial occasions.[3] Sterne, by tracing great events back, not to the will of God or the hostility of a demon but to the mispronunciation of a maidservant or the slip of an obstetrician's hand, has discovered the cosmology appropriate to farce. No-one can appear heroic whose felicity depends upon such things.

The fact that Sterne finds a comic use for such concatenations of causes does not necessarily mean that he doubted their existence. In *Tristram Shandy* they are both remorseless and

---

[1] See his *A Philosophical Essay on Probabilities*, trans. F. W. Truscott and F. L. Emory, 1902, p. 4.

[2] Wilkie Collins, *The Moonstone*, 1873, Part I, Ch. xii, p. 92.

[3] *Treatise*, III.xiv, p. 171.

trivial, but they never seem unreal. One senses that they are rather productive of satire than its object.

There is a further, more tenuous analogy between the artistic method of Sterne and the practice of contemporary natural philosophers which I myself hardly know whether to trust. Nevertheless, it may be mentioned as a bare conjecture. Once more, however, my explanation must be devious. I must link Sterne's technique with that of the visual arts before I relate both to the scientist.

One of the most marked characteristics of Sterne's way of telling a story is the freedom with which he manipulates tempo. A journey across half France will be swallowed up in a dozen pages, but the clearing of a throat can fill a chapter. Sometimes this arises from the mad scrupulousness with which Tristram sticks to the principle that everything–even to the precise inflection of Uncle Toby's voice as he suggests that they ring the bell[1]–must be exhaustively explained. At other times it is due to a more mysterious impulse to give a minute physical description of an individual figure. The twentieth-century reader, accustomed to fiction which steers a decent middle course between these extremes, can turn slightly giddy. One has just told oneself that this is an eighteenth-century novel in which we are to be given little or no description of the physical appearance of things–and forthwith one is presented with an account[2] of, say, Trim's precise attitude, as he prepares to read a sermon, which is far more elaborate than anything we should find in a modern novel. Naturally, the passage is too long to quote, but it includes such observations as that Trim's body was bent forwards just so far as to make an angle of 85 degrees with the horizon, his right leg was firm and supporting seven-eighths of his weight, his left leg somewhat advanced, one hand held before his breast and the other hanging at his side. One registers the parody of the kind of scientist (by this time old-fashioned) who wished wholly to reduce the world to its mathematically expressible properties, one mentally compares it with Swift's story of the tailor on Laputa who took his customer's attitude by a quadrant before he cut his cloth,[3] and then, having noticed all this, one realises

[1] *Tristram Shandy*, I.xxi, p. 63–II.vi, p. 99.   [2] *Ibid.*, II.xvii, pp. 120–3.
[3] *Gulliver's Travels*, III.ii, in Harold Williams's edn., 1941, p. 146.

that there is something more. In fact, one perceives a residuum of sheer naturalism in Sterne which is absent from Swift. Swift's *attention* is all upon the Royal Society, Sterne's *eye* is on Trim.

Now this sort of attentiveness to the purely phenomenal is something we are more accustomed to find in the visual arts than in literature. I suppose the nearest written equivalent will be found in several attempts made in the eighteenth century to capture the technique of actors. A key-passage (which post-dates *Tristram Shandy*) is Lichtenberg's description of Garrick.[1] Sterne (himself a reasonably accomplished draughtsman) frequently directs our attention to painters or engravers at these moments in his book. Mrs Shandy, who is frozen for our visual dissection as she bends to listen at a door, is compared with an intaglio,[2] Walter Shandy with a figure in Raphael's *School of Athens*:

> My father instantly exchanged the attitude he was in, for that in which *Socrates* is so finely painted by *Raffael* in his school of *Athens*; which your connoisseurship knows is so exquisitely imagined, that even the particular manner of the reasoning of *Socrates* is expressed by it—for he holds the fore-finger of his left-hand between the fore-finger and the thumb of his right, and seems as if he was saying to the libertine he is reclaiming—'*You grant me* this—and this: and this, and this, I don't ask of you—they follow of themselves, in course.'
>
> So stood my father, holding fast his fore-finger betwixt his finger and his thumb, and reasoning with my uncle *Toby*, as he sat in his old fringed chair, valanced around with party-coloured worsted bobs—[3]

Sterne is naturally inclined—it is part of his comic rhetoric—to draw his similes from the classic art of antiquity or Renascence Italy. It does not follow that these periods will provide the closest analogies to what Sterne, as an artist, was really doing. Sudden enlargement and intensification of the trivial is foreign to the homogeneous lucidity of classical art. Even Turner's

---

[1] See the second of his *Letters from England* (October 10th, 1775), in *Gesammelte Werke*, ed. Wilhelm Granzmann, Baden–Baden, 1944, vol. I, pp. 976–87. See also J. P. Stern, *Lichtenberg: a Doctrine of Scattered Occasions*, 1963, pp. 28 f.

[2] *Tristram Shandy*, V.v, p. 357.   [3] *Ibid.*, IV.vii, p. 278.

'interiors' at Petworth, in which, say, the corner of a sofa is dimly discerned through the oceanic spray of tempestuous light, is in certain respects closer than anything by Raphael to what Sterne is getting at. But the best analogy is with the genre painting of Holland. We may recall how the young Rembrandt liked to give point to his lovingly observed scenes of common life by echoing in them the grand postures of the Italian Renascence.[1] But, just possibly, we may think of Vermeer.

It was at one time fashionable (it was a period of reaction against Victorianism) to draw a harsh contrast between the art of the novelist, laden with morality and ideas, and the art of the painter, austerely concerned with pure appearance. Vermeer was thought an example especially favourable to this view. Today we are beginning to see how Vermeer's paintings were enjoyed in his own day from a far more moralistic point of view than we had supposed. To be sure, Vermeer, the country-man and contemporary of the great Huygenius who half-transformed, half-created the science of optics, is interested in the minute, empirical exploration of light. But he is also interested in the object illuminated, and, where that object is human, he is interested in its humanity. Thus the same painting combines a treatise on the diffusion of light with a sermon on drunkenness. He places his severe, defining right angle with the instinct of a master of form, but he chooses his moment—the opening of a letter, or the raising of a glass—with the instinct of a novelist. Thus, if we fairly acknowledge both the human interest of Vermeer and Sterne's minute analysis of the phenomenal, the two artists will be found to have moved surprisingly close together. Of course the nervous hilarity of Sterne continues to divide them; yet both artists—and this is the point—seem to bring to bear on their material a sort of electrically brilliant attention. It suggests the specialised observation of the scientist rather than the social awareness of the ordinary man. Thus, although Sterne could not comprehend the mystery of any piece of mechanism, he could, when he chose, see like a scientist. I have said that Sterne's picture of the funeral of Uncle Toby is like something glimpsed at the end of a tunnel. It would be more precise to say that it is like something

[1] See Sir Kenneth Clark, *Rembrandt and the Italian Renaissance*, 1966, Ch. 1.

c

examined through a telescope—more precise, since by means of
this analogy we catch the peculiar quality of an object, in
itself remote, suddenly subjected to close-up scrutiny. Vermeer,
we know, delighted in the use of the *camera obscura*. Sterne
writes as though he were using some mysterious equivalent
device. It was his tragedy (but also his triumph) that he lived
before the invention of the tape-recorder, the machine which
actually enables us to retrieve fragments of conversation from
fugitive or forgotten situations.

To find a literary analogue to this special intensity of perception is much harder. Pope's *The Rape of the Lock* is a possible
case; Pope, like Sterne, grows at times so spellbound with the
surfaces of things that he forgets his satirical duty (which is,
of course, to strip away, to flay and to expose):

> For lo! the Board with Cups and Spoons is crown'd,
> The Berries crackle, and the Mill turns round.
> On shining Altars of *Japan* they raise
> The silver Lamp; the fiery Spirits blaze.
> From silver Spouts the grateful Liquors glide,
> While *China's* Earth receives the Smoking Tyde.[1]

This passage, the critics tell us, mocks the pretentiousness of
polite society. Yet it is also a rendering of pure sheen and
texture which anticipates impressionism. The allusion to far-off
places is of course a satirical device designed to intensify by
contrast the superficiality of the coffee-party. Yet at one
imaginative level (and I cannot feel that it is the least
important) it has had an opposite effect: it has exalted a glittering eighteenth-century group of ladies and gentlemen to the
level of a sort of vision; the fragile porcelain (which has, after
all, really come from China) becomes an exotic marvel, the object
as much of a delighted visual wonder as of intellectual mockery.
It is strange that satire, which is the art of penetrating the
superficies, should be transcended by an art confined to mere
surface, yet it is so. Pope found that the vistas provided by
seeing through things can be less ample than those we get from
just seeing.

But Pope, though he goes beyond Sterne in his preoccupation

[1] Canto III, 105–10, in Geoffrey Tillotson's second Twickenham edn.,
1954, p. 173.

with light, scarcely merits a comparison, however conjectural, with the contemporary scientist. For one thing, he lacks Sterne's half-humorous fascination with the precision afforded by mathematics. For another, the method of expansion and contraction, magnification and diminution is not pursued by him with anything like Sterne's virtuosity. When Sterne wrote the account, which Paul Stapfer discovered, of his dream about an orchard, he quoted Pope's 'And now a Bubble burst, and now a world', but as soon as we read the whole passage, we see that this is not Sterne drawing strength from Pope. It is rather the other way round; Pope's line takes on an added power from its remarkable context. It is Sterne who propels the reader's imagination from the armies of Alexander to the insects on a leaf, and thence to 'a huge noise and fragor in the skys'.[1]

In *Tristram Shandy* this technique is ubiquitous. At the beginning of the book we are invited to consider the bizarre possibility that human spermatozoa consist of minute human beings—*homunculi*—and are thus introduced at once to the mind-stretching alternation of macro- and microscopic writing which is to prevail from here on. At one level, Uncle Toby's miniature campaigns on the bowling green are a tiny replica of the great Duke of Marlborough's campaigns, at another Dr Slop's forceps are blown up by the writer to fill as much space as Tristram's entire formal education. Attention can assume many forms. In Sterne it constantly recalls that *redisposition of reality which suggests itself to a scientist working with lenses.*

There is indeed one place where Sterne's imagination actually overtakes the specialised empiricism of science, and runs ahead into the undiscovered country of science-fiction. He begins with an essentially satirical idea; that if people were made of glass one could read their inmost thoughts; but, just as Swift became engrossed with the mere wonder of 'big men and little men' (as Johnson scornfully put it[2]) so Sterne's eye is caught and held by the picture of people made of glass:

> —But this is an advantage not to be had by the biographer in this planet,—in the planet *Mercury* (belike) it may be so,

[1] See Paul Stapfer, *Laurence Sterne, sa Personne et ses Ouvrages*, Paris, 1870, pp. xi, xvi–xlix.

[2] See Boswell's *Life*, March 24, 1775, in G. Birkbeck Hill's edn., 1935, vol. II, p. 319.

if not better still for him;—for there the intense heat of the country, which is proved by computators, from its vicinity to the sun, to be more than equal to that of red hot iron,— must, I think, long ago have vitrified the bodies of the inhabitants, (as the efficient cause) to suit them for the climate (which is the final cause); so that, betwixt them both, all the tenements of their souls, from top to bottom, may be nothing else, for aught the soundest philosophy can shew to the contrary, but one fine transparent body of clear glass (bating the umbilical knot);—so, that till the inhabitants grow old and tolerably wrinkled, whereby the rays of light, in passing through them, become so monstrously refracted,—or return reflected from their surfaces in such transverse lines to the eye, that a man cannot be seen thro';—his soul might as well, unless, for more ceremony, —or the trifling advantage which the umbilical point gave her,—might, upon all other accounts, I say, as well play the fool out o'doors as in her own house.[1]

IV

It begins to look as if Sterne's relation to the natural philosophy of his time is far from simple. In a way he is its court-jester, nourished by the benevolently powerful object of his mockery. I have argued that the determinism of *Tristram Shandy* is to be distinguished, as being 'scientific', from the teleological schemes of older philosophers. Yet it may be that at a deeper level this description would have to be reversed. Although the scientists of the seventeenth century were almost unanimous in rejecting the final causes of the Schoolmen, their real enemy was not teleology as such but merely that form of it which predetermined every investigation to a Christian conclusion. And even in this, if Whitehead is right, they may have been guilty of a certain ingratitude. Whitehead claimed[2] that the scientific revolution was, at bottom, the natural consequence of mediaeval Christianity; the reason is comparatively simple. If a man believes that the universe is a mere complex series of fortuitous events, he has little motive for sustained investigation. But if he believes that the universe was made by an

---

[1] *Tristram Shandy*, I.xxiii, pp. 74–5.
[2] In his *Science and the Modern World*, 1936.

intelligent and purposeful God, he has every reason for looking beneath the surface of things for their latent rationale. On such a view it must appear that David Hume's philosophy, that strange grandchild of seventeenth-century empiricism, is ultimately less friendly to the progress of a growing science than is the philosophy of Aquinas. This view is not extravagant. E. A. Burtt has observed[1] that a modern empiricist, transported to the time of Galileo and Copernicus, would not have advanced science an inch. It appears that the greatest scientific discoveries, though ultimately confirmed by experiment, are founded on an extra-empirical expectation of design. Nor did this fact wholly escape the eighteenth century. Dr Johnson made his Imlac say, 'What reason did not dictate reason cannot explain.'[2] And indeed the whole horror of the Humian universe is that it can only be described, and can never be explained. The scientist who does not explain is scarcely worthy of the name, which is one reason why Linnaean botany is so far below physics in the modern hierarchy of the sciences. The principle that nature does nothing in vain is a teleological myth which is fundamental in the structure of scientific thought.

There is no doubt that such an account would surprise many of the scientists themselves. It certainly implies that numerous pronouncements, by scientists, designed to protect intellectual integrity, were anti-scientific in their unconscious tendency. Thus we classed Sterne's levelling of causes as an instance of his harmony with contemporary science, and this is true in so far that many scientists would have been willing to endorse it. But by Whitehead's theory, any such reduction of the universe to a chain of causally potent trivia must ultimately prove fatal to the proper aspirations of science. How, then, are we to classify the following paragraph?

> We live in a world beset on all sides with mysteries and riddles – and so 'tis no matter – else it seems strange, that Nature, who makes every thing so well to answer its destination, and seldom or never errs, unless for pastime, in giving such forms and aptitudes to whatever passes

[1] *The Metaphysical Foundations of Modern Physical Science*, 2nd edn., 1932, p. 25.
[2] *Rasselas*, Ch. xlvii, in R. W. Chapman's edn., 1927, p. 213.

through her hands, that whether she designs for the
plough, the caravan, the cart—or whatever other creature
she models, be it but an asse's foal, you are sure to have
the thing you wanted; and yet at the same time should so
eternally bungle it as she does, in making so simple a thing
as a married man.[1]

Here a solemn exordium on the theme of *Natura nil agit
frustra* (momentarily qualified by the confession that she also
enjoys her *lusus*—'unless for pastime') is overturned by the
counter-example of the married man, a topsy-turvy phenomenon
for which there is no accounting. Here, oddly enough, it is the
teleological passage which 'sounds scientific' and the confession
of anomaly which sounds like surrender. If all animals were
lusus naturae, that is, freakish products of her 'pastime' rather
than her serious design, there could be no biology, for there
would be no species and no ground for assuming even that one
skeleton would resemble another.

In the second century BC the librarian of Pergamum, one
Crates of Mallos, engaged in a philosophical dispute with the
librarian of Alexandria, the famous Aristarchus.[2] The two men
differed over the nature of language. Aristarchus held the
'theory of analogy' according to which the structure of language
is an intelligible system of repeatable relations. Crates upheld
the 'theory of anomaly' according to which language is a
merely random assemblage of speech units. Crates was able to
present a spuriously impressive front, which combined disarming intellectual modesty with an appearance of cynical sophistication. His pervasive scepticism was utterly unfruitful.
Aristarchus on the other hand had the faith which moves
mountains. He persistently sought the latent, unifying principle
beneath the seemingly chaotic surface and laid the basis of all
subsequent philology.

This far-off war of the grammarians is curiously instructive.
Aristotle held that knowledge which dispensed with the intel-
ligible reason of things was scarcely worth calling knowledge.
To our awareness of the 'that' of things must be added a

---

[1] *Tristram Shandy*, IX.xxii, p. 625.
[2] A brief account of the controversy can be found in Sir John Edwin
Sandys's *A History of Classical Scholarship*, 1921, vol. I, pp. 156 f.

penetration of the 'wherefore'.[1] He was very clear that this went for the scientist, just as much as it went for the metaphysician. The fate of Crates of Mallos may make us pause and wonder whether the scientists of the seventeenth century who so clamorously disclaimed interest in the 'wherefore' of things were not cutting the ground from under their feet. When their position was carried to its natural conclusion by Hume it proved intellectually paralysing.

It may seem that we have wandered a long way from Sterne. But look again at the paragraph in which reverence before the majestic design of Nature is gradually broken up in chuckles at her frivolity. Sterne knows which way the wind is blowing. We shall never find in him the petrific clarity of Hume, but we easily discover an instinctive awareness that if we lose our faith in the coherence of the world we lose our capacity for constructive natural philosophy. It is no accident that the writer who first mapped the farcical universe of interlocking trivia should also be the prophet of intellectual abdication. The great irony here lies in the fact that the instrument with which Sterne dethroned the scientific intellect is a world-view drawn from the scientists themselves. But we are now in a position to resolve this paradox. The cosmology the scientists bequeathed to Sterne was not the cosmology they had presupposed at the time of their greatest glory. Sterne has merely achieved a vague echo of that more incisive irony of Hume's whereby the completed principles of empiricism were to quell the ambitions of empirical science.

The ways in which Sterne's picture falls short of the radicalism of Hume's have already been noted. Sterne levelled causality, but did not, like Hume, uproot it. Sterne turned the intellect into an object of affectionate fun, by cutting off its practical efficacy and licensing it to ramble impotently over the web of reality, understanding the part but never the whole. But Hume withdrew even this poor freedom, and denounced the intellect as merely imagination so effectively disguised that it had fooled itself.

V

But if the intellect is powerless in Sterne, sentiment, it is said, is strong. The lamp of reason is virtually extinguished, but the

[1] *Posterior Analytics*, 76a, 78a–f.

sub-rational faculties of feeling, humour, social intuition and affection irradiate the world from below. What heart so chilled with scepticism that it cannot be warmed with contemplation of the good Toby? No book which so successfully combats intellectual despair with a faith in human charity should be described as pessimistic. So runs the argument.

Yet there is something wrong. I can gladly acknowledge the hilarity of Tristram Shandy, I can readily admit its heart-warming power, but I cannot believe it to be an optimistic book in the sense required. Perhaps it is because charity means more than a warm heart that we sense a breath of nihilism behind even the most affectionate exchanges of the brothers Shandy. We may even begin to suspect that real morality, so far from being preserved by the power of sentiment, has rather been discarded together with the competent intellect. Uncle Toby is a dear good soul, but it would be rash to call him a saint. Is this as high as human nature will reach? It is curious that before the eighteenth century the good characters in literature tend to unite an intelligent perceptiveness with a keen moral sensibility. Lear's moral regeneration on the heath involves an opening of the eyes. After the close of the seventeenth century, however, the road divides. One way leads to the warm-hearted, lovable innocent, the other to the moral vigilante—naturally, for it was in this century that subjective feeling was firmly detached from cognitive sensation. Jane Austen, who chose the way of knowledge, actually gave the choice a definition and a name, and used it as a title for her first novel. I suppose if I were myself forced to choose between Jane Austen's Mr Knightley or Edmund on the one hand and Fielding's Parson Adams or Sterne's Uncle Toby on the other, I might weakly opt for the second alternative. On the other hand (to set up the same choice of principle with fresh examples) it is hard to believe that Mr Pickwick, say, is morally superior to George Eliot's Mary Garth. Which shows, presumably, that more factors are involved than are included in the terms of our antithesis. Again, there are sheer exceptions, figures to whom the distinction is in any case inapplicable: a huge real-life one in Boswell's Dr Johnson and a less potent one in Smollett's Matthew Bramble. But the choice remains oddly workable. The antithesis tends to resolve itself into the division between those who see morals as essentially a matter of rational insight (these exalt such virtues as consideration, justice, discretion) and those who feel that morality is properly a matter of passion, warm or cold, benevolent or malignant. It might be argued that a rationalist philosophy will favour the first of these, and empiricism the second. After all, Plato, the prince of rationalists, believed that to commit a sin is rather like making an intellectual error.[1] It seems no great step from this to the familiar example of a Jane Austen character scoring seven out of ten for morals at the end of a novel. On the other hand, it was Hume who wrote at the head of Book III of the *Treatise*, 'Moral distinctions not derived from reason', and in Book II, Part iii, § 3, 'I shall endeavour to prove *first*, that reason alone can never be a motive to any action of the will, and secondly, that it can never oppose passion in the direction of the will.' Again, it was Hume who wrote the sentence (so easily construed as the clarion call of romanticism), 'Reason is, and ought only to be the slave of the passions.'[2]

The constant danger of the anti-rationalist morality is that it should degenerate into mere sensibility, the ethic of 'warm feelings'. Has this already happened to Sterne? A good example of Sternian morality in action is provided by the episode in which Uncle Toby learns of the plight of Le Fever, lying desperately ill at the local inn. Le Fever himself is of course no more than a convenient vessel, and is remarkable chiefly as showing how desperately simple Sterne can be if his interest is not engaged. On this ground the critic led the master: in point of moral subtlety Sterne's narrative compares unfavourably with Ferriar's story of Sorlisi,[3] a tale which strangely combines the bawdy of Uncle Toby's wound and the pathos of Le Fever, coasts dangerously near the Kitsch emotionalism of *Eloisa to Abelard* yet emerges triumphantly in the clear light of good feeling and charity. But, however faint Sterne's regard for Le Fever, towards Uncle Toby, who never *deserves*, always *feels*, he is all attention.

Toby's first reaction to Trim's news is an impulse to set off and visit the poor fellow. Then he says, 'I wish I had not

---

[1] *Protagoras*, 356c–357e.

[2] *Treatise*, II.iii.3, p. 415.

[3] *Illustrations of Sterne*, 1798, pp. 145–63.

known so much of this affair.'[1] The moral tone of this disarming remark is very delicate. Uncle Toby is certainly acknowledging the existence of a practical obligation. After all, he has already arranged to send a couple of bottles round to the inn. In the circumstances it may seem churlish to complain that he has taken a moment to consider his own feelings. However, when Trim returns with more news, Toby says, 'I wish, Trim, I was asleep.'[2] Sterne is very skilful, but I fancy that this time he has over-reached himself. The reaction he wants from his reader is, 'Ah, good soul, how he feels it, and how innocent he is of any pride in his own feelings!' In fact Trim, the loyal servant, *has* this reaction: 'Your honour is too much concerned.' But the implied direction to the reader is too peremptory, and he can easily rebel: 'How he feels it—but why must he *revert* to his own feelings—even if he is not proud of them he certainly has a tender regard for them.' The truth is that Sterne as a moralist is more interested in subjective than objective problems or crises, and that some of the author's subjectivist bias has infected his creature. It came naturally to every eighteenth century empiricist to assume that all questions should be reduced as far as possible to the data immediately confronting the sensitive mind. Indeed, from Locke to Hume, the constant tendency to reduce epistemology to a psychological description of mental contents was a simple consequence of empiricist principles. Instead of asking, 'What is this for?' or 'What is the logic of the public situation?' they would ask, 'What, here and now, can I taste, feel or see?'

The elegant writings of the third Lord Shaftesbury are very relevant here. His famous dictum, 'The most ingenious way of becoming foolish is by a system',[3] might almost replace Epictetus's as a motto for *Tristram Shandy*. Leslie Stephen writes of him: 'The main purpose of his writings is to show how, amidst the general wreck of metaphysical and theological systems, a sufficient base may still be discovered on which to construct a rational scheme of life.'[4] Shaftesbury's way of doing

[1] *Tristram Shandy*, VI.vi, p. 418.

[2] *Ibid.*, VI.vii, p. 423.

[3] *Advice to an Author*, iii.1, in his *Characteristics of Men, Manners, Opinions, Times* (1711), Library of Liberal Arts 1964 reprint of the 1900 edn. of J. M. Robertson, vol. I, p. 189.

[4] *History of English Thought in the Eighteenth Century*, vol. II, p. 21.

this was to concentrate his attention on those impulses towards the good and the beautiful which work, below the level of reason, in the human breast. Again, we think of *Tristram Shandy*. Hume felt a degree of admiration for Shaftesbury which the modern philosopher finds hard to understand. The most probable reason for this reverence was given by Henry Sidgwick when he observed that Shaftesbury was 'the first moralist who distinctly takes psychological experience as the basis of ethics'.[1]

If Shaftesbury is the clue to the nature of sentimental affection in Sterne, the moral force of *Tristram Shandy* may be something less than the healing agent for which we had hoped. The fundamental bias of Shaftesbury's ethics can best be shown by quotation:

> One who aspires to the character of a man of breeding and politeness is careful to form his judgment of arts and sciences upon right models of perfection. If he travels to Rome, he inquires which are the truest pieces of architecture, the best remains of statues, the best paintings of a Raphael or a Caraccio . . .
>
> 'Twere to be wished we had the same regard to a right taste in life and manners. What mortal being, once convinced of a difference in inward character, and of a preference due to one kind above another, would not be concerned to make his own the best? If civility and humanity be a taste; if brutality, insolence, riot, be in the same manner a taste, who, if he could reflect, would not choose to form himself on the amiable and agreeable rather than the odious and peverse model?[2]

Shaftesbury, it will be observed, is a moral aesthete. It would not be difficult to add to this quotation many more of the same kind. Confronted with the stark problems of ethics, he everywhere has recourse to the language of artistic taste. His solution to the Christian problem of evil is the aesthetic one; the black areas in the creation are analogous to those odd minglings of woven flowers and background which are essential to the total

---

[1] *Outlines of the History of Ethics*, 1967, p. 190.
[2] *Advice to an Author*, III.iii, *op. cit.*, vol. I, pp. 217–18.

effect of a rich tapestry.[1] A little later he argues[2] that it is
because of the harmonious order from inferior to superior
things that we are able to admire the universe, and is prepared
to apply this analysis to such things as monstrous births.

Of course one never catches Sterne in a stance so vulnerable.
But he has inherited the taint of aestheticism for all that. In
my discussion of the Le Fever episode I confined my expression
of unease to the reactions of Uncle Toby. In fact all is not well
even with Trim's narrative. What is wrong here is the same as
what is wrong with Uncle Toby: it is artful in the wrong way;
this, for instance:

> . . . he was lying in his bed with his head raised upon his
> hand, with his elbow upon the pillow, and a clean white
> cambrick handkerchief beside it:–The youth was just
> stooping to take up the cushion, upon which I supposed
> he had been kneeling,–the book was laid upon the bed,–
> and as he rose, in taking up the cushion with one hand,
> he reached out his other to take it away at the same time.
> –Let it remain there, my dear, said the lieutenant.[3]

We sense, beneath the soldierly compassion, the relish of the
connoisseur.

Sterne further shares with Shaftesbury a quality which can
perhaps be best described as cosiness. Shaftesbury, his attention fixed upon the experiencing human heart rather than on
the public world, could never rise above the ethic of warm
feelings. A poignant example of this is his attempt to form a
conception of disinterested virtue. He eagerly affirms that 'to
be bribed only or terrified into an honest practice, bespeaks
little of real honesty or worth.'[4] But, for all his hatred of
Puritans who refer all to reward, it soon emerges that there is
one pressing reason why we should follow virtue: it is inherently
so beautiful that the man who unites himself with its principles
will find himself filled with a kind of joy, whereas it is only too
plain that 'to be wicked or vicious is to be miserable and

---

[1] *The Moralists*, I.ii, *ibid.*, vol. II, p. 14.

[2] *Ibid.*, I.iii, vol. II, pp. 20–1.

[3] *Tristram Shandy*, VI.vii, p. 422.

[4] *Sensus Communis: an Essay on the Freedom of Wit and Humour*, II.iii,
op. cit., vol. I, p. 66.

unhappy'. For Shaftesbury's morally cultured man, virtue is in a very real sense its own reward.[1]

Such an ideal, naturally, could never survive imaginative realisation. Let us suppose we are reading a novel in which a detailed character is presented to us; the character of a man who behaves virtuously because he believes that thereby he will become happy. The novelist who attempted such a characterisation would discover, pragmatically, that he had not portrayed a good man. It is not that goodness and happiness are incompatible; it is just that the goal of happiness must not be allowed to appear among the motives for goodness. Thus Toby is both good and happy, but Sterne could never allow Toby to be actuated by an egoistic hedonism. Nevertheless, the resulting picture is open to criticism of a less radical sort: we may find Toby's unseeing benevolence uncomfortably close to complacency, yet Toby is never the moral mercenary.

Thus, of the two most disquieting features of Shaftesbury's ethics, his aestheticism and his moral egoism, the first only is discernible in *Tristram Shandy*. If this were all, it would scarcely justify a comparison between the two writers. But, as I have implied, they have more fundamental things in common. Much that is distressing in Shaftesbury's moral theory can be traced to his distinctive psychological approach, to his tendency to refer all moral questions to subjective sentiment rather than to objective consequence. And this basis, for all that Sterne's greater tact eliminates the worst results, is present in *Tristram Shandy*. 'They differ from nuns in this,' says Trim, describing the Beguines of the Spanish Netherlands, 'that they can quit the cloister if they choose to marry; they visit and take care of

---

[1] This account of Shaftesbury, which places him in the empiricist tradition, may appear to contradict the account given by Ernst Cassirer (*The Platonic Renaissance in England*, trans. J. P. Pettegrove, 1953) according to which Shaftesbury belongs to the anti-empiricist Platonic tradition. The contradiction can be resolved by observing that Shaftesbury is a true descendant of the Cambridge Platonists as long as he successfully maintains his theory of disinterested morality (this is the Shaftesbury in whom Cassirer is interested—see *op. cit.*, pp. 191–2) but turns empiricist as soon as he falls back upon the delighted analysis of psychological contents. Since the publication of Norman Kemp Smith's *The Philosophy of David Hume* (1941) it has not been possible to doubt what Hume himself tells us (*Treatise*, Introduction, xxi n.) that Humian moral philosophy descends from Shaftesbury and Hutcheson.

the sick by profession'. Uncle Toby's reply is revealing: 'I had
rather, for my own part, they did it out of good-nature.'[1]
The heart is all. It is hard to avoid the sense that in the world of
Tristram Shandy virtue is *essentially* impractical. Toby is the
saint of this world and Toby (imagine him working for Oxfam)
is a bumbling idiot. His goodness illuminates the whole man
from within, and shines from his countenance, but its rays
scarcely reach the outside world of suffering.

In such a situation it is tempting to clutch at straws: to
discover in the proved inefficacy of sentiment a revival of
ethical rationalism. Could not Sterne be telling us, it is suggested,
that the old doctrine of rational conduct is the only thing that
can save us from this plight? After all Sterne in his sermons
is prepared on occasion to exalt the moral role of reason above
that of feeling: 'Could they [the Israelites] learn to weigh the
causes and compare the consequences of things, and to exercise
the reason, which God has put into us for the Government and
direction of our lives,–there would be some hopes.'[2] But
Tristram Shandy has already squashed any such hopes of
reformation. The continuity of thought between Sterne's
sermons and his fiction is indeed striking, but it does not
amount to an identity. The sermons, unlike the more strenuous
Tristram, frequently settle on the soothing platitude. If, in
some corner of Sterne's mind, ethical rationalism remained as
some sort of ideal, *Tristram Shandy* tells us that it was it was
finally, like the asceticism of Bernard de Mandeville, that
peculiar sort of ideal which is never actually practised. We
have seen, through the exaggerating medium of Sterne's art,
reason reduced, in Humian fashion, to ratiocination, and
thence to fatuity. The subsequent reduction of sentiment can
only in the circumstances imply a kind of despair. Even
A. H. Cash, who has argued cogently for the rationalist in
Sterne, concedes that a certain moral shift is observable from
Sterne's sermons to *Tristram Shandy*, 'from clerical optimism
to humorous pessimism'.[3]

Of course Sterne does, on occasion, make fun of Shandean

[1] *Tristram Shandy*, VIII.xx, p. 571.

[2] *The Sermons of Yorick*, II.xiv, in the Shakespeare Head edn., 1927,
vol. I, p. 160.

[3] *Sterne's Comedy*, Pittsburgh, 1966, p. 126.

benevolence, but behind these passages (which are often hilarious) lies something very cold, something more like nihilism than rationalism. The best example can be found, surprisingly, in the rather dreary continental journey. Tristram, filled with sentimental affection for an ass he has met at Lyons, endeavours to feed the beast a macaroon. The reader is slowly reconciling his heart to the fact that it will shortly be warmed in the usual way when suddenly the mood is broken by a glorious confession: '. . . at this moment that I am telling it, my heart smites me, that there was more of pleasantry in the conceit, of seeing *how* an ass would eat a macaroon–than of benevolence in giving him one, which presided in the act.'[1] To be sure, the mere choice of a macaroon, of all things, ought to have warned us, but nevertheless the effect of this sentence is not just to make us laugh. It also seems to let in fresh air.

But the passage is not typical of the book. There is finally no mockery behind Uncle Toby's celebrated address to the fly which 'tormented him cruelly all dinner-time': '. . . go, poor devil, get thee gone, why should I hurt thee?–This world surely is wide enough to hold both thee and me.'[2] If Toby is a fool here, he is an Erasmian holy fool; what is absurd in the eyes of the world is unequivocally good in the eyes of Sterne. We may think for a moment of that other, more dangerous, Erasmian fool who, at the end of his travels, thought the human race so stank that the society of horses was preferable to the love of wife and child. Yet the Swiftian vision, while it is more frightening, is also more ambiguous; 'sanity' and 'folly' as mere words will never be quite the same again. But in Sterne we look eagerly for some hint of radical asceticism, and are disappointed. A social awareness of absurdity here co-exists, in naive harmony, with full sentimental simplicity. This passage is the true *locus classicus* for the ethics of *Tristram Shandy*. The action which by its very smallness the more effectively reveals a charitable heart–that is the one to choose. We should ask ourselves, 'Why is it that, say, a flashback to Toby in the field, assisting the wounded at risk to his own life, is clearly so much less suitable as a display of Shandean

---

[1] *Tristram Shandy*, VII.xxxii, p. 524.
[2] *Ibid.*, II.xii, p. 113.

charity?' Might not one reason be that it would lack the
piquant flavour? The story of Toby and the fly is, before all
else, an episode to be relished by the morally fastidious reader.
Tristram himself, though only ten years old at the time, found
that the incident 'instantly set my whole frame into one
vibration of most pleasurable sensation'.[1] The aesthetic, subjective bias is clear. Moreover, there is a hint of what lies beyond
such subjectivism of the ethical emotions, namely the obscure
excitement of the schizophrenic. 'I laugh till I cry,' wrote
Sterne in a letter to Garrick,[2] 'and in the same tender moments
cry till I laugh.'

We are left with the sense that the incompetence of reason
is not after all made good by the power of sentimental affection.
For, although the affection is real enough, somehow competence
is not its strongest point. In *Tristram Shandy* all things, though
they set out bravely, somehow issue in a kind of futility. It is
revealing that the fundamental, recurring images of the book
are, first, the spider,[3] spinning impalpable structures from his
own interior, and, second, the image of impotence, beginning
with the impaired conception of Tristram in the first chapter and
ending with the incapacity of Walter Shandy's bull at the close
of volume IX. It is curious that even Walter, the father-figure
of the book, is delicately twitted by the author with his sexual
inadequacy. A laconic exchange[4] between husband and wife as
they watch Toby setting off to do battle with the widow
Wadman is sufficiently clear in its implications. Christopher
Ricks was wise to pitch his moral defence of *Tristram Shandy*
at the subliminal level of character-creation. The book's overt
morality—sentiment, issuing in eccentricity, symbolised by
sexual incapacity—is more vulnerable.

But if the ethics of *Tristram Shandy* can be defended 'from
below' in the manner of Ricks, might not a similar defence be

[1] *Tristram Shandy*, II.xii, p. 114.

[2] April 19th, 1762, in *Letters of Laurence Sterne*, ed. L. P. Curtis, 1935,
p. 163.

[3] The stock image in the eighteenth century for subjectivity. Key
passages are Bacon, *Novum Organum*, I.xcv, in the edn. of Spedding, Ellis
and Heath, vol. I, 1857, p. 201, and Swift, *Battel of the Books*, printed in
A. C. Guthkelch and D. Nichol Smith's edn. of *A Tale of a Tub*, 1958, pp.
228–32.

[4] *Tristram Shandy*, IX.xi, pp. 613–4.

extended to the notion of sentimental affection? Can it be that the sentimental qualities of Sterne's characters, though they never feed the hungry nor heal the sick, have never the less certain real salutary powers of a less obvious kind? The point was argued by J. B. Priestley, in a light-hearted essay which has proved seminal:

> . . . each follows his own nose and takes care that his mind keeps all its doors and windows closed. Such a notable want of intellectual sympathy and understanding, such a slavish devotion, on every hand, to a certain fixed set of ideas, such a rigid determination to shut out all thought that appears in a new form, deal death to philosophies and sciences and all reasonable intercourse and call up a horrible vision of humanity as a set of puppets worked on the wires of a few instincts. A satirist, loathing his species, could have taken such tragicomical little creatures, each in the separate mechanical box of his mind, and made out of them a scene or narrative that would have jangled the nerves of a dozen generations. Sterne, however, having shown us this want of even the most ordinary intellectual sympathy, preserves the balance by emphasising what we might call the emotional kinship of his people. If the Shandies cannot share one another's thoughts, they can share one another's feelings.[1]

Sterne himself deliciously underlines the point by showing us what counts as an intellectual argument at Shandy Hall: 'He was a very great man! added my uncle *Toby* (meaning *Stevinus*) –He was so, brother *Toby*, said my father (meaning Peireskius).'[2] Yet all the while, as Priestley observes, there is a sense in which Walter and Toby really are at one.

Bathed in the warmth of such common affection, the Shandys can easily endure the imprisonment of reason. But to be shut out of the circle of intuitive benevolence–now *that* is something not to be contemplated. We are allowed an occasional glimpse of what such exclusion means, and these are the real dark patches in the book. They tend to involve a reference to the

---

[1] *The English Comic Characters* (first published 1925), London, 1963, p. 136.

[2] *Tristram Shandy*, VI.ii, p. 410.

harshly caricatured figure of the papist Dr Slop. The difference in tone between the mutual incomprehension of Walter and Toby and Dr Slop's failure in sympathy is considerable. One of the finest examples of the novelist's art in the whole book is the arrival of Dr Slop in the middle of Trim's hobby-horsical account of what is meant by radical heat and moisture.[1] Walter, Toby and Yorick make the audience, filled with an affectionate wonder at the phenomenon, Trim. Dr Slop, whose intuition is not attuned to Shandy Hall, misinterprets their mood as one of contemptuous amusement. His own 'knowing' attempts to patronise Trim result in his instant alienation from the rest at the unspoken level of sentiment. It is all very delicately done–almost, but not quite, imperceptibly. Sterne smiles on the strangely comfortable impotence of the shattered soldier and the failed philosopher, but he does not smile at Dr Slop.

VI

If we glance back at Priestley's description of *Tristram Shandy* as it would be *were it not for* its unifying emotional sympathy, we find ourselves in a strangely familiar place–a mind with 'doors and windows closed', each person in 'the separate mechanical box of his mind'–this is the architectural head from which we began. This is all the more remarkable in that Priestley seems to have arrived at his diagnosis without any prior research into the history of ideas. He got that vision out of *Tristram Shandy*, so some of it must have got into *Tristram Shandy* out of Locke.

We, on the other hand, have come by the more laborious route. We have even noted the way in which Shandean isolation differs from Lockian. Locke's epistemology, if carried to its conclusion, makes the ordinary world of chairs and tables into a mysterious, inaccessible realm. Of this there is little trace in *Tristram Shandy*. Public physical objects occasionally become objects of a kind of wonder, the essentially penetrable mysteries beloved of the scientist, but never the intrinsically unobservable object of the philosopher. Sterne rather confines himself to the less radical position whereby the minds of other people are

[1] *Tristram Shandy*, V.xxxix–xl, pp. 400–2.

inaccessible to us, though their bodies are not. What is pre-supposed by such a picture is, of course, a Cartesian dualism of mind and body. *Tristram Shandy* stands as a marvellously rich and detailed embodiment of the Cartesian view—mediated by Locke—that the mind is a mysterious, fugitive, invisible substance, interpenetrating and acting upon the extended world of matter. The sense of duality is in one respect stronger in Sterne than in Descartes, for in *Tristram Shandy* the power of mind to govern the animal spirits and so to move the body is comically diminished. We receive a vivid sense of the imprisoned souls of the Shandys, eccentric ghosts, fluttering inside mechanically determined machines. This is the philosophy of the age and it is also the philosophy of *Tristram Shandy*. But to say this is not to state an analytic truth. Richardson's *Pamela* does not follow, and can scarcely be said to presuppose such a philosophy, for the simple reason that *Pamela* is not philosophical at all. Sterne added to his qualities of humour, imagination and insight the less purely literary quality of cleverness. He could not help being fascinated by the world of clockwork-plus-human unpredictability which was offered by the philosophers of the day. And, in the main, he was not only fascinated but also dominated by it.

In the main, certainly, but not entirely. There are two strands in *Tristram Shandy* which show less philosophical docility. We may place the first under the heading The Comic Spirit, the second under Sterne the Lisping Behaviourist.

The way the Comic Spirit works is as follows. He cannot help seeing the picture of the immaterial inhabiting the material as funny. It is funny because it is grotesque, and grotesque because improbable. Should we, then, believe in it? Thus laughter can, by its own impetus, almost transform itself into philosophic criticism. I have praised the artist who drew our picture of the boy imprisoned in the head, because his very simplicity resulted in a salutary exposure of improbabilities. A cartoonist, struck more by the comic potential of the scene than by any philosophic scepticism, might redraw it in such a way as to make the critical point still clearer.

Something of this sort had already befallen the psycho-physical picture at the hands of Jonathan Swift, long before the Muse disturbed the asthenic sloth of Sterne. This is how

Swift did it (there are numerous examples: I choose this one on the ground that anticipations of Freud are usually amusing):

> ... I am apt to imagine, that the Seed or Principle, which has ever put Men upon *Visions* in Things *Invisible*, is of a Corporeal Nature: For the profounder Chymists inform us, that the Strongest *Spirits* may be extracted from *Human Flesh*. Besides, the Spinal Marrow, being nothing else but a continuation of the Brain, must needs create a very free Communication between the Superior Faculties and those below: And thus the *Thorn in the Flesh* serves for a *Spur* to the *Spirit*.[1]

It is sometimes useful to ask, 'What is the least suitable epithet to apply to X?' In the case of Sterne's humour, the least suitable epithet is 'robust'. This learned, we can begin to predict the differences between Swift's and Sterne's use of comic physiology (we use the same technique when we elicit the difference between Sterne and Rabelais by examining the Rabelaisian passages in Sterne). All of which points to the episode of Phutatorius and the Chestnut as a candidate for comparison. The reader may need to be reminded that a hot chestnut, without Phutatorius's knowledge, has fallen down the front of his trousers, affecting him first with a remote sensual pleasure and then with considerable pain. Sterne takes it upon himself to explain why Phutatorius did not instantly perceive what was amiss:

> –the soul of *Phutatorius*, together with all his ideas, his thoughts, his attention, his imagination, judgment, resolution, deliberation, ratiocination, memory, fancy, with ten batallions of animal spirits, all tumultuously crouded down, through different defiles and circuits, to the place in danger, leaving all his upper regions, as you may imagine, as empty as my purse.[2]

As Traugott observes,[3] this passage parodies Cartesian theory. It does so by admitting an acid realism which the philosopher would instinctively exclude. Moreover, Sterne has cheated very

---

[1] *A Discourse concerning the Mechanical Operation of the Spirit*, in *The Tale of a Tub, etc.*, ed. A. C. Guthkelch and D. Nichol Smith, 1958, p. 287.
[2] *Tristram Shandy*, IV.xxvii, p. 321.
[3] *Tristram Shandy's World: Sterne's Philosophical Rhetoric*, 1954 p. 49.

ingeniously. According to the system he is mocking, our becoming aware of *anything* involves an equally turbulent deployment of miniscule agents. But Sterne has smuggled in a suggestion of incongruity between the plight of Phutatorius, crippled with a Cartesian psycho-physiology, and the ordinary man, who would just notice what was up. The system of soldiers and messengers would not seem grotesquely elaborate if there were not an implied contrast with the simply evident *fact* of the chestnut. It is as if there were a direct route to the fact, and an indirect one by way of Cartesian epistemology. And this means that Sterne is endangering not only the Cartesian dualism but also that radical separation of the mind from the external world which he normally does not touch on. It is, of course, unlikely that Sterne knew he was doing this. Yet such ridicule is a potent weapon, and not in a merely literary way. When Gilbert Ryle announced that he was going to refer to the Cartesian system, 'with deliberate abusiveness', as 'the dogma of the ghost in the machine',[1] he had already drawn first blood in a philosophical war. Such forays recur. We may think of the deliberate domestic realism in Sterne's account of Dolly and the sealing-wax[2] (which exposes an irreducible metaphor in the term 'impression') or the 'tactless' clarity with which the workings of Uncle Toby's imagination are anatomised: '. . . this identical bowling-green instantly presented itself, and became curiously painted, all at once, upon the retina of my Uncle *Toby's* fancy;—which was the physical cause of making him change colour.'[3] Again, Locke, casually assuming a quiescent imagination in his reader, had said that reasoning consists in finding out the agreement or disagreement of ideas by means of a *medius terminus*,[4] to be used as a measuring rod. Naturally, Sterne's imagination proved irrepressible.[5] One is tempted to pursue Tristram's account of the electrified communication between a man and his hobby-horse[6] but we must not be seduced from the most important example of all:

If the fixture of *Momus's* glass, in the human breast, according to the proposed emendation of that arch-critick,

[1] *The Concept of Mind* (first published 1949), 1963, p. 17.
[2] *Tristram Shandy*, II.ii, p. 86. [3] *Ibid.*, II.v, p. 98.
[4] *Essay*, IV.xvii.2.11, pp. 387, 406.
[5] *Tristram Shandy*, III.xl, pp. 237–8. [6] *Ibid.*, I.xxiv, p. 77.

had taken place,—first, This foolish consequence would
certainly have followed,—That the very wisest and the very
gravest of us all, in one coin or other, must have paid
window-money every day of our lives.

And, secondly, That had the said glass been there set up,
nothing more would have been wanting, in order to have
taken a man's character, but to have taken a chair and
gone softly, as you would to a dioptrical beehive, and
look'd in,—view'd the soul stark naked;—observ'd all her
motions,—her machinations;—traced all her maggots from
their first engendering to their crawling forth;—watched
her loose in her frisks, her gambols, her capricios; and after
some notice of her more solemn deportment, consequent
upon such frisks, &c.—then taken your pen and ink and
set down nothing but what you had seen, and could have
sworn to:—But this is an advantage not to be had by the
biographer in this planet,—in the planet *Mercury* (belike)
it may be so, if not better still for him . . .

But this . . . is not the case of the inhabitants of this
earth;—our minds shine not through the body, but are
wrapt up here in a dark covering of uncrystalised flesh
and blood; so that if we would come to the specifick
characters of them, we must go some other way to
work.[1]

Sterne is here at once deeply traditional and ingeniously
topical. He has taken from Hesiod—or more likely from Lucian—
or still more likely from some dictionary of mythology the story
of how Momus, the god of fault-finding, complained to Vulcan
that no window had been placed in the human breast, to make
his work easier. The story, which must always have carried a
metaphysical twinge, has been transformed into something like
surrealism by Sterne's ostentatiously physiological approach.
The whole metaphor of a window on the soul has become a
degree less metaphysical. An eighteenth century man might
wonder, as a fourteenth century man would not, what it would
be like if one could apply a lens to a trepanned cranium, and
actually see the thoughts. What colour would they be? What
shape? Would a memory of a horse be horse-shaped? Or is

---

[1] *Tristram Shandy*, I.xxiii, pp. 74–5.

there some mistake here? Sterne manages his grotesque apparatus with a fine carelessness. He at first suggests that one glance will satisfy Momus. Christopher Ricks has commented[1] on the casual phrase, 'take a man's character', and noted that the status of 'take' is determined by its recurrence in the following words, 'take a chair'. But the phrase has also a vaguely scientific flavour; it recalls the idiom, 'take an observation', or 'take a temperature'. In a curious way, the closest analogy is with an idiom which in Sterne's day did not yet exist: 'take a photograph'. The basis was however already in the language; the limner employed with such disastrous results by the Vicar of Wakefield 'took likenesses for fifteen shillings a head'.[2] But we soon learn that things are not quite so simple. For when we look inside a human being we find, it seems, another human being, now frivolous, now solemn, but presumably as enigmatic, ultimately, as the person with whom we began. Everyone who tinkers with Lockian epistemology stumbles upon an infinite regress in the end, but few extract such cool enjoyment from the fact as Sterne. He even turns his Investigator into a delighted Peeping Tom for an instant. 'Can't you see,' the Comic Spirit is saying to us, 'that it is all absurd?' But, considered as philosophy (if we may do such a thing), the criticism is merely negative. It supplies nothing to replace the system it derides.

The second strand of scepticism in *Tristram Shandy* is, however, a little more positive. One great vice of Lockianism is its tendency to generate new universes. Berkeley, it will be remembered, accused Locke of duplicating the world. In fact the charge is too mild. He triplicated it. There is the world of external objects, there are ideas, and there is language. These, we are assured, correspond to one another, but as soon as we enquire how, we find ourselves inspecting not a relation but a hiatus. This is the farcical situation which Sterne exploited, where the universe of discourse refuses to attach itself to the real world. But here he is not content with laughter. There is a sort of embryonic Wittgenstein inside Sterne, who constantly

---

[1] Introduction to the Penguin *Tristram Shandy*, p. 14.
[2] Oliver Goldsmith, *The Vicar of Wakefield* (1766), Ch. xvi, in *The Collected Works of Oliver Goldsmith*, ed. A. Friedman, 1966, vol. IV, p. 82.

emphasises those situations in which language is not a separable picture of the world, but rather a special mode of acting, or doing within the world. That this should happen anywhere in the eighteenth century is astounding. Two things in Sterne equipped him for the step: a sense of the preposterousness of Locke and a novelist's eye for the realities of human intercourse. Indeed there are signs that Wittgenstein himself half-saw like an artist before he could demonstrate like a philosopher. His attack on the picture theory of language is almost entirely in figurative terms—tool-kits, games, levers in a signal-box, knobs on a wireless-set, pointing fingers. The delicate and arduous task of rethinking all this in a logically explicit fashion has fallen to Bernard Harrison.[1] It is said that Wittgenstein was once halted in his exposition of the picture theory by Sraffa's making a sudden gesture: what, after all, was *that* a picture of?[2] The Shandean flavour is unmistakable. The same question might be asked of Toby's *argumentum fistulatorium*—his habit of whistling *Lillabullero* when Walter transgresses the bounds of credibility.[3] We can work out a 'representative' account of what Toby is saying if we wish: something like 'Enough of that, brother Shandy, it is intuitively obvious that your reasoning has gone astray'—but this, apart from the fact that it is already out of character, does not explain the *force* of what Toby actually does. For we feel that Toby has not pictured some set of ideal considerations so much as he has *done something* to his brother. He has in fact anchored him to the earth. We are, even as minds, wedged into the world, and the seeming freedom of Lockian representative discourse is an illusion. Hence, perhaps, Sterne's keen delight in pragmatic refutation: '. . . the Philosopher would use no other argument to the sceptic, who disputed with him against the reality of motion, save that of rising up upon his legs, and walking a-cross the room . . .'[4] His deep interest in the quasi-linguistic efficacy of gesture is similar. Fluchère has noted[5] most of the relevant passages.

[1] *Meaning and Structure: an Essay in the Philosophy of Language*, 1972.

[2] See Norman Malcolm, *Ludwig Wittgenstein: a Memoir*, 1958, p. 69.

[3] *Tristram Shandy*, I.xxi, pp. 69–71.

[4] *Ibid.*, I.xxiv, p. 78.

[5] *Laurence Sterne: de l'homme à l'œuvre*, pp. 484–7, in Barbara Bray's translation, pp. 279–81.

Trim 'strikes the end of his stick perpendicularly on the floor, so as to give an idea of health and stability'.[1] The Widow Wadman's violent kick[2] on being tucked up in bed speaks eloquently of her passion for Toby. The book itself is full of typographic gestures; for example:

'——Shut the door.——'[3]

Gesture is also seen as activating mental performance. Trim is unable to repeat the Ten Commandments until he is put through a ritual series of military postures.[4] To be sure Walter dismisses this performance as no true knowledge but a mere scaffold, but he is wrong. Trim prevails in the end. Locke's view of language seems to have been modelled on the noun, which, as we were told at school, is always the name of something. His theory is unfriendly to those primitive particles of language, alarm-signals, interjections, warnings, exhortations, which seem more deeply embedded in behaviour. It is Sterne's great delight to use the lower forms of language as arrows to pierce the airborne balloon of Walter's Lockian discourse. It is peculiarly delicious, in view of what follows, that it is Walter who is interrupted (as Ricks says) in a non-verbal communication.[5] The fashionable view of language as, properly speaking, a system corresponding in detail to that great set of 'things' which is the world had already been satirised by Swift, whose learned Balnibarbian philosophers had perceived that, if discourse was merely a set of *ersatz* things, it would be altogether better to converse with the things themselves—and accordingly crept about under huge burdens of miscellaneous objects.[6] The passage is a good example of the destructive philosophical genius of the Comic Spirit (for I am not sure that Swift himself knew, philosophically, what was wrong; he knew only that it was funny). But Sterne, assiduously goading Locke from below with jokes, pinches, gestures, is a degree more positive. He has not only half subverted the secular orthodoxy of the day; he has also told us where to look for our next philosophy. We need not doubt that Sterne is really aware that gesture rivals

[1] *Tristram Shandy*, V.vii, p. 361.   [2] *Ibid.*, VIII.ix, p. 548.
[3] *Ibid.*, I.iv, p. 8.
[4] *Ibid.*, V.xxxii, pp. 392–3.
[5] Introduction to the Penguin *Tristram Shandy*, p. 19.
[6] *Gulliver's Travels*, III.v, in Harold Williams's edn., 1941, pp. 169–70.

abstract discourse as a paradigm of human discourse. He
deliberately stressed, not so much its accuracy as its efficacy:

> Whilst a man is free—cried the Corporal, giving a
> flourish with his stick thus—

> A thousand of my father's most subtle syllogisms could
> not have said more for celibacy.[1]

Yet even here I am unsure how far Sterne is conscious of the
philosophical *implications* of what he has done. In a sense, of
course, he has a Shaftesburian[2] answer all ready for us. Wit
and humour are themselves cognitive faculties and their findings
need not be translatable into the language of sobriety. An
ounce of wit can end a protracted, absurd, rationalistic lawsuit.[3]
Fluchère has argued[4] convincingly that Sterne is sincere in his
violent opposition[5] to Locke's disparagement[6] of wit at the

---

[1] *Tristram Shandy*, IX.iv, p. 604. It is regrettable (from my point of view)
that Sterne has here aimed his satire at the Scholastic ('syllogisms' implies
Aristotelianism) rather than at Locke. The reader who wishes to try the
gesture should begin at the *lower* end.

[2] See Ernst Cassirer, *The Platonic Renaissance in England*, Ch. VI, pp.
170–85.

[3] *Tristram Shandy*, III, Preface (following Ch. xx) p. 199.

[4] *Laurence Sterne: de l'homme à l'œuvre*, p. 287, in Barbara Bray's translation p. 82. I am not sure that Fluchère is right in the motive he ascribes
to Sterne—'because that is where the shoe pinches' (car c'est bien là où le
bât le blesse). Sterne's defence of humour is not merely Luddite.

[5] *Tristram Shandy*, loc. cit., pp. 200–2.

[6] *Essay*, II.xi.2, vol. I, pp. 202–4.

expense of judgment. If his humour has done more damage (and real, philosophical damage) to the great Locke than his reason ever could, he might well feel confidence in this opinion.

This, then, is the second and more positive strand of opposition in Sterne to the dominant philosophy of his time. We should never have had it but for Sterne's instinct for comedy, but because it is never allowed to develop beyond its comic origins the great breach for which we had hoped is never effected. The incisive criticisms are all mere sparks, which drift from us and are lost in darkness. They are never marshalled; their collective force is never assessed. To be sure, if they had been, *Tristram Shandy* would not be the literary masterpiece it is. The moments when the unremittingly introspective criteria of the age are exchanged for an interest in the logic of the public situation—as when Walter observes, 'Love, you see, is not so much a SENTIMENT as a SITUATION, into which a man enters, as my brother *Toby* would do, into a *corps* . . .'[1] —these moments remain untypical. The slow empiricist erosion of the public (remember Hutcheson's suggestion, which so delighted Hume,[2] that morality is a sentiment) is here momentarily reversed, but the reversal is, because instinctive, impotent. *Tristram Shandy* remains, not the destroyer of the fashionable world-picture, but, with its chaotic determinism, its biological psychology and its microscopic observation, its one adequate literary monument.

[1] *Tristram Shandy*, VIII.xxxiv, p. 589.
[2] In T. H. Green and T. H. Grosart's edn. (1875) of the *Inquiry*, which they present under the title *Essays Moral Political and Literary of David Hume*, vol. II, p. 10n. This forms the fourth volume of their edition of *The Philosophical Works*. This note is not in Selby-Bigge's edn.

CHAPTER 3

Sentiment and Sensibility

I

Locke's philosophy is an empiricism founded in the subjective experience of the perceiver. Descartes too started from the solitude of his own mind but his thoughts held, even before he began to respond to the external world, a pre-empirical content, namely the idea of God; further, this was a peculiarly potent idea; its infinity and perfection showed that it could not be the product of the finite subject and must therefore refer to an objective existent; and a perfect God who really exists guarantees in advance the testimony of the senses. The external world brings to the Cartesian mind a letter of introduction, so to speak, from the Supreme Being, and by this means both parties are protected, bound in an authorised epistemological contract. With Locke it is otherwise. His empiricism, as it is purer, so it is more naked, more defenceless. The precognitive mind from which he begins is not stamped with the validating image of God; on the contrary it bears no image whatever; it is a *tabula rasa*. A man who knows nothing of foreign countries is not in a good position for evaluating his own. A man who has nothing to go on but experience is scarcely in a position to evaluate experience. In the ordinary way of things so bizarre a wish does not arise, but if you are committed to the meta-physical habit of referring to the 'testimony' of senses which mediate between an 'external' and an 'internal' world, it can. Locke could not tell whether his senses were telling him the truth or not. Thus the effect of his philosophy was to separate man from the real world. But neither Locke nor his reader perceived that he had been peremptorily disinherited. Sterne, as we have seen, travelled only the first stage with Locke; that is to say, he acquiesced in the inaccessibility of other minds but did not seriously suspect that objective reality itself was similarly unknowable. And to be sure his acquiescence in the first stage was not really philosophical. Berkeley, indeed, had gone to the root of the matter, but the common reader remained unimpressed. It is not difficult to see why. Berkeley, with all his saintly simplicity of character, with all his deep religious conviction, was not fully serious about the inexhaustible world before him. This imparts to his most brilliant work an air, ultimately, of frivolity. He turned the universe inside out, but somehow the very ease with which he did it suggested not so much a true metaphysical revolution as a conjuring trick. With so little dust and heat, men felt, nothing could really have changed. Berkeley thus remains a sort of amazing mirage in the intellectual life of the age.

But with David Hume a new sort of strenuousness enters philosophy. Throughout his life Hume retained a profound reverence for common sense. To depart from it caused him the greatest distress and whenever he could, at some cost to the consistency of his philosophy, he gave it an authority higher than that of his own speculations. With more than monastic devotion, he submitted all his works to the judgment of nature. Yet in Hume the shadow of solipsism lengthens.

The last sentence is no doubt old-fashioned, and not only in style. In 1941, when Norman Kemp Smith published his formidable book, *The Philosophy of David Hume,* our picture of Hume the supreme sceptic was destroyed and instead we were given Hume the Naturalist (as opposed to Supernaturalist). Many think of Hume as the man who resolved 'cause' into 'habitual concurrence', denied the validity of inference or induction, ascribed a fictitious status to the self and to public objects. Those who think thus may well experience some relief on reading Kemp Smith's book; but I fancy that the relief will be not unmixed with a purely intellectual disappointment. For one thing the naturalistic philosophy is so much weaker, as philosophy, than the old scepticism.

The classic statement of the old view of Hume, the view so laboriously overthrown by Kemp Smith, can be found in Leslie Stephen's *History of English Thought in the Eighteenth Century:*

> . . . with Hume the three substances [soul, God, matter] disappear together. The soul is dissolved by the analysis which has been fatal to its antithesis. All grounds for an

a priori theology are cut away, though this conclusion is, for obvious reasons, not so unequivocally displayed in the treatise. All our knowledge is framed out of 'impressions' and 'ideas', ideas being simply decaying impressions. The attempt to find a reality underlying these impressions is futile, and even self-contradictory. We are conscious only of an unceasing stream of more or less vivid feelings, generally cohering in certain groups. The belief that anything exists outside our mind, when not actually perceived, is a 'fiction'. The belief in a continuous subject which perceives the feelings is another fiction. The only foundation of the belief that former coherences will again cohere is custom. Belief is a 'lively idea related to or associated with a present impression'. Reason is 'nothing but a wonderful and unintelligible instinct in our souls, which carries us along a certain train of ideas, and endows them with particular qualities according to their particular situations and relations'. Association is in the mental what gravitation is in the natural world. The name signifies the inexplicable tendency of previously connected ideas and impressions to connect themselves again. We can only explain mental processes of any kind by resolving them into such cases of association. Thus reality is to be found only in the ever-varying stream of feelings, bound together by custom, regarded by a 'fiction' or set of fictions as implying some permanent set of external or internal relations, and becoming beliefs only as they acquire liveliness. Chance, instead of order, must, it would seem, be the ultimate objective fact, as custom, instead of reason, is the ultimate subjective fact. We have reached, it is plain, the fullest expression of scepticism, and are not surprised when Hume admits that his doubts disappear when he leaves his study. The old bonds which held things together have been completely dissolved. Hume can see no way to replace them, and Hume, therefore, is a systematic sceptic.[1]

One relatively small point can be cleared out of the way at once: Hume did not believe that each and every operation of

[1] *Op. cit.*, vol. I, pp. 36–7.

reason was a mere instinctive ritual of the mind; on the contrary he thought that reason retained all its old status so long as it concerned itself with relations of ideas and left matters of fact alone; let us then make the necessary adjustment: it was not ratiocination but inference that Hume attacked. That is to say, although Hume showed that all our knowledge of past, present and future was baseless and irrational, he did not show that logic and mathematics were in the same plight.[1] This modification is not alone enough to overthrow Stephen's contention that Hume is a sceptic. To make a clean sweep of the traditional view Kemp Smith employs a different sort of criticism: Stephen's account, he says, is not so much inaccurate (except for its conclusion) as incomplete. All that he says about the critique of substance is well enough as far as it goes, but by leaving out all the positive, constructive elements in Hume's thought it ends in misrepresentation. The reader may well wonder what possible 'positive' repairs could ever make good the metaphysical destruction he has just witnessed.

II

Kemp Smith's answer is brilliantly simple and we had better confess at once that Hume would probably have been very pleased by it. Hume restored the *status quo*, he says, by reversing the roles hitherto played by reason and feeling respectively. Hume is first and last a moralist. It is no accident that in his brief autobiography the work which Hume described as 'of all my writings, historical, philosophical or literary, incomparably the best' was the *Enquiry concerning the Principles of Morals*. The driving force behind the *Treatise* itself is ethical. To be sure, the term 'moral' bore in the eighteenth century a broader meaning than it has today, but the subtitle of the *Treatise*–'An Attempt to introduce the experimental Method of Reasoning into Moral Subjects'–tells the same tale. Hume's early philosophical reading was in the rationalist ethics of Latin antiquity. It led to a sort of philosophical trauma for which Shaftesbury and Hutcheson provided the only adequate therapy. It was

[1] See his *Inquiry*, I.iv, p. 25. Hume is not, however, absolutely consistent on the point. In the *Treatise* (I.iii.14, p. 166) numbers are seen as empirical objects, having no intrinsic relations, to be arranged according to notions of identity, *etc.*, exerted spontaneously by the mind.

from these writers that Hume learned to repose his aching brows on the indulgent pillow of sentiment. Hence Hume derived his famous ethical theory, 'Reason is, and ought only to be the slave of the passions.' Once this truth is recognised, philosophic man can rest his itching intellect. Hume, far more than Locke, was concerned to explore the limits of human understanding, and certainly to discover that the foundation of morals is not rational but sentimental—just the way we are made—is to find oneself at the end of a road. That which has no rational structure is not amenable to metaphysical analysis. Readers of the *Treatise*, pulverised by the destructive criticism of the first book, have seldom struggled on to the long withheld refreshment of the third. But in truth the later part of the *Treatise* makes an essential part of its dialectic. Hume is but clearing the ground before raising a new structure. Once this is understood it becomes clear, says Kemp Smith, that the pattern of Hume's epistemology mirrors the pattern of his ethics. The movement of thought is not towards a nihilistic scepticism but towards a positive goal, which may be represented by the catch-phrase, 'Reason is and ought to be subordinate to our natural beliefs.'[1] Such, in crude summary, is Kemp Smith's thesis.

We may begin by acknowledging that there is a sense in which it is absolutely right. Kemp Smith knows more about Hume than anyone else and can find a reference for each particle of his interpretation. Hume is historically 'placed' with a weight of scholarship so far unmatched, and at the same time Kemp Smith can be seen as the first writer properly to respect the *ipsissima verba* of the philosopher. Yet a feeling remains that his book is not truly critical; he is the chronicler, not the historian of Hume's thought. He chides previous readers of Hume for neglecting the *Enquiries*, the third book of the *Treatise*, the professed intention of the philosopher as expressed in his correspondence, to say nothing of the immediate influences on his writings. Meanwhile, amid all this careful exegesis, philosophy is forgotten.

This phenomenon has one obvious parallel. Students of literature have grown accustomed to the fact that there are

[1] Kemp Smith, *The Philosophy of David Hume*, p. 11.

two sorts of criticism, one written by poets and one by scholars. The poets tell us that Virgil wept with Dido when Aeneas sailed from Carthage, that Shakespeare shrank from the newly made King Henry V when he rejected Falstaff. The scholars tell us that, attuned as they were to the conventional morality of their times, Virgil and Shakespeare knew no such inward crisis. One is grateful to both parties. The scholars do well to remind us of the ethico-political situation, but their arguments tend to flatten the idiosyncrasies of an author, to merge him too completely with his 'background'. If the 'world-picture' enjoys uncontested authority, is to be the last criterion of meaning, the final court of appeal, then how is a writer to be unconventional, and how is the world-picture itself to develop and change? Such changes, we all know, often originate in the back of the mind. The poet, better trained perhaps than the scholar to ask 'What is the important action here?' may often smell out the personal, subversive tendency of a passage which the writer himself would describe in the most conventional terms. Note that it is characteristic of the poet to attend to the inner structure of the published poem. It is the scholar who longs to ask the author what he meant. Thus Kemp Smith is what is known in the literary world as a scholarly intentionalist. The author says he is a moralist and Kemp Smith the pure exegete naturally submits to the authorial view. But real philosophers are less easily subdued. Kemp Smith strives to cover the whole variegated surface of Hume's thought. Bertrand Russell (who corresponds to the poet in my literary analogy) is, on the contrary, unashamedly exclusive:

> David Hume (1711–76) is one of the most important among philosophers, because he developed to its logical conclusion the empirical philosophy of Locke and Berkeley, and by making it self-consistent made it incredible. He represents, in a certain sense, a dead end: in his direction, it is impossible to go further. To refute him has been, ever since he wrote, a favourite pastime among metaphysicians. For my part, I find none of their refutations convincing; nevertheless, I cannot but hope that something less sceptical than Hume's system may be discoverable.

His chief philosophical work, the *Treatise of Human*

Nature, was written while he was living in France during
the years 1734 to 1737. . . . Hume's *Treatise of Human
Nature* is divided into three books, dealing respectively
with the understanding, the passions and morals. What is
important and novel in his doctrines is in the first book,
to which I shall confine myself.[1]

To Russell, as to nearly every working philosopher, Hume,
whether he liked it or not, was a sceptic. As soon as we drop
the scholar's blanket question: 'What did Hume say?' and ask
instead the philosopher's question 'What in the philosophy of
Hume is fundamental?' we shall grow impatient with Kemp
Smith's account. For the sharp edge of Hume's destructive
reasoning is no less fatal to his own constructive philosophy
than it had been to previous metaphysics.

Indeed it is surely very odd to claim that a man who reduces
knowledge to a psychologically conditioned sentiment, forever
separated from the real, can ever be anything but a sceptic.
Kemp Smith seems to imagine that Hume discovered an antidote to ethical scepticism in the Hutchesonian notion 'that
Morality is nothing in the Abstract Nature of Things, but is
entirely relevant to the Sentiment or mental Taste of each
particular Being; in the same Manner as the Distinctions of
sweet and bitter, hot and cold, arise from the particular feeling
of each Sense or Organ. Moral Perceptions, therefore, ought
not to be class'd with the Operations of the Understanding,
but with the Tastes or Sentiments'.[2]

This is no antidote; on the contrary it is scepticism of the
most devastating kind. To give up the quest for a *justification*
of ethical opinions, and to seek instead merely a psychological
explanation, is to give up ethics for psychology. It is difficult
to resist the conclusion that what Hume did with knowledge
is essentially similar. We may say if we like that Hume
preserved the plain man's 'certain knowledge' by detaching
that certainty from insight and ascribing it to belief, but we
must end by granting that such invulnerability is dearly
bought. We just cannot say, 'It's all right, I know Rational

[1] *History of Western Philosophy,* pp. 634–5.
[2] Quoted by Kemp Smith from the 1748 and 1751 edns. of the *Enquiry
Concerning Human Understanding.* This passage is not given in Selby-
Bigge's edn.

Insight has collapsed, but look, here are Feeling and Imagination who can do the same job just as well!'

'Insight' and 'imagination' are not proper names, like Dobbin and Dapple. They both denote and connote. They say something *about* the thing to which they refer, and as soon as we ask what they say we shall see that the whole question of scepticism turns on it. If we say that a thing results from insight we are saying that it is founded in reality. If we say that a thing is the product only of imagination we are saying it is unreal. No doubt Coleridge would not agree but Coleridge lived late enough to be bemused by Kant. Coleridge does seem to have believed that the imagination was *constitutive* of knowledge and that, somehow, the imagination was equal to its task; but one cannot believe in a Coleridgian Hume. Yet this, it would seem, is exactly what Kemp Smith wants us to do, for he quotes a typical passage from Coleridge as epigraph to his chapter on abstract ideas. The truth is that Coleridge was only able to think as he did because he had an *inflationary* mind; it came naturally to him to blow up imagination to the status of insight; but Hume's mind was on the contrary reductive. The phrase 'nothing but' resounds petrifically through the *Treatise*. Thus, for Hume, to assimilate knowledge to imagination was an act of reduction. And indeed any other interpretation is foreign to the spirit of the age. It is true that Shaftesbury, with his smiling contempt for the maker of systems, could view with pleasure the substitution of sentimental fiction for rational fact. But Hume could never match the intellectual complacency of a Shaftesbury.

Kemp Smith is not unaware of this difficulty. In order to resolve it he notes that Hume distinguishes two concepts of imagination: first the capricious fictive faculty of individuals and second the shared faculty which goes to form knowledge. Certainly Hume acknowledges this distinction,[1] but it is not the distinction between fact and fiction which Kemp Smith requires for his argument; it is merely the difference between the idiosyncratic and the common; the common imagination is no less fictive than the idiosyncratic. Thus the distinction between fact and fiction is still to be sought. In the end Kemp

---

[1] *Treatise*, I.iii.9, p. 117 n.

Smith meekly acquiesces[1] in the Humian claim that fact and fiction 'taste different'. To say 'We *do* know and there's an end on't' is not to resolve the philosophical problem. Rather, it is a refusal to do any more philosophy.

III

It is curious how recent writers on Hume, overwhelmed by the weight of Kemp Smith's learning, are nevertheless frequently seduced from the straight road of naturalism by the sheer inner impetus of the philosophical material before them. An ironic specimen of this can be found in A. H. Basson's *David Hume*[2] — ironic because what at first appears as a fake rebellion against Kemp Smith ends by implying a real rebellion. Basson tells us that Hume *was* a sceptic[3] but at once makes it clear that he is using 'sceptic' in a technical, not to say an obsolete, sense: something like 'committed to the piecemeal examination of phenomena opposed to dogma, assenting to nothing that is occult'. This gives us, it would seem, a positivistic Hume to which Kemp Smith could readily agree. Basson adds that Hume's scepticism is qualified by the fact that he held one basic metaphysical dogma, concerning the limits of human understanding. This exception made, he feels that the rest is straightforward enough:

> First, the sceptic is particularly concerned to avoid dogmatical opinions on occult or hidden matters, as opposed to those which are objects of sense experience. Such matters, he says, cannot be decided, and our only hope is to arrive at a suspense of judgment, a kind of indifference, about them. Second, the sceptic does not suspend judgment on matters of immediate sense experience, nor does he attempt to deny those sentiments and beliefs which are the necessary and *involuntary* products of sense experience.[4]

As soon, however, as Basson examines Hume's one, negative dogma, he burns his fingers. What confronts him is not, as one might have guessed, the delicate irony whereby any positivist who says 'I am a positivist' proves that he is no such thing (for

[1] *The Philosophy of David Hume*, p. 462.
[2] 1958. [3] *Op. cit.*, p. 141. [4] *Ibid.*, p. 141.

to say 'I am a positivist' is to codify one's position in meta-physical terms; the ostentatious hostility of positivism to meta-physical beliefs is itself a metaphysical belief; the fact that it is negative does not alter the fact that it is metaphysical *in kind*). No, what we have here is a bolder irony. The truth is that Hume's one, negative dogma on the limits of knowledge proves fatal, not only to metaphysical beliefs but also to common sense. The paragraph quoted is at first sight very reassuring; it suggests that ordinary knowledge is to be un-touched. But its power to reassure entirely depends on our not perceiving the ambiguity of 'experience'. 'Experience' as a *subjective* phenomenon was certainly never doubted by Hume. That we have perceptions is indisputable; the darkness drops when we ask what they are perceptions *of*. Hume did not dis-believe in the existence of the witness (seeing's believing!) only his *testimony* was suspect. Thus we begin to see that Hume was not such a cosy, sensible fellow after all. Within five pages Basson can write, 'Hume and the sceptics tell us in effect that we can know only what seems to be so, and never what is really so. We are, as it were, bound to appearances and separated forever from the real nature of things.' Suddenly we realise what has happened. The metaphysical doctrine which prevented Hume from being a full sceptic in the old sense proved just enough to turn him *into* a sceptic in the modern sense. Hume the Positivist ducks out of sight and Hume the Platonist Unparadised takes his place.

We realise in retrospect that Basson had to tread very care-fully in the paragraph I quoted. To be sure 'sentiments' and 'beliefs' go unchallenged, but only so long as they make no claim to cognitive status. Knowledge on the other hand *is* challenged, fails to present the password and is shot full of holes.

It is evident that Hume is deeply committed to the empiricist dualism of subject and object which I have traced from seven-teenth century science. He thus remains a good deal further from positivism than Berkeley.[1] It is true that he explicitly rejected

[1] I am inclined to agree with G. J. Warnock that Hume learned astonish-ingly little from Berkeley. See Warnock's introduction to Berkeley's *The Principles of Human Knowledge and Three Dialogues between Hylas and Philonous*, 1962, pp. 35–6. Berkeley and Hume were, I fancy, tempera-mentally antipathetic.

the quasi-scientific 'causal' theory of perception, that is the
theory that material objects are not themselves perceptions but
are capable of causing perceptions. Unlike Berkeley, however,
he produced no radical alternative, but continued to oppose
common sense by distinguishing perceptions from material
bodies (now deprived of any causal connexion with mind).[1]
We have only to watch him exploring the nature of moral
sentiment to see how deeply the seventeenth century scientific
world has sunk into his mind:

> But can there be any difficulty in proving, that vice and
> virtue are not matters of fact, whose existence we can infer
> by reason? Take any action allow'd to be vicious: Wilful
> murder, for instance. Examine it in all lights, and see if
> you can find that matter of fact, or real real existence,
> which you call *vice*. In which-ever way you take it, you find
> only certain passions, motives, volitions and thoughts.
> There is no other matter of fact in the case. The vice
> entirely escapes you, as long as you consider the object.
> You never can find it, till you turn your reflection into your
> own breast, and find a sentiment of disapprobation, which
> arises in you, towards this action. Here is a matter of fact;
> but 'tis the object of feeling, not of reason. It lies in your-
> self, not in the object. So that when you pronounce any
> action or character to be vicious, you mean nothing, but
> that from the constitution of your nature you have a
> feeling or sentiment of blame from the contemplation of it.
> *Vice and virtue, therefore, may be compar'd to sounds,*
> *colours, heat and cold, which, according to modern philo-*
> *sophy, are not qualities in objects, but perceptions in the*
> *mind* . . .[2]

The distinction between primary and secondary qualities,
thrown out of the front door, soon finds its way in at the back.
It is ironic that he should support his assertion that value is
subjective—a thesis only vaguely opposed by common sense—
by appealing to a view with which common sense can have no
sympathy whatsoever. 'You say this action is wicked, but can
you *point* to the characteristic you call "wicked" any more than

[1] See Basson, *op. cit.*, p. 117.
[2] *Treatise*, III.i.1, pp. 468–9. My italics in the last sentence.

you can point to whatever it is that makes you call that pillar-box "red"?' The man in the street might well be puzzled by so plausible a use of the *a fortiori*.

Hume differs finally from Berkeley in his refusal to transfer 'real' from the material to the mental sphere, and it is this, ironically, which makes him the greater sceptic as regards the contents of experience. The term 'idea', used by Locke and Berkeley indifferently to cover perceptions or purely mental contents is by Hume reserved for inner phenomena. For perceptions of the external world he coined the term 'impressions'. But, as is well known, he steadfastly refused to acknowledge that impressions were distinguished from ideas in virtue of the fact that they were objectively true. To reason thus was for Hume to go beyond experience, and Hume was an empiricist. He was therefore driven back on a sort of desperate psychologism—impressions differ from ideas in their greater vivacity, or their different flavour. It is at this point in his reasoning that one might look for the Berkleian revolution; 'if neither idea nor impression can be conjoined with reality, it is plain that the term "real", as hitherto understood by philosophers, has no use; may we not therefore set it to work once more *within* the world of mental objects?' Hume shrank from such a conclusion, and adopted instead the sceptical alternative. Reality is not in the mind; both impressions and ideas are in the mind; we have nothing but impressions and ideas; therefore we know nothing.

There remains a sophistical refutation of the claim that Hume was a sceptic. It all depends on a carefully prearranged definition of the word 'sceptic' and is formally, but only formally, satisfactory. It runs as follows: a sceptic is one who believes nothing; Hume attacked, not belief but knowledge; alongside his assertion that we cannot know that the sun will rise tomorrow runs a recurring insistence that we believe it will (Hume himself no less than the rest of us). The first answer to this argument is that 'scepticism' as ordinarily understood applies quite as much to knowledge as belief. Indeed, it is only in the artificial atmosphere of Hume's philosophy that the two are so entirely separate; this is in itself instructive and brings us to the second stage of our answer. The belief which Hume leaves us is a hollow substitute for what he took away. It is not, for example, anything like 'rational conviction'; it cannot pretend to a greater or less probability, for it has no probability at all. It is, in short, a sort of religious faith. And we know from the *Dialogues Concerning Natural Religion* with what contempt Hume could view such an attitude, if aimed at the Almighty. One longs for Berkeley to appear at Hume's elbow, armed with the shaft with which Hylas transfixed Philonous, proving his material world to be but a theological illusion.[1]

Bernard Williams is not Berkeley, but is perhaps the next best thing. He noted[2] the analogy between the 'strained and unnatural' religious scepticism of Philo in the *Dialogues* and that refusal to believe in a material world which is in the *Treatise* described as equally strained. It is evident, Williams feels, that Hume believed that the charge was unfairly applied to the religious sceptic but entirely fair in its application to the man who refused to believe in common-sense materialism. Williams resolves the difficulty by observing that Hume probably did not really think that *religious* scepticism was strained and unnatural at all. It is an answer in the tradition of Kemp Smith and, as exegesis, is probably just. But as soon as we ask 'In what *sense* is the word "strained" applied to disbelief in the material world?' we shall find that the answer is not logical but psychological. If Hume thought that atheism was less strained than immaterialism, he meant by this that it came more naturally; he did not mean that it was in any way more probable. Thus, if we are willing to read the logical implications of what is before us, a darker resolution emerges; our belief in a material world is no better founded than our belief in a personal God, so irresistibly demolished in the *Dialogues*. Hume, in fact, knew very well that the effect of his reasoning was to leave the bluntest empiricism level with the wildest metaphysical speculation:

> Let men be once fully perswaded of these two principles, *That there is nothing in any object, consider'd in itself, which can afford us a reason for drawing a conclusion beyond it;* and, *That even after the observation of the frequent or constant conjunction of objects, we have no reason to draw any inference concerning any object beyond those of which we have had*

[1] See above, pp. 35–6.

[2] 'Hume on Religion', in *David Hume: a Symposium*, ed. D. F. Pears, London, 1966, pp. 79–81.

experience; I say, let men be once fully convinced of these two principles, and this will throw them so loose from all common systems, that they will make no difficulty of receiving any, which may appear the most extraordinary.[1]

Yet it must be confessed that Hume's faith in the material world was real faith. So far from being a disingenuous profession of piety, it was an ineluctable necessity of his constitution. Indeed, its reality could be tested very simply: by arranging a wager. Let a physicist be introduced to Hume and bet him a hundred guineas that the next time he heats a kettle of water it will boil at 212° Fahrenheit. Hume, without hesitation, would refuse the bet. Temperamentally he has nothing in common with Sartre's Roquentin, who thought his tongue might at any moment turn into a centipede. Thus, as soon as it becomes a question of hard cash, Hume's celebrated scepticism, it may be said, flies out of the window. True, but we tested not the philosopher, but the man. Hume's philosophy brought him to a pitch of scepticism which was simply impracticable–or, if one prefers, intolerable–and the result was a kind of schizophrenia. Everyone knows the celebrated passage in which Hume describes what it was like to leave off philosophising and revert to ordinary life, but it will bear repetition:

> The *intense* view of these manifold contradictions and imperfections in human reason has so wrought upon me, and heated my brain, that I am ready to reject all belief and reasoning, and can look upon no opinion even as more probable or likely than another. Where am I, or what? From what causes do I derive my existence, and to what condition shall I return? Whose favour shall I court, and whose anger must I dread? What beings surround me? and on whom have I any influence, or who have any influence on me? I am confounded with all these questions, and begin to fancy myself in the most deplorable conditions imaginable, inviron'd with the deepest darkness, and utterly depriv'd of the use of every member and faculty.
>
> Most fortunately it happens, that since reason is incapable of dispelling these clouds, nature herself suffices to that purpose, and cures me of this philosophical melancholy

[1] *Treatise*, I.iii.12, p. 139.

and delirium, either by relaxing this bent of mind, or by some avocation, and lively impression of my senses, which obliterate all these chimeras. I dine, I play a game of backgammon, I converse, and am merry with my friends; and when after three or four hours' amusement, I wou'd return to these speculations, they appear so cold, and strain'd, and ridiculous, that I cannot find in my heart to enter into them any farther.[1]

It is not accurate to describe this passage as a philosophical analysis of the rival efficacy of two human organs of belief, the first called Reason and the second Nature; the two are not co-ordinate, and the second is powerless to heal the sickness of the first, simply because it is not that sort of thing. A schoolboy who is at first baffled by the proper geometrical method of bisecting an angle is not helped by the teacher who suggests that he can do it well enough by using his eyes and guessing–at least, he is not helped with his *geometrical* difficulty. Nature can indeed help Hume with his emotional troubles; she is strong to dispel melancholy, but she cannot, *ex hypothesi*, answer a single argument. Thus the clouds which Nature drives away are not identical with those called up by Reason, but are rather their emotive shadows. This is why I spoke of schizophrenia. This passage is not philosophical to the end. A change of mood is not an argument. Hume finds his *ataraxia* only by ceasing to philosophise.

Perhaps we are now in a position to attend with proper respect to the great utterances of the isolated mind which we find in Book I of the *Treatise*. At first it is the relations between things which are dissolved (and this is peculiarly the work of Hume):

All the perceptions of the mind are of two kinds, *viz.* impressions and ideas, which differ from each other only in their different degrees of force and vivacity. If you make any other changes on it, it represents a different object or impression. The case is the same as in colours. A particular shade of any colour may acquire a new degree of liveliness or brightness without any other variation. But when you

[1] *Treatise*, I.iv.7, pp. 268–9.

produce any other variation, 'tis no longer the same shade or colour. So that as belief does nothing but vary the manner, in which we conceive any object, it can only bestow on our ideas an additional force and vivacity. An opinion, therefore, or belief may be most accurately defin'd, A LIVELY IDEA RELATED TO OR ASSOCIATED WITH A PRESENT IMPRESSION.[1]

Belief, it seems, has been surrendered. But the mind, we may feel, though it can no longer judge of reality, is still allowed a sort of response to it. But the structure of Hume's argument is disquieting to the realist As we have seen, it is significant that while he readily defines 'idea' as a copy of 'impression', he refuses to define 'impression' as a copy of 'real object'. The first relation is within his purview, the second is extra-empirical. Thus the discerning reader can already see that Hume is imprisoned in the psychology of the individual.

The same forces are at work in another celebrated passage:

> Thus all probable reasoning is nothing but a species of sensation. 'Tis not solely in poetry and music, we must follow our taste and sentiment, but likewise in philosophy. When I am convinc'd of any principle, 'tis only an idea, which strikes more strongly upon me. When I give the preference to one set of arguments above another, I do nothing but decide from my feeling concerning the superiority of their influence. Objects have no discoverable connexion together; nor is it from any other principle but custom operating upon the imagination, that we can draw any inference from the appearance of one to the existence of another.[2]

Here again relations are dissolved, and the immediate cause of their dissolution is a distinctively Humian critique: there is no object such that it is logically inconsistent to conceive it as not existing. But again the psychologizing flavour directs us to a more fundamental cause. My third quotation should make the nature of the underlying cause sufficiently clear (I have, in a

[1] *Treatise*, I.iii.7, p. 96.
[2] *Ibid.*, I.iii.8, p. 103.

manner, cheated, since this quotation in fact is the earliest of the three in the order of the *Treatise*):

> Now since nothing is ever present to the mind but percep-
> tions, and since all ideas are deriv'd from something ante-
> cedently present to the mind; it follows, that 'tis impossible
> for us so much as to conceive or form an idea of any thing
> specifically different from ideas and impressions. Let us fix
> our attention out of ourselves as much as possible: Let us
> chace our imagination to the heavens, or to the utmost
> limits of the universe; we never really advance a step
> beyond ourselves, nor can conceive any kind of existence,
> but those perceptions, which have appear'd in that narrow
> compass. This is the universe of the imagination, nor have
> we any idea but what is there produc'd.[1]

This is distinctively Humian in its force and clarity, but in all else it is utterly traditional. The tradition is, of course, Lockian empiricism. All that is needed is for that easy first person plural to resolve itself into a first person singular.

Nevertheless, it might be said, Hume was not the man to evade plain facts. We do believe, and Hume did not shrink from incorporating this element into his philosophy. But we have now seen enough to know that this so-called positive element in his thought cannot buy back the real world for us. Everyone knows how Hume's empiricism provided the ground and method of his destructive work; it is not always noticed that it is the same empiricism which ultimately deprives the constructive philosophy of any real curative power. For however carefully we savour our opinions we shall never discover in differences of taste a guarantee of their veracity or probability. Sentimental naturalism, in short, can remind us of the fact of belief, but can never explain its justification. Thus the very thing for which the sceptic is hungry is systematically withheld.

What, then, was the effect of Hume? One is tempted to answer: 'None whatsoever.' The *Treatise*, in Hume's own words, 'fell dead-born from the press'.[2] The celebrity enjoyed by Paley's famous 'watch-maker' argument for the existence of God seems

---

[1] *Treatise*, I.ii.6, pp. 67–8.

[2] 'My Own Life', in Kemp Smith's 2nd edn. (1947) of the *Dialogues Concerning Natural Religion*, p. 234.

conclusive proof that the arguments of the *Dialogues Concerning Natural Religion* were either forgotten or not understood. Leslie Stephen, in his great *History of English Thought in the Eighteenth Century*, admitted the force of these objections, yet resisted the conclusion. He wrote:

> If Hume impressed men of mark so slightly, we are tempted to doubt whether he can have affected the main current of thought. Yet, as we study the remarkable change in the whole tone and substance of our literature which synchronised with the appearance of Hume's writings, it is difficult to resist the impression that there is some causal relation. A cold blast of scepticism seems to have chilled the very marrow of speculative activity. Men have lost their interest in the deepest problems, or write as though paralysed by a half-suppressed consciousness of the presence of a great doubter.[1]

Of course such a penumbra of influence as this is not, as Stephen acknowledges, reducible to precise determination as to what is cause and what effect. Between the man who says that it was Hume who, seeping slowly into the intelligence of the better heads, and thence to the worse, transformed the mind of England, and the man who says that Hume is simply a symptom like the rest, who shall adjudicate? My own impulse is to say that Hume was both symptom and stimulus, like a man who finds himself in a boat and begins by powerful strokes to propel it in the direction in which it is already moving. Yet this opinion, for all its appearance of judicious moderation, is as much a guess as either of the others. Thus, if in the following pages I speak of an opinion or an assumption as Humian, the term should not be construed as meaning 'caused by Hume', but only as meaning 'like Hume's'. Leslie Stephen, when he decided that there were many others besides Hume who were in some sense Humian, seems to have concentrated on the explicit scepticism of the first book of the *Treatise*. But it may be worth asking whether the so-called constructive philosophy called forth any echoes. My answer will be that it did, and that they will be found among the great romantics. I shall further argue that if the

[1] *Op. cit.*, vol. I, p. 1.

remedy of sentiment appears less factitious in them than in Hume, this is only because they were less clear-headed than he.

I have already broached this topic in two places; first when in my discussion of *Tristram Shandy* I called Hume's 'Reason is, and ought only to be the slave of the passions' the clarion-call of romanticism, and second when I described Kemp Smith's interpretation of Hume as Coleridgian.[1] To be sure, I said that in Shandy Hall sentiment supplied the place of rational com-munication, but 'sentiment', so used, was not yet a technical term. It was Hume who strove to give sentiment a cognitive status. The man in the street is familiar with the 'sentiments' of compassion or of affection, and this is the sense in which the word applies to *Tristram Shandy*. But the 'sentiment of belief' and the 'sentiment of disapprobation' are the work of Hume, and are less easily digested. In just the same way the ordinary man is familiar with 'imagination' as the organ of fantasy, but is less happy with 'imagination' as the organ of knowledge. Yet it is the second—that is the peculiar and Humian—sense of 'sentiment' and 'imagination' that is most deeply relevant to English romanticism.

In Coleridge's famous distinction between the primary and secondary imagination, two things are obvious at once—first a certain affinity with Hume's distinction between two sorts of imagining, and second a complete dissimilarity of tone:

> The IMAGINATION then, I consider either as primary, or secondary. The primary IMAGINATION I hold to be the living Power and prime Agent of all human Perception, and as a repetition in the finite mind of the eternal act of creation in the infinite I AM. The secondary Imagination I consider as an echo of the former, co-existing with the conscious will, yet still as identical with the primary in the *kind* of its agency, and differing only in *degree*, and in the *mode* of its operation. It dissolves, diffuses, dissipates, in order to recreate; or where this process is rendered impos-sible, yet still at all events it struggles to idealise and to unify. It is essentially *vital*, even as all objects (*as* objects) are essentially fixed and dead.[2]

[1] See above, pp. 73 and 99.

[2] *Biographia Literaria*, ed. J. Shawcross, the 1954 corrected reprint of the first edn. of 1907, Ch.xiii, vol. I, p. 202.

Countless literary readers have seized eagerly on this paragraph, only to discover, when they had read it through, that they did not quite know what to do with it. The primary imagination sounds exciting, with its mysterious cognitive powers, but evidently all that is something to do with metaphysics and has no very obvious connexion with literature. On the other hand, if the secondary imagination is not cognitive, in what sense is it an echo of the primary? And is there no difference between it and Coleridge's 'fancy', apart from the fact that since fancy amuses itself with 'fixities and definites' the material of the secondary imagination is somehow more fluid? These are not easy questions and their answer requires an eccentric preparation.

IV

In Istanbul in 1944 there appeared an essay called *'Figura'*,[1] which dealt with the structure of mediaeval literature in general and Dante in particular. It was by Erich Auerbach and has since become famous. In this essay Auerbach proposes a distinction between what he calls (following mediaeval usage) *allegoria* and *figura*. If you are writing an *allegoria*, you invent a set of persons and a story to represent a preformulated abstract meaning. For example, you might wish to celebrate the triumph of thrift over extravagance and carry out your design by describing a fight in which a poorly clad knight (called Thrift) succeeded in unhorsing a richly clad knight (called Extravagance). That is *allegoria*. *Figura*, on the other hand, is in the literary sphere a rarer and more interesting phenomenon. The writer of a figural poem does not frame a fictitious series of persons to convey the Significance; instead he encounters, in real life, a person or thing which is felt to be quite objectively significant, and this the poet need only describe, literally. Thus, whereas in *allegorial* poetry the overt story is fictitious though the Significance may be seriously asserted, in *figural* poetry both the representing figure and the thing figured are felt to be equally real. *Allegoria* can readily be seen as complex narrative metaphor, and the metaphor is the work of the poet as *fictor*, feigner. The figural poet, on the other hand, finds his metaphors walking about the real world, the streets of Florence or the

[1] Printed in *Scenes from the Drama of European Literature*, New York, 1959.

Cumbrian fells, and so has no need to invent metaphorical structures of his own. The great figural poet for Auerbach is, as my last sentence hinted, Dante.

From the beginning of the *Vita Nuova* to the end of the thirtieth canto of the *Paradiso*[1] Beatrice was for Dante an image of God.[2] But he did not invent her. He met her. Admittedly, some critics have tried to argue that Beatrice is an allegorical fiction, but they are recent, and of small authority. As Scartazzini writes, 'for four centuries no biographer and no commentator, with the exception of the worthy Giovan Maria Filelfo, whom our modern allegorists will scarcely care to recognise as their spiritual father, doubted the physical reality of Beatrice'.[3] The truth is clear enough. In 1274 two Florentine children met, Beatrice Portinari and Dante Alighieri. Beatrice was eight and Dante was nine. T. S. Eliot has written[4] that the only thing which puzzles him about the story is that they both seem just a little too old for what happened. The child Dante, at the sight of the little girl in the red dress, suffered an inrush of love into his spirit which the rest of his life was not so much a growing out of as a growing into. He tells us how his heart suddenly said to him 'Here is a lord stronger than I', how his perception told him, 'Your blessing has now appeared', and how his guts (he says 'the place where our food is digested') began to weep.[5] They met again nine years later in a street and then several times before Beatrice's death at the age of twenty-four or twenty-five. At her death Dante wrote the *Vita Nuova* in which he explains with an astonishing simplicity (though at the same time perhaps a certain shrillness) how Beatrice was an image of God. But the reader does not meet her face to face until the thirtieth canto of the *Purgatorio*:

> Guardaci ben: ben sem, ben sem Beatrice
> Come degnasti d'accedere al monte?
> Non sapei tu che qui e l'uom felice?[6]

---

[1] Here the contemplative Bernard takes over.

[2] Though he dissembled in the *Convivio*.

[3] G. A. Scartazzini, *A Companion to Dante*, trans. A. J. Butler, 1893, p. 182.

[4] 'Dante', III, in his *Selected Essays*, 3rd. edn., 1951, p. 273.

[5] *Vita Nuova*, I, in the edn. of T. Casini, revised C. Segre, Florence, 1962, pp. 8–10.

[6] 'Look well at me. I really am, I really am Beatrice. How did you ever

From this we move upward until we come to the place where
Dante, reunited with the girl he met forty-odd years before in
the house of Portinari, forgets her in his contemplation of the
light that shines from behind her, and Beatrice rejoices to be
forgotten.[1]

It is not altogether clear how far Auerbach's distinction
between *allegoria* and *figura* was framed by him and how far it
was found by him in the writings of mediaeval theorists.
Certainly the writers he puts forward as the authors of the
antithesis prove again and again to have been themselves
confused about it. But fortunately the question of the origin of
a critical distinction is separate from the question of its use and
its usefulness. The importance of the distinction between
allegoria and *figura* is, I submit, very great, greater perhaps than
Auerbach himself realised. Its relevance to mediaeval literature
is, I suppose, undisputed. Any contrivance which so adequately
distinguishes de Lorris from Dante is not to be rejected. But
Auerbach has devised a critical tool which is applicable to other
literatures than the mediaeval. In particular it applies (and this
is why I mentioned the Cumbrian fells a few pages back) to
Wordsworth. As the work of Dante is the great monument of
the figural mode in Italian, so the poetry of Wordsworth is in
English.

But here we must pause. It may be that when we turn from
scriptural exegesis (where Auerbach's distinction probably
originated) to literature, our distinction must lose some of its
starkness. For some, it will doubtless appear too crudely biographical. After all, if reference to real persons or events is to be
the sole criterion of figural status, then the most trivial poem
may be proved figural by antiquarian research ('The cherry tree
mentioned in line six may still be seen in the poet's back
garden . . .') and conversely Beatrice herself (Scartazzini not-
withstanding) is in principle open to the simplest historical
disproof. Thus the identification of figural poems becomes a
biographical rather than a critical task. Moreover it must be
conceded that as soon as we begin to read the *Comedy* we must

deign to come to the mountain? Did you not know that here man is happy?'
Purgatorio, XXX, in *La Divina Commedia* di Dante Alighieri, ed. S. A.
Chimenz, Turin, 1963, p. 584.

[1] *Paradiso*, X.61, p. 708; c.f. *Paradiso*, XXI.22–4, p. 813.

modify our original contention. Cato is historical enough, but Dante never really met him on the shores of Purgatory. Dante was not above inventing his dialogue. With Wordsworth we must concede still more. The grey-haired schoolmaster described in the Matthew poems[1] is in fact a mere composite, and so is the 'stout but hale' Wanderer:[2] 'Like the Wanderer in "The Excursion", this Schoolmaster was made up of several both of his class and men of other occupations. I do not ask pardon for what there is of untruth in such verses, considered strictly as matters of fact.'[3] But all this can be answered. Our literary responses are not immune to influences from sources outside literature itself. Few readers can lay their hands on their hearts and say that our knowledge of the impending death of Keats has no effect on our reading of his poems. Still fewer can read the line 'Dark, dark, dark, amid the blaze of noon' with complete indifference to the blindness of the poet. The line itself is the stronger for the sufferings of the poet *in his life*, and it certainly follows that if Milton's blindness be ever proved to have been an imposture that line will be diminished for all readers who are not themselves blinded by theory. But this does not mean that criticism can relax. Reality does not figure in literature as mere referent, either mentioned or not mentioned. Great art and attention are needed to encompass the real, and its presence in a work is a matter of degree. Rembrandt's own face is more fully present in his self-portraits than Van Dyck's is in *his*. Thus literary criticism will still be needed to distinguish fully figural art from that which is minimally figural. Since 'figural' was never offered as a criterion of merit there is nothing vicious in this.

As for the suggestion that Cato is less than fully figural, we simply agree. Much of the confusion about the nature of Dante's poetry arises from a failure to accept the fact that he worked in a mixed mode. Thus Cato is figural in that he once lived and the character in the *Comedy* is firmly derived, by a kind of imagina-

---

[1] 'Matthew', 'The Two April Mornings', 'The Fountain', *Poems of Sentiment and Reflection*, X, XI, XII, in *The Poetical Works* of William Wordsworth, ed. E. de Selincourt and H. Darbishire, vol. IV, 1947, pp. 68–73.

[2] *The Excursion*, I.34, *Poetical Works*, vol. V, 1949, p. 8.

[3] From the notes dictated by Wordsworth to Isabella Fenwick in 1843, printed in *Poetical Works, ed. cit.*, vol. IV, 1947, p. 415.

tive extension, from the historical man. But the fact that even so much 'imaginative extension' is involved is enough to make him less fully figural than, say, Beatrice. Not that Beatrice herself is, so to speak, *total figura*. She had died years before. Dante never met her in Purgatory, he only imagined it. And no doubt he deceived himself in the imagining. I told the story of Dante and Beatrice, after all, with too much faith, too little scepticism. The real difference between Virgil and Beatrice in the *Comedy* is that Dante knew Virgil very well indeed (though he never met him) and Beatrice—perhaps—scarcely at all (though he met her several times). Which makes Virgil more fully figural than Beatrice; which is not absurd.

As for Matthew and the Wanderer, they never even looked like true *figurae* anyway. They too are examples of a mixed mode. The faint tang of real experience which attaches to Matthew is wholly explicable in terms of the theory. Real memories of the Reverend William Taylor and others are confusedly operative in the poems. But this is not enough, at the level of literary genetics, to compose a solid *figura*, and, predictably, a solid *figura* we do not find. The great *figurae* of Wordsworth's poetry are *objects* of perception. But both the Wanderer and Matthew are projections of the perceiving subject. The style in which they are described readily takes on the accent of the ballad, which, as we shall see, proved unsuitable for Wordsworth's greatest poetry. Both men are dream selves, thinly disguised as remembered *figurae*, described in language of *ersatz* simplicity.

Thus far, then, the critical insight and the 'biographical' conception of *figura* harmonise. But it is surely possible to imagine a situation in which they would not. Let us think of one of the great encounters of *The Prelude*, a passage which we have assumed, before any hard biographical evidence has come in, to be a grand example of the figural mode (purer indeed than anything in Dante). Now let us suppose that evidence turns up which proves conclusively that what we took for description was really invention. Would we be right, in such a case, to drop the rich response of years? In fact we could not help doing so. The passage would be importantly modified by such a piece of information. And this is not so very strange. If one takes a piece of pious Victorian verse and writes at the foot of it 'by

John Betjeman' it instantly takes on a mysterious atmosphere of ironic self-love. Again, it must be said: our poetic responses are not immune to attack from the world of fact and faking. The poetry of the *Prelude* makes serious and simple claims upon the real of an astonishing kind. Wordsworth felt some sort of need to apologise for the 'lack of fact' in the Wanderer; the very idea of defending the practice of fiction would scarcely have occurred to an earlier poet. A seventeenth century verse meditation can often be transferred, without violence, from a book of lyrics to a scene in a play, where it becomes the opinion of a fictitious personage. But in Wordsworth the choice of genre (or rather, in the end, the refusal to accept any conventional genre at all) is crucial. The case of Wordsworth is a sort of reversal of the case of Milton. We can, with a great effort, imagine what it would be like to learn that the author of *Samson Agonistes* had never gone blind. We can, with a great effort, imagine what it would be like to learn that the author of *The Prelude* had never seen the things he described. The effect of this on Wordsworth is in fact very curious. It almost turns him into a verse novelist. But Wordsworth belongs to an earlier phase of the imagination. Before the novel understood itself it appeared as fake-history, a kind of ingeniously circumstantial mendacity. The writer could, by acknowledging the fiction, finally elude the charge of lying; or else he could adhere to the harsh, factual line, in which case lies will beset his progress, since this low kind of truth is in some ways harder to attain than the hypothetical universal of Aristotle.[1] Wordsworth chose the factual, and it is no accident that, as his highest virtue is a sort of candour of the eye, so his most frequent vice is a certain humbug. But he chose the more difficult course. They jest at scars that never felt a wound.

Wordsworth's greatest poetry is not fiction. How could it be? Why should he invent images to express a given meaning when in his ordinary life he encountered men, trees, and rocks which were *objectively* significant? This explains something which would otherwise be puzzling: the fact that Dante and Wordsworth, separated as they are by centuries of history and hundreds of miles of geography, are curiously alike. Charles

[1] History tells us 'What Alcibiades did'; poetry 'what would happen'. *Poetics*, 1451b.

Williams, who was a good intuitive critic of Dante, repeatedly compared the two poets.[1] I am told by a friend that once when he was on a journey some lines of poetry were running in his head; he strove persistently to trace them to a source in the *Inferno*; but they proved to be from 'The Leech Gatherer'.

The similarity between the two poets can be traced, microscopically, in their styles. Eliot, in his 1929 essay on Dante, praised the Italian poet for writing 'the greatest poetry . . . with the greatest economy of words, and with the greatest austerity in the use of metaphor . . .'.[2] Wordsworth's own Preface to *Lyrical Ballads* is a sustained plea for a renewed austerity in poetic diction. The Preface is very puzzling, even vulnerable, until it is read as the personal plea of the figural poet. If you are a figural poet you may, in the course of a walk, come to a wood which you instantly apprehend as numinous. The wood is, literally, a wood, is itself, and is 'significant'. It is a *figura*. You go home and try to write a poem about the real wood with its extra spiritual dimension. Now one of the first things you will discover is that it is no use trying to write about, say, Dryads.

In the handbooks a Dryad is a wood-spirit, but almost for that very reason it cannot represent your wood. When Dryads first entered Greek mythology it may well be that they derived from some real encounter with numinous woods. But by the end of the eighteenth century they are *tabu* to the figural poet simply because they proclaim their metaphorical status. The reader who opens a book and begins to read about Dryads will not have his perceptions enlarged; he will settle back comfortably to be diverted by the play of poetical fancy.

Now this is the point to which we have been working (and it involves an extension of *allegoria* to metaphorical writing in general). If you *meet* your metaphors (or perhaps we had better say your significant objects) walking about the public world, you have no need to construct elaborate metaphors of your own. On the contrary, you have a strong motive for avoiding as otiose all metaphor which is not strictly tied to the task of conveying the object's appearance. To write 'The Leech Gatherer' with a Shakespearian technique would be to pile

---

[1] See his *The Figure of Beatrice.*
[2] 'Dante', II, *Selected Essays*, p. 252.

Pelion upon Ossa. The reader's response would be clotted and confused by the simultaneous presence of two profoundly different poetic modes. Since for the figural writer all the significance, all the resonance is located in the object rather than in the fictions of the poet, he will want as far as possible a merely descriptive style. All the 'poetry' is in the object. Therefore the mysterious object must simply be transcribed, as lucidly as possible.

The result of this necessity will be, so to speak, a style-less style. This is just what Wordsworth achieved at his best. It will be evident from this analysis that the translucent episodes of *The Prelude* are the great Wordsworth, and that the ostentatiously simple ballads are, at bottom, a mistake. Wordsworth needed the style-less style, the formless form, the unencumbered voice of the 'man speaking to men'. The ballad, though linguistically simple, is in fact one of the most formal of poetic kinds. If you are a sincere animist, you will not be understood as long as you write in language which can be taken as 'merely metaphorical'. Your talk of speaking rocks will be enjoyed as personification, your talk of wood-spirits as fictitious mythology. For this reason the figural mode becomes the enemy and not the friend of metaphor.

Auerbach has shown us that there are two kinds of poetry: first a poetry made with words, and second (and more rarely) a poetry which, before it becomes verbal, is *made with perceptions*. Metaphor, which Aristotle held[1] to be the most crucial feature of poetry, while still supreme in the poetry of verbal fiction, finds a cool reception in the poetry of perception.

We are told in the fourth chapter of *Biographia Literaria* that the distinction between imagination and fancy first grew in Coleridge's mind as a result of his encounter with the original genius of Wordsworth. It seems that at first he was at a loss to say just what it was that made Wordsworth's poetry so different.[2] In Coleridge's account of the effect Wordsworth's poetry had on him we can distinguish two stages: the first a plain empirical record,[3] the second much more heavily loaded with a presupposed metaphysic.[4] In the earlier passage Coleridge

---

[1] *Poetics*, 1459 a.
[2] *Biographia Literaria*, IV, in Shawcross's edn., vol. I, p. 60.
[3] *Ibid.*, vol. I, p. 58.   [4] *Ibid.*, vol. I, p. 59.

is interested, above all, in the bareness of Wordsworth's poetry; in fact, he isolates precisely those features which we isolated a few pages back when we applied Auerbach's distinction:

> There was here no mark of strained thought, or forced diction, no crowd or turbulence of imagery . . . The occasional obscurities . . . had almost wholly disappeared, together with that worse defect of arbitrary and illogical phrases at once hackneyed, and fantastic, which hold so distinguished a place in the *technique* of ordinary poetry . . .

This was the poetry to account for which Coleridge's conception of imagination was originally framed. The question which now seems to be worth asking is this: how far does Coleridge's thought mirror Auerbach's, evolved as we have seen in response to a closely similar critical task?

V

A reading of D. G. James's *Scepticism and Poetry* (1937) helps to answer this question. *Scepticism and Poetry* is not so much a book about Coleridge's views on imagination as a book on imagination by a disciple of Coleridge. James felt called upon to fight the notion that poetry typically consists of systems of emotive utterance attaching to a universe of hard, given particulars. Rather, he thought, poetry is essentially cognitive, is a mode of apprehending the world. The mind (and here lies the crux) is not merely passive but is active in perception. The psychological fact that an observer can 'see' a set of lines on a page *either* as a flight of steps *or* as an overhanging cornice betrays the larger fact that there is an interpretative element unconsciously present in all perception. This informing, schematising property of the perceiving mind is most naturally classified under the heading of imagination. Such, in summary, was D. G. James's view. In his fight against the 'emotivists' he felt, not unnaturally, that he had Coleridge on his side.

For Coleridge, as we have seen, divides the imagination into primary and secondary, describes the primary as the prime agent of all human perception, and the secondary as an echo of the primary.

To begin with, we cannot doubt that James is right to place

Coleridge with those who see the mind as active in forming what we call real, perceivable things, who see the mind even as partly constitutive of reality. This is of course a radical philosophical idea; it would clearly be possible to trace it to the dialogues of Plato, or else, with equal cogency, to the work of Kant, Schelling and Fichte. The argument of this book requires that we track the idea among English thinkers of the seventeenth century. The promiscuity of Coleridge's reading easily permits all three.

Thus we can say that Coleridge, no less than Hume, fretted at the epistemology of Locke, but was more willing than Hume to adopt the Platonist way out. Locke wrote:

> These simple ideas, the materials of all our knowledge, are suggested and furnished to the mind only by those two ways above mentioned, viz. sensation and reflection. When the understanding is once stored with these simple ideas, it has the power to repeat, compare, and unite them, even to an almost infinite variety, and so can make at pleasure new complex ideas. But it is not in the power of the most exalted wit, or enlarged understanding, by any quickness or variety of thought, to *invent* or *frame* one new simple idea in the mind, not taken in by the ways before mentioned . . .[1]

Locke's language here instantly recalls Coleridge's account of fancy, which 'has no other counters to play with but fixities and definites' and 'must receive all its materials ready made'. But what for Coleridge is a subordinate function of the mind, typically exercised by inferior poets, is for Locke the mind itself. To Coleridge the human understanding was something much more interesting than a *tabula rasa*.

But if Locke was his great seventeenth century foe, Coleridge nevertheless had an ally in Locke's own century–namely, Ralph Cudworth, the greatest of the Cambridge Platonists. In his *True Intellectual System of the Universe* (1678) Cudworth wrote to confute the 'sottish conceit of Atheists . . . that not only sense, but also knowledge and understanding in men, is but a tumult, raised from corporeal things without pressing

[1] *Essay*, II.ii.2, vol. I, p. 145.

upon the organs of their body'.[1] Human knowledge is 'not a mere passion from sensible things';[2] sensible things themselves (as for example light and colours) are not known or understood either by the passion or fancy of sense, nor by anything merely foreign or adventitious, but by intelligible ideas exerted from the mind itself . . .[3] There is abundant evidence that Coleridge was acquainted with the *True Intellectual System*. The Gutch notebook contains a cluster of references to it which suggest a sustained reading of Cudworth in 1796.[4] A verbal reminiscence of Cudworth appears in Coleridge's sonnet on the birth of Hartley in the same year.

At first sight, then, D. G. James appears to be an excellent Coleridgian. In stressing the vital activity of the mind in perception and proceeding from this to the conception of poetry as embodying an act of apprehension, he would seem to have seized on the fundamental question. Yet his assertion of the special, cognitive property of poetry soon brings him into collision with a certain difficulty, and that difficulty is: metaphor. The collision is nowhere explicit in James's book; he writes as if it were not there at all.

The most important chapter for our purpose is his third, in which he makes the following statement of the position so far reached: '. . . the essence of poetry, of its creation and enjoyment, consists of creative prehension of an object.'[5] A little later he writes: 'The business of poetry then is to make conveyance of imaginative objects.'[6] Although James is speaking here of the secondary imagination, the word 'objects' bears a strong sense. The fact that these objects are created by the imagination does not mean that they are not real, since all objects, chairs, tables, trees, people, are likewise created—by the primary imagination. The principal difference between them is that the process whereby the primary imaginary forms its objects is

[1] In the edn. of 1845, vol. III, p. 61. See Basil Willey, *The Seventeenth Century Background*, 1953, pp. 155–7.

[2] *True Intellectual System*, p. 65.

[3] *Ibid.*, p. 62.

[4] It is not certain that Coleridge read beyond the first book of the *True Intellectual System*. However, the notebooks make it clear that he swiftly found his way to the doctrine he craved; see K. Coburn's edn. (1957) of *The Notebooks, 1794–1804*, esp. entry no. 200 and her comment on it.

[5] *Scepticism and poetry: an Essay on the Poetic Imagination*, 1937, p. 75.

[6] *Ibid.*, p. 81.

unconscious. Thus 'objects' has a high cognitive status. Certainly there is a sense in which the poet makes the things he sees; but only the sense in which we all make everything we see. We may therefore legitimately set on one side for a moment the language of creation and ask instead what poets in particular, in their special act of prehension, *see*. James is plainly sensible of the pressure to answer this question: what is the cognitive content of the secondary imagination? The answer he offers is this: '. . . by the secondary imagination the world is constantly represented as "vital".'[1] The secondary imagination is an animist. Thus Shakespeare speaks of 'the marigold that goes to bed wi' th' sun and with him rises, weeping'.[2] To defend the special cognitive status of this James enlists the aid of Bacon, Schopenhauer and Whitehead,[3] all of whom, it seems had their animistic moments and high I.Q.s too.

The tendency of Professor James's argument is plain. Like Auerbach's it tends to the exclusion of metaphor. For if 'bright Phoebus in his strength' embodies a serious animism it ceases to be an example of that species of metaphor known as 'personification'. Certainly the secondary imagination loves to indulge the pathetic fallacy, but if James's analysis is correct it ceases to be a fallacy and becomes a fact, the evidence for which may be examined in the works of Bacon, Schopenhauer and Whitehead. Ruskin, who coined the phrase 'pathetic Fallacy', has plenty of room for metaphor (though he strangely insists that the greatest poets do not use such metaphors) yet he has no room for animism. D. G. James, who *has* room for animism, cannot really afford room for metaphor (though he writes as if he could). The two categories are mutually exclusive. In so far as a passage is asserting animism so far must we take its personalising of nature as literal statement. And *vice versa*.[4]

Thus we arrive at the same point that we reached through a

[1] *Scepticism and poetry: an Essay on the Poetic Imagination*, 1939, p. 82.
[2] Quoted *ibid.*, p. 85.   [3] *Ibid.*, p. 86.
[4] These remarks may be thought to contradict the argument of my *Two Concepts of Allegory* (1967), since I there disputed C. S. Lewis's contention that allegory and Platonism were opposites, and mutually exclusive. I replied that a serious assertion of Platonism might still be allegorical, or metaphorical, for the special reason that a literal account of the transcendent is impossible. I applied the same argument to allegories of the inner life, or of mental events. But these remain special cases (though they loom large in the history of allegorical poetry). I could not reason in this way of

consideration of *figura*. To demonstrate this I need only repeat from earlier in this chapter a sentence describing the difficulties of the figural poet who, instead of framing his significant structures by means of poetic devices, finds the significance located in the object. This was the sentence: Your talk of speaking rocks will be enjoyed as personification, your talk of wood-spirits as felicitous mythology.

Both Auerbach's thesis and Coleridge's as expounded by James yield a poetic of percept as opposed to a poetic of literary construct; both seem profoundly relevant to the work of Wordsworth; both tend to the exclusion of metaphor.

Now if we are right so far it would seem that we have an important criticism to make of James (and also, apparently, of Coleridge); namely that, compared with Auerbach, he is fatally undiscriminating in the choice of his poetic examples, and fatally over-ambitious for the scope of his theory. Auerbach at least realised that a figural analysis is properly applied only to a figural poet, like Dante. But James was rash enough to apply his theory to the greatest non-figural, constructive poet, Shakespeare. One senses the difference as soon as James shifts from his consideration of Wordsworth's 'Leech Gatherer' (which fits his case admirably) to Shakespeare's lines on marigolds. The truth is that it *is* relevant to the Wordsworth poem to argue seriously for an extension of the province of organic vitality, in such a way that a stone and an old man have the same status. Philosophical talk about the substitution of an organic for a mechanist world-view *is* relevant to the work of the great romantic. But as soon as we turn to

> The marigold that goes to bed wi' th' sun
> And with him rises, weeping

we feel the crass irrelevance of the solemn citation of Schopenhauer and Whitehead. The crucial difference lies in the fact that Shakespeare is working (as he always worked) within a world of *metaphor*. There is a difference of principle between Bacon's obscure and tentative ascription of minimal consciousness to natural objects and the exuberant anthropomorphism

---

animism, since its assertion does not in fact require metaphorical language. Lewis's argument which does not work where he most wishes it to—on De Lorris, say—works perfectly here.

of Shakespeare's lines. The O level student who says that they are an example of personification gets his mark; but when that same student comes to apply that same rhetorical concept to Wordsworth, he will (if he has any critical vigilance) experience a certain discomfort. The discomfort springs from an intuition that Wordsworth means what he says, has experienced the mysterious vitality of which he speaks.

The latent conclusion of James's argument must be dragged into the light; it is that poetic personification and metaphor in general (except for a few 'pupillary' tropes and metaphors designed to present vividly the appearance of a thing) must be relegated to the category of fancy; and that those elements in a poem which we can unhesitatingly term imaginative will be those in which a special perception of the world is seriously asserted. James's theory thus becomes (like Auerbach's) a good Dante-Wordsworth theory but a bad theory of poetry.

Must we make the same criticism of Coleridge? Is Coleridge's account relevant only to the poetic revolution inaugurated by his friend, or did James mishandle the precepts of his master? I shall argue that the second alternative is the right one. Coleridge is one of the most complex minds in the history of English literature, and it is no light matter to assume his critical armour. James involved himself in a critical situation that was more intricate than he knew.

First of all, there is no escaping the fact that, even if Coleridge's notion took origin from the encounter with Wordsworth's poetry, it at once attached itself to Shakespeare's. Certainly the date given in the *Biographia* for its genesis precedes any written record we have: he says it happened in his twenty-fourth year (Coleridge was born in 1772). But it remains a fact that in all the early versions we possess the distinction appears in connexion, not with the poetry of Wordsworth but with the poetry of Shakespeare. For example, according to Crabb Robinson's *Times* report,[1] Coleridge in the fourth lecture of the 1811–12 series stressed the poet's need for *imagination*, in addition to *mere association* and *sensibility*, and drew his examples from the source he used for chapter 11 of

[1] See Shawcross's edn. of the *Biographia* already cited, vol. I, pp. l–li. The report itself is given in S. T. Coleridge, *Shakespearian Criticism*, ed. T. M. Raysor, 2nd edn., 1960, vol. II, pp. 158–9.

the *Biographia*: Shakespeare's *Venus and Adonis*. The notion can be chased yet further back in the twenty-fifth notebook where there is a whole section which probably belongs to the lectures of 1808.[1] Here the antithesis between fancy and imagination appears explicitly, and the examples are the Shakespearian ones of the *Biographia*. Again, there is no mention of Wordsworth. The very earliest reference I am aware of occurs in a letter of 1802[2] to W. Sotheby where Coleridge is drawing a distinction between Greek and Hebrew poetry (in favour of Hebrew). There is a good deal about Pindar but, again, nothing about Wordsworth. All these passages are sketches of what is later defined as the *secondary* imagination.

Perhaps we can now begin to see where James went wrong. First of all, Coleridge makes the difference between the primary and secondary imagination much more firmly than James does; in particular, he observes that the secondary imagination 'dissolves, diffuses, dissipates in order to recreate.' This at once suggests Shakespeare. It also suggests metaphor, and (what was surely one of the principal goals of the distinction) the difference between a live, quickening metaphor and a lifelessly clever one. We have only to think of the etymology of *metaphor* –'transference'–to see how a theory of the secondary imagination naturally becomes a theory of metaphor; the secondary imagination must necessarily take its terms from the realm of the primary imagination, and transfer, or even wrench them to its own purposes.

James's mistake lay in his attempt to treat the secondary imagination as a mere extension of the primary. Let us remember: it is the primary imagination which gives us our ordinary world of percepts, of individuated objects. Now it is surely true that almost all philosophers (Plato in his early dialogues is a possible exception) have been concerned with the world of the primary imagination. The secondary world has been left to the poets, and both parties have been for the most part content. But Wordsworth is an exception: he is a poet

---

[1] See *Shakespearian Criticism*, ed. Raysor, vol. I, p. 188.

[2] *Collected Letters of Samuel Taylor Coleridge*, ed. E. L. Griggs, 1956, vol. II, pp. 459–60: 'At best it is but Fancy, or the aggregating faculty of the mind–not Imagination, or the *modifying*, and *co-adunating* Faculty.'

who works in the primary imagination. It is often said that *any* good book makes the world look different to the man who has just read it. But when people say this they usually intend a moral transformation of the world rather than a modification of our actual categories of perception. But Wordsworth's poetry pleads continually for something resembling an epistemological conversion in the reader.

Laurence Lerner has noted[1] the prevalence in Wordsworth of the 'whether . . . or' construction, the recurrent nervousness lest the thing he thought he saw should prove a mere projection of his mind; for example;

> My seventeenth year was come
> And, whether from this habit, rooted now
> So deeply in my mind, or from excess
> Of the great social principle of life,
> Coercing all things into sympathy,
> To inorganic natures I transferr'd
> My own enjoyments, or, the power of truth
> Coming in revelation, I convers'd
> With things that really are, I, at this time
> Saw blessing spread around me like a sea.[2]

Here the lines are up-beat: confidence follows and almost cancels the doubt. But sometimes we find the opposite order:

> To every natural form, rock, fruit or flower,
> Even the loose stones that cover the high-way,
> I gave a moral life, I saw them feel,
> *Or linked them to some feeling* . . .[3]

But strangest of all is the outright suppression of the 'or' clause, resulting in a sort of syntactic aposiopesis:

> Now, whether it were by peculiar grace,
> A leading from above, a something given,
> Yet it befell that, in this lonely place,

[1] See his *The Truest Poetry*, 1960, pp. 140 f.

[2] *The Prelude*, II.405–14. This and all subsequent quotations from *The Prelude* are taken, unless otherwise stated, from the text of 1805–6 as given in the 2nd edn. of E. de Selincourt (revised by Helen Darbishire), 1959.

[3] *Ibid.*, III.124–7 (my italics).

When I with these untoward thoughts had striven,
Beside a pool bare to the eyes of heaven
I saw a Man before me unawares:
The oldest man he seemed that ever wore grey hairs.[1]

Here perhaps the vision was too peremptory, and left no leisure for the sceptical alternative. But sometimes the vision itself proved unstable; not only its status but its very contents shifted; in the Immortality Ode the transfigured world of childhood is suddenly seen as:

Fallings from us, vanishings;
Blank misgivings of a Creature
Moving about in worlds not realised[2]

Wordsworth can hardly believe his own vision, and its very significance is insecure, but all this only increases the harrowing urgency with which he pleads for our conversion.

Thus, to the man who is trying to understand what Coleridge meant by '*secondary* imagination', Wordsworth is a red herring. James generalised from Wordsworth when he should have generalised from Shakespeare. The poetry of Wordsworth has certain philosophical consequences. The poetry of Shakespeare has none. When we say, 'has philosophical consequences' we *mean* 'modifies our picture of the real world', that is to say, the world of the *primary* imagination. Thus Wordsworth is, what most poets are not, a poet of the primary imagination. Indeed, he is almost alone. But Shakespeare is at the head of a great company; he is master of the secondary imagination. The discomfort we feel when we try to apply Schopenhauer and Whitehead to Shakespeare's personifications arises from the covert wrenching of a poetry operating in the mode of the secondary imagination out of that mode and into the world of percepts, the ordinary province of philosophical discourse. Trying to find support for Shakespeare's personifications in the writings of animistic philosophers is like looking for Heaven with a space-ship; that is, it involves a confusion of levels.

It seems that Coleridge's secondary imagination is something at once more mysterious and more familiar than we had

---

[1] 'Resolution and Independence', 50–56, in the de Selincourt and Darbishire edn. of the *Poetical Works*, vol. II, 1952, p. 237.

[2] 143–7, *Poetical Works*, vol. IV, 1947, p. 283.

guessed. The whole point of saying that a poet works in the
secondary and not the primary imagination is to make it clear
that he is not modifying the individuational or ontological
structure of this public world. He is making/seeing something
in a secondary realm. It follows that if the secondary imagination is cognitive it is a secondary cognition that is involved,
operating independently of the ordinary knowledge discussed
by philosophers. What emerges from our enquiry is that in a
real sense Wordsworth actually was the philosophical poet
Coleridge insisted on taking him for.[1] Of course Wordsworth
was no match for Coleridge in dialectical acuteness, and indeed
took a very English pride in never having 'read a word of
German metaphysics, thank Heaven!'[2]

But a man can be interested in metaphysics without having
opened a book in his whole life. It may be that more than one
learned don asked his last metaphysical question at the age of
ten, and lost his philosophy with his innocence. It may be that
Wordworth's simplicity of mind, while it unfitted him for
dispute with Coleridge, nevertheless saved him from some
Coleridgian absurdities. Certainly, Coleridge was disappointed
in Wordsworth–largely, it seems, because Wordsworth's
philosophy failed to mirror his own–yet he never ceased to feel
that there was a sense in which his mind was utterly transcended
by Wordworth's.

It is interesting to read Coleridge's account of what he
expected from Wordsworth's projected poem, *The Recluse*:

> Then the plan laid out, and, I believe, partly suggested
> by me, was that Wordsworth should assume the station of
> a man in mental repose, one whose principles were made
> up, and so prepared to deliver upon authority a system
> of philosophy. He was to treat man as man–a subject of
> eye, ear, touch, and taste, in contact with external nature,
> and informing the senses from the mind, and not com-
> pounding a mind out of the senses; then he was to describe

---

[1] 'I think Wordsworth possessed more of the genius of a great philosophic poet than any man I ever knew, or, as I believe, has existed in
England since Milton,' *Table Talk*, July 21st, 1832, in the Oxford edn. of
1917, p. 189.

[2] *Correspondence of Crabb Robinson with the Wordsworth Circle*, ed. Edith
J. Morley, 1927, vol. I, p. 401.

the pastoral and other states of society, assuming something of the Juvenalian spirit as he approached the high civilisation of cities and towns, and opening a melancholy picture of the present state of degeneracy and vice; thence he was to infer and reveal the proof of, and necessity for, the whole state of man and society being subject to, and illustrative of, a redemptive process in operation, showing how this idea reconciled all the anomalies, and promised future glory and restoration. Something of this sort was, I think, agreed upon. It is, in substance, what I have all my life been doing in my system of philosophy.[1]

It is indeed. Of course we cannot say with confidence what Wordsworth would really have written if he had finished *The Recluse*. But we may suspect some significance in his very failure to finish it. As it is, the first instalment, *The Prelude*, scarcely fulfils the grand Coleridgian design. The interesting thing is that Coleridge's description is accurate enough as long as it remains true to the Locke tradition. Man as 'a subject of eye, ear, touch and taste, in contact with external nature'—this is the alpha and omega of *The Prelude*. The word 'informing' strikes the first false note, with its 'cultured', glib assumption of a Greek metaphysic—an Aristotelianism of convenience. Thereafter the excursion into theological sociology is pure Coleridge.

Time did nothing to heal the division between the two men. Wordsworth never demonstrated the Christian God in the structure of nature in quite the way Coleridge wanted. Coleridge grew more doctrinal, more metaphysical, more theological as the years went by. Wordsworth remains a philosophically inarticulate member of the school of Locke. The scepticism of Hume and the precise status of Hume's pseudo-cognitive sentiment is never explicit in Wordsworth, but as Hume was a psychologising philosopher, Wordsworth was a psychologising poet.

VI

'The Old Cumberland Beggar'[2] makes a good introduction to Wordsworth. I have always found that it sorted out the

---

[1] *Table Talk*, July 21st, 1832, p. 188.
[2] *The Poetical Works*, vol. IV, pp. 234–40.

E

Wordsworthians from the non-Wordsworthians admirably. The non-Wordsworthian reads the poem as social moralising, and indeed there is social morality (of a curious kind) in the poem. Wordsworth describes the old man as he moves slowly from village to village, the object of a considerate charity wherever he goes. Destitution has reduced him almost to unconsciousness; his eyes never move from the ground before his feet. The reader, who was prepared to pity or to sympathise, may be surprised at the abrupt imperative which follows:

> But deem not this Man useless—

A strange argument then unfolds. By 'nature's law' every creature, however humble, has a function. The utility of the old Cumberland beggar consists in his power to call forth acts of charity, to stimulate feelings of benevolence, followed by self-congratulation (the word is Wordsworth's). From this Wordsworth concludes that the old man ought not to be taken into the workhouse, but rather

> let his blood
> Struggle with frosty air and winter snows;
> And let the chartered wind that sweeps the heath
> Beat his grey locks against his withered face.

But, to be sure, workhouses were vile places. A man might commend a vagrant to the rough elements rather than to the workhouse, and still be humanitarian. Wordsworth, after all, seems first to have conceived the poem in a fit of generous indignation[1] inspired by reading extracts from Crabbe's *The Village* in the *Annual Register*. The word 'useless' is, presumably, partly explained by historical context. It is aimed at the 'Utilitarian' legislation, which by the act of 1722 had raised the number of workhouses. Yet one has only to glance at Crabbe's poem to see that there is a difference between it and Wordsworth's.

[1] A feeling that there may have been something theoretical about Wordsworth's indignation is enhanced by his curious comment to the effect that Crabbe was not correct as far as his (Wordsworth's) experience went; for in the North imbeciles were usually left at large, and were 'too often the butt of thoughtless children'. That 'too often' suddenly sends the argument in the opposite direction. See Mary Moorman, *William Wordsworth; the Early Years*, 1957, p. 55.

Theirs is yon house that holds the parish poor,
Whose walls of mud scarce hold the broken door;
There, where the putrid vapours, flagging, play,
And the dull wheel hums doleful through the day;—
There children dwell who know no parents' care;
Parents, who know no children's love, dwell there![1]

The difference is simple; Crabbe's interest in the subject is truly humane whereas Wordsworth's is not. For, really, arguments about the comparative hardship of life inside and life outside the workhouse are not relevant to Wordsworth's poem. One has only to attend to the connexions of thought to see that he is taking quite another line. The reason why the old man should not enter the workhouse is not that he will be happier outside, but that if he were taken in he could not discharge his curious ethical function. The 'Utilitarianism' of the legislators is indeed strangely transformed.

Thus there is a moralising argument and I had better confess at once that I find it repellent. It turns on an inversion of the normal order of ethical discourse. Instead of saying that charity is good because it relieves distress, Wordsworth is virtually saying that distress is good because it provides stimulus and scope for charity. Thus a sort of meta-ethical realm is introduced. It is important that men should be happy, but it is far more important that charity should *exist*. It is an argument congenial to the right-wing mind, and especially to the right-wing Christian mind. If we want an analogue to Wordsworth's reasoning, we must look in the works of Roman Catholic apologists; Newman, for example:

> The Church aims, not at making a show, but at doing a work. She regards this world, and all that is in it, as a mere shadow, as dust and ashes, compared with the value of one single soul. She holds that, unless she can, in her own way, do good to souls, it is no use her doing anything; she holds that it were better for sun and moon to drop from heaven, for the earth to fail, and for all the many millions who are upon it to die of starvation in extremest agony, so far as temporal affliction goes, than that one

[1] *The Village*, Book I, in *The Poetical Works of George Crabbe*, ed. A. J. Carlyle and R. M. Carlyle, 1908, p. 37.

soul, I will not say, should be lost, but should commit one
single venial sin, should tell one wilful untruth, though it
harmed no-one, or steal one poor farthing without excuse.
She considers the action of this world and the action of the
soul simply incommensurate, viewed in their respective
spheres.[1]

But it is hardly less important to distinguish Wordsworth from
Newman than it was to distinguish him from Crabbe. The
difference here is that Newman's mind works theologically.
Thus, whereas Wordsworth stresses the importance of feeling,
Newman stresses the importance of spirit. If Newman's ethics
smell of scholasticism, Wordsworth's smell of subjectivity.

But, as I have hinted, the morality of 'The Old Cumberland
Beggar' is not all there is to that poem. It is not even the most
important thing. We may feel, as we read Wordsworth's
strangely untroubled, strangely pitiless description of the
beggar, that all is explained by the depraved ethical argument.
But there is a kind of negative power in the treatment of the
central figure that leaves one dissatisfied with such an explanation.

> The aged Man
> Had placed his staff across the broad smooth stone
> That overlays the pile; and from a bag
> All white with flour, the dole of village dames,
> He drew his scraps and fragments, one by one;
> And scann'd them with a fix'd and serious look
> Of idle computation. In the sun
> Upon the second step of that small pile,
> Surrounded by those wild unpeopled hills,
> He sat, and ate his food in solitude;
> And ever, scattered from his palsied hand,
> That, still attempting to prevent the waste,
> Was baffled still, the crumbs in little showers
> Fell on the ground; and the small mountain birds,
> Not venturing yet to peck their destined meal,
> Approached within the length of half his staff.

[1] *Difficulties felt by Anglicans in Catholic Teaching*, Part II, Lecture viii,
4th edn., 1876, pp. 210–11. C.f. Evelyn Waugh, who, when interviewed by
the BBC on June 26th, 1960, said he thought it would be a good thing if
the world were blown up, provided that the thing was done inadvertently.

It is in a way sad to see Crabbe's verse, decent and compassionate as it is, so thoroughly eclipsed by Wordsworth's amoral poetry. Wordsworth's lines, no doubt, are full of tenderness. But all the tenderness is lavished on the act of seeing, none on the human figure himself. Social indignation really has nothing to do with what is going on here. Neither 'pity' nor 'admiration' is a useful term to describe Wordsworth's relation to the beggar; 'fascination'—and perhaps 'envy'—come a good deal nearer. The solitude of the beggar is not for Wordsworth a social fact, nor in any ordinary sense is it an ethical fact; it is phenomenal in the Greek sense of the word: that is, it is a matter of the way the figure impinges on the perceiving mind. So far from being interested in the human predicament, he is really moved above all by the inhumanity of the figure before him, by its stillness, by its continuity with the surrounding landscape. The good Wordsworthian, who knows how Wordsworth is often at his best when at his worst—when giving with lunatic pedantry the dimensions of a pond or tracking the Idiot Boy—will not be surprised to find that a characteristically odd passage betrays the profounder meaning of the poem. I mean the lines where Wordsworth tells how charitable villagers do not place their gifts in the old man's hand but instead—so submerged and decrepit is he—they 'lodge' them in his hat. The verb suggests an action like that of fixing a message in the crook of a tree. But of course Wordsworth is also capable of conveying his meanings in lines which are straightforwardly and incontestably superb:

> Thus, from day to day.
> Bowbent, his eyes for ever on the ground
> He plies his weary journey, seeing still,
> And seldom knowing that he sees, some straw,
> Some scattered leaf, or marks which, in one track,
> Nails of cart or chariot wheel have left
> Impressed on the white road,—in the same line,
> At distance still the same. Poor Traveller!
> His staff trails with him; scarcely do his feet
> Disturb the summer dust; he is so still
> In look and motion, that the cottage curs,
> Ere he has passed the door, will turn away,

Weary of barking at him. Boys and girls,
The vacant and the busy, maids and youths,
The urchin newly breeched–all pass him by:
Him even the slow-paced waggon leaves behind.

Note how in the last line a sort of metrical *rigor mortis* sets in.
Precisely those things which to the practical intelligence seem
otiose–the marks in the dust, the passing waggon–are the
essence of the poem.

There are, of course, many analogues in Wordsworth to the
experience of this poem. Most people, on seeing a corpse fished
out of a lake, feel horror at what has happened to the unfortunate man. Wordsworth, to use his own words–which
should be respected–felt no such 'vulgar fear', but rather a
kind of aesthetic awe.[1] Most people on meeting an emaciated
discharged soldier[2] at the point of death by sickness or starva-
tion are moved by horror or pity. Wordsworth certainly behaves
to the soldier as a charitable man must, though it might be said
that he satisfies only the minimum requirement (he takes the
soldier to a cottage and instructs the labourer who lives there
to give the soldier a place to sleep and some food). But it is
clear that his mind is elsewhere. In fact, as always, it is following the movement of his eye, observing the moonlight on the
mouth and hands, the unmoving shadow. When he leaves the
soldier Wordsworth is not in any of the ordinary states of mind,
deemed appropriate to such an occasion. On the contrary, his
condition can be described as distinctively Wordsworthian.
As I understand it, it is something like an exalted inner
peacefulness. Even when Wordsworth's moralising is at its most
abstract, his phraseology betrays the same strange temper:

> . . . the *soothing* thoughts that spring
> Out of human suffering.[3]

One suspects that this bizarre observation, for all its un-
exceptionable context, happens at the same time to express,
with an unguarded simplicity, a real peculiarity in Wordsworth's
emotional make-up.

[1] *The Prelude*, V.460–18.
[2] *Ibid.*, IV.400 f.
[3] 'Ode: Intimations of Immortality from Recollections of early Child-
hood', 184–5, *Poetical Works*, vol. IV, p. 284 (my italics).

But what makes the solitary soldier particularly relevant to the old Cumberland beggar is his parting remark:

> '. . . my trust is in the God of Heaven
> And in the eye of him that passes me.'[1]

The last words of 'The Old Cumberland Beggar' are these:

> As in the eye of Nature he has lived,
> So in the eye of Nature let him die!

What does 'in the eye of' mean in these passages? The phrase, given gnomic authority by Wordsworth, obviously bears some relation to popular idiom. We speak still of living in the king's eye, when we mean living under the king's observation. We also use 'in the eye of' to mean 'subjectively related to' ('Beauty is in the eye of the beholder'). Obviously of the two idioms the first is central here. But can we say with confidence that the second is utterly irrelevant? For, if the soldier's words mean *only* that he relies on other people noticing his distress, why does Wordsworth point the lines as he does, and why, within his own narrative, does he react the way he does? In either poem the phrase conceals a metaphysical frisson: the old beggar (who, whatever else became of him, would cease to exist as an object of Wordsworthian vision the moment he entered a work-house) is held in a kind of perceptual field of force; he is there, the focus of the landscape, because Nature herself is watching him. In the episode of the solitary soldier the subjective reference has narrowed; the soldier owes his visionary identity to the watching eyes of Wordsworth, the everlasting passer-by, *spectator haud particeps*. Shakespeare, it is generally agreed, could write most kinds of poetry better than anyone else before or since; but we shall search the works of Shakespeare in vain for anything like Wordsworth's swift translation of every public event into the distinctive terms of his own reaction. It is inconceivable that Shakespeare should have introduced the Dark Lady into his Sonnets by observing that it was through meeting her that he first experienced a certain kind of elevated thought, contempt, mingled with a kind of devotion. Yet this is just what Wordsworth would do. In Shakespeare the poet's emotions are both expressed and analysed; they are never

---

[1] *The Prelude*, IV.494–5.

solemnly noted in a kind of separation from the public object. This is poetic psychologising, and is the proper domain of Wordsworth.

VII

Once committed to the Wordsworthian method there is no escape via metaphysical conjuring tricks. That is, once one has adopted the practice of treating each event as the mere occasion of one's own reactions, it is no good claiming that what your reactions tell you is that the inner world is united with the outer; if *your* reactions tell you that, then this is just another of *your* reactions. Readers of Hume are, or ought to be, aware of the predicament. The existence of a subjective sentiment, whatever its content, cannot resolve epistemological scepticism. If we awake within a dream, we have not really awoken.

It is sometimes said that this charge of egotism is unfairly applied to *The Prelude* because Wordsworth's mind mirrored the universe; so that to explore 'the growth of a poet's mind' was in this case simply to explore the world. It will be evident from what I have said so far that I believe this view to be mistaken. A kind of loss of innocence has occurred and the result is that we never feel we are looking at public objects. Rather we are admitted to a new kind of theatre, where we watch the mental images of a fellow creature. Hence the sense of dream which pervades the poem. For Hume, dreams and mental images were distinguished from percepts by their comparative lack of vividness. The time was to come when Wordsworth would casually reverse this assumption, urging that once his percepts had had all 'the glory and the freshness of a dream'.[1] Nothing in Wordsworth is ever simply vivid; instead it is *poignantly* vivid, *strangely* vivid; the intervening adverbs betray the same truth. In various early passages of *The Prelude* Wordsworth wrestled honestly with his problem. Let us look again at the crucial passage:

> My seventeenth year was come
> And, whether from this habit, rooted now
> So deeply in my mind, or from excess
> Of the great social principle of life,

---

[1] Immortality Ode, 5, *Poetical Works*, vol. IV, p. 279.

> Coercing all things into sympathy,
> To unorganic natures I transferr'd
> My own enjoyments, or, the power of truth
> Coming in revelation, I convers'd
> With things that really are, I, at this time
> Saw blessings spread around me like a sea.[1]

Here Wordsworth is plainly bewildered. He is afraid that his insights are merely projections, hopes that they are telling him about external reality. But the important thing is that, whatever the final decision (and here none is taken), the categories of his thought are Lockian. But Wordsworth, unlike Locke, has a distinctive psychology, a peculiar cast to his mind, and is therefore afraid, as Locke was not, that his ideas are not truly representative of the world. He has two possible ways of resolving the situation. One is traditional. The universe is so ordered that the psychology we inherit is precisely fitted to reflect the structure of reality. This pious commitment finds expression in these lines:

> Nor, sedulous as I have been to trace
> How Nature by extrinsic passion first
> Peopled my mind with beauteous forms or grand,
> And made me love them, may I well forget
> How other pleasures have been mine, and joys
> Of subtler origin; how I have felt,
> Not seldom, even in that tempestuous time,
> Those hallow'd and pure motions of the sense
> Which seem, in their simplicity, to own
> An intellectual charm, that calm delight
> Which, if I err not, surely must belong
> *To those first-born affinites that fit*
> *Our new existence to existing things,*
> And, in our dawn of being, constitute
> The bond of union betwixt life and joy.[2]

Obviously, if this view is to have any cogency, its piety must be more than piety; it must be religion. We need to believe that the universe is *divinely* ordered to ensure that just correspondence. In other words, we need the divine guarantor of Cartesian philosophy. Take away the divine authority and we

[1] *The Prelude*, II.405–14. [2] *The Prelude*, I.571 f (my italics).

have no reason whatever to trust in the existence of so minute
a system of correspondences. And in Wordsworth's lines that
authority is indeed nowhere to be found. Instead we are left
with the numinous, quasi-allegorical figure of Nature, which
obviously is in no position to guarantee *itself*. Wordsworth is
in this respect a true member of the psychologising, empiricist
tradition; he has no time for entities which are the product of
a purely ontological necessity. With all his great capacity for
worship, he was always readier to reverence the proliferating
Effect than the First Cause.

The other method is to reject the dualism fathered by
seventeenth century science, and to opt for a union of mind
with its immediate objects; that is to invert the old disparagement of secondary qualities at the expense of the primary:

> Those incidental charms which first attach'd
> My heart to rural objects, day by day
> Grew weaker, and I hasten on to tell
> How Nature, intervenient till this time,
> And secondary, now at length was sought
> For her own sake. But who shall parcel out
> His intellect, by geometric rules,
> Split, like a province, into round and square?
> Who knows the individual hour in which
> His habits were first sown, even as a seed,
> Who that shall point, as with a wand, and say,
> 'This portion of the river of my mind
> Came from yon fountain?' Thou, my Friend! art one
> More deeply read in thy own thoughts; to thee
> Science appears but, what in truth she is,
> Not as our glory and our absolute boast,
> But as a succedaneum, and a prop
> To our infirmity. Thou art no slave
> Of that false secondary power, by which,
> In weakness, we create distinctions, then
> Deem that our puny boundaries are things
> Which we perceive, and not which we have made.
> To thee, unblinded by these outward shows,
> The unity of all has been reveal'd . . .[1]

---

[1] *The Prelude*, II.203–26.

This, of course, is very clever, and it comes as no surprise when Wordsworth tells us that he got it all from Coleridge. We may suspect that the doctrine is too polemical for its own good. It is easy (and indeed correct) to claim that the objects of scientific discourse are further abstracted than those of ordinary conversation, but to turn the degree of abstraction into a degree of subjectivity can scarcely be done without undermining the objects of ordinary knowledge. But we may further suspect that in any case Wordsworth has not really assimilated the doctrine of his friend. I imagine that a man who believes in the unity of subject and object will talk, supposing the mysterious theory allows of his talking at all, in the most down-to-earth terms—'Of waist-coats Harry has no lack, good duffle grey and flannel fine'—but this is not the way Wordsworth speaks, at least in *propria persona*. Instead he theorises about the 'river' of his mind (which at once recalls William James's 'stream of consciousness') and its 'fountain' (meaning 'source') which suggests psychological genesis rather than external validation. In fact it is clear from the way the passage begins that Wordsworth is following his usual egotistical method. If we say that a tree decays it is clear that we are talking about a change in a public object. But when Wordsworth says that 'charms . . . grew weaker' is he talking about the outer world or about a change in him, William Wordsworth? Most people would say the second.

But one other passage must be noted:

> . . . so wide appears
> The vacancy between me and those days,
> Which yet have such self-presence in my mind
> That, sometimes, when I think of them, I seem
> Two consciousnesses, conscious of myself
> And of some other Being.[1]

The curious thing about this passage is the way it suggests Berkeley. If *esse* is *percipi*, the only way to preserve objective existents is to propose an unsleeping divine perceiver to hold them in position, so to speak, when one's own beam of attention is extinguished. But really this is not so much like Berkeley at all. 'Being' with a capital B can fool us only for a second.

[1] *Ibid.*, II.28–33.

In fact the vigilant God of Berkeley is as far removed from Wordsworth's thought as is the ontological God of Descartes. Nevertheless, we may say, at least Wordsworth has got rid of the two-dimensional world of the solipsist dream; if an object can be sighted from two points at once, it fills out, becomes three dimensional. But this is hardly what Wordsworth has done. He has not—for who can, once the question is posed in these terms?—escaped from his own perspective into someone else's; he has only stepped out of William Wordsworth II into William Wordsworth I. If we read on we find that the two perceiving minds, different and yet the same, are in any case not trained upon the same object; the earlier mind is bent upon 'a grey stone/of native rock', the latter on 'A smart Assembly-room that perk'd and flar'd'. Each dreams his proper dream. Thus the tendency of this fission of the subject is towards a scepticism blacker than that of solipsism. The solipsist can still believe in a continuing self; Wordsworth's *subjective* world is falling to pieces. It is not of course in danger of that disintegration into atoms that can be followed out in Hume's *Treatise;* instead we have a division into two chunks, each tolerably coherent and continuous in itself. And of course what separates the halves of Wordsworth's mental life is not the failure of causality. Yet there is a sense in which, in the terms of Hume's philosophy, it is a more radical separation than anything in the *Treatise*. In Hume, feeling remains the last criterion. When every other support has failed, this has strength to sustain us. The *sentiment* of identity is not in question. Yet in Wordsworth it is just this which has failed. He does not feel the same as he once felt; his consciousness 'tastes different'. Thus from one amoeba-like subject, two subjects can be generated, but never an object.

In 'The Garden' Marvell wrote

> Society is all but rude,
> To this delicious solitude

and we applaud the metaphysical conceit. In the Prelude (II.313–317) Wordsworth writes

>   . . . solitude
> More active, even, than 'best society',
> Society made sweet as solitude

> By silent inobtrusive sympathies,
> And gentle agitations of the mind

and we recognise a thought which is, as its serious awkwardness betrays, half-metaphysical. We watch Wordsworth deliberately retreating into the soft interior of his shell. Thus far, of course, the very fact that we can speak of a gradual withdrawal shows that Wordsworth cannot have adopted the fully metaphysical position which identifies public and private facts. As long as Wordsworth makes it clear that he knows he is preferring subjective feelings to objective facts, he must believe, if his preference is to make any sense, that the two are distinct. It is only after the preoccupation with the private has extended its scope to cover all the material of the mind that it can deserve to be called fully metaphysical.

Thus we have a tendency rather than an accomplished fact. But it is always the objective which is eroded by the subjective, never the other way round. A few quotations should make this clear.

> . . . in my thoughts
> There was a darkness, call it solitude,
> Or blank desertion, no familiar shapes
> Of hourly objects, images of trees,
> Of sea or sky, no colours of green fields;
> But huge and mighty Forms that do not live
> Like living men mov'd slowly through my mind . . .[1]

This may be called dualist; the mysterious subjective ideas (to use Locke's word) are strongly distinguished from those ideas which represent the external world. But gradually this model —the subjective ousting the objective—is replaced by one more sinister—the subjective *usurping* the objective:

> But ere the fall
> Of night, when in our pinnace we return'd
> Over the dusty Lake, and to the beach
> Of some small island steer'd our course with one,
> The Minstrel of our troop, and left him there,
> And row'd off gently, while he blew his flute
> Alone upon the rock; Oh! then the calm

[1] *The Prelude*, I.420–6.

And dead still water lay upon my mind
Even with a weight of pleasure, and the sky
Never before so beautiful, sank down
Into my heart, and held me like a dream.[1]

Now, dream and daylit experiences are no longer antithetical;
instead one silently engulfs the other.

Odd echoes of the Berkeleian solution occur, but they are
robbed of all force by the context. In one place Wordsworth
seems for a moment to combine the Platonic strain of Locke's
philosophy—the belief in the ulterior reality of 'real essences'—
with Berkeley's reinforcing divine intelligence. One seems to
see Wordsworth's mind twitching this way and that like a
wounded snake—any solution *except* ordinary realism, now, it
would seem, irrecoverably lost:

> . . . In tranquil scenes, that universal power
> And fitness in the latent qualities
> And essences of things, by which the mind
> Is mov'd by feelings of delight, to me
> Came strengthened with a superadded soul
> A virtue not its own.[2]

But, again, our presentiment was less than accurate. The full
epistemological force of Locke's latent essence is scarcely
grasped, and, as for Berkeley's God, one is tempted to replace
him with Wordsworth's own unconscious (Wordsworth II
again!)—'a virtue not its own but mine'. Plainly our best course
is to wait for the next occurrence of that distinctively Wordsworthian phenomenon, the visionary anecdote, and, when it
comes, to watch and diagnose. It seems clear that lines 367 to
371 (in the 1805–6 text) give us the next aesthetic crisis:

> Oft in those moments such a holy calm
> Did overspread my soul, that I forgot
> That I had bodily eyes, and what I saw
> Appear'd like something in myself, a dream,
> A prospect in my mind.

The withdrawal into the 'tender inward' of the skull, behind
the optic nerves, is stronger still.

---

[1] *The Prelude*, II.170–80.   [2] *Ibid.*, II.343–8.

VIII

It is perhaps worth recalling at this point that Wordsworth's original title for the great poem of which *The Prelude* represents a mere preliminary fragment was *The Recluse*. To be sure, a very prosaic interpretation of this title is available, and it is Wordsworth who gives it:

> . . . the result of the investigation which gave rise to it was a determination to compose a philosophical poem, containing views of Man, Nature, and Society; and to be entitled, The Recluse; as having for its principal subject the sensations and opinions of a poet living in retirement.[1]

This shows plainly enough that 'recluse' meant for Wordsworth what it means for any man: 'person living a retired life'. However, the attentive reader of *The Prelude* will not readily believe that such a short answer exhausts the significance of the word. The eye is caught by the phrase 'sensations and opinions' and one observes the ways in which the public, Coleridgian theme, 'Man, Nature and Society', is swiftly reduced, and collected within the purview of a single perceiving subject. Clearly, the perceiving poet's retired condition must be more than a pure social accident, must be related to the content of this audaciously philosophical poem, or there would be no sense in his fixing on it, and nothing else, for a title. Why, after all, did he not call his poem *Man, Nature and Society*?[2] It is hard to resist the obvious answer. Wordsworth's Poet is not only socially but epistemologically recluded. The movement of thought is sufficiently clear: let us make a universal poem (here Coleridge's voice is loudest); yes, but let it be clearly shown how all is transmitted through the egotistical glass of the poet's perceiving mind (Wordsworth's voice taking over); yes, and let us grant that the perceiving mind, contemplating its private objects in a strange and poignant isolation, is the real subject of the poem.

[1] Wordsworth's preface to *The Excursion*, 1814, in *Poetical Works* vol. V, ed. de Selincourt and Darbishire, 1949, p. 2.

[2] In his letter to James Losh of March 11th, 1798 (*The Letters of William and Dorothy Wordsworth* ed. de Selincourt, vol I, 2nd edn. revised by K. L. Shaver, 1967, p. 214) Wordsworth in fact offers this as an alternative title; but *The Recluse* prevailed.

We are now in a position to account, to some extent at least, for a recurrent feature of Wordsworth's poetry; we may call this feature 'nostalgia for the object'. I have already suggested that in Wordsworth's attitude to the old Cumberland beggar there may be something like envy, and this is *prima facie* extremely puzzling; how can a man, alive and sensitive at every pore, envy another creature who is not only old and destitute, but also, through age and destitution, almost unconscious? The answer is that it is the very unconsciousness that Wordsworth envies. It was almost inevitable that the slow progress of subjective isolation should have, as one of its psychological consequences, a compensatory obsession with the objective condition. The poet, inhabiting an increasingly mental world, grows hungry for 'thinghood'. For the Cartesian rationalist articulate thought is the foundation of our confidence in reality. For Wordsworth one suspects that articulate thought and reality are in some way inimical to one another. This may partly be traced to Wordsworth's own strange spiritual development in which articulateness was attained at the very time when his grip on the object became infirm. Certainly, we have to do here with a development which is more psychological than rational. Also, we are no longer discussing Wordsworth's intuitive epistemology. When we say that Wordsworth is interested in the beggar as pure object we are no longer exploring the question whether the beggar enjoys a real existence, independently of Wordsworth's perceptions; rather, Wordsworth is interested in what it must be like to *be* a pure object, undistracted by the non-stop spectacle which Sensibility provides. The reaction is indeed extreme. Wordsworth's mind is not content to plead, 'Let me be assured that the tree I contemplate is real and substantial'; instead it cries, 'Let me *become* a tree!' The alienation of the subject can be ended only by suicide. This is the death-wish of romanticism.

Thus it is a mistake to think that the poet, the man of keen sensibility, represents a romantic ideal. No doubt the great romantic writers conform to this picture, but (for this very reason) it was not the thing they most desired. It is typical of the bourgeois philistine, or of the pre-romantic intelligence of a Byron, to make a cult of this sort of thing. To each his proper compensation. Keats's view is very different: 'A poet is the most unpoetical of any thing in existence.'[1] When he wrote these words Keats was thinking of the contrast between the poet and the philosopher (or man of profound convictions) rather than of the contrast between the poet and the substantial object. But though the standard of comparison may vary, both Wordsworth and Keats have the same fear for the poet; it is his power (so like weakness) to become anything and everything (which is very like being nothing) that appals them both. When Keats wrote, in the same letter, how the poet is a kind of nothingness, even when he is in a room full of children, we can smell something epistemological in the disquiet. Wordsworth's interest in his fellow creatures was normally in inverse proportion to the degree of consciousness they displayed. At Cambridge his poetic gift languished; but a lonely leech-gatherer could revive it. It is true that the figure of Coleridge appears in Wordsworth's verse again and again, but he is not, and cannot be, the subject of a Wordsworthian poem. His status is rather that of a god, or a muse: invoked, but never described.

The phenomenon extends from Wordsworth as far as the disintegrating romanticism of Nietzsche. Nietzsche, though he sought in his artist hero to glorify consciousness, often found himself celebrating the *object* of consciousness. When his rhetorical energies are employed in the service of the subject he will praise celibacy[2] (because it sharpens the intellectual energies); when they are employed in the service of the object he will praise sexuality.[3] In truth he thought a poet was not so fine a thing as a tiger.

Thus one strange result of the romantic movement was the inversion of 'the Elizabethan World Picture'. Shakespeare assumed that cabbages were superior to stones, horses to cabbages and men to horses. But Blake clearly felt that to cease to be a fretful, thought-ridden man and become a tree was a sort of metaphysical promotion: 'The apple tree never asks the beech how he may grow.'[4]

[1] Letter to Richard Woodhouse, October 27th, 1818, in *The Letters of John Keats*, ed. H. E. Rollins, Cambridge, Mass., 1958, vol. I, p. 387.
[2] *Genealogy of Morals*, III.ix, in *The Complete Works of Friedrich Nietzsche*, ed. Oscar Levy, vol. XIII, 1910, pp. 142–6.
[3] *Ibid.*, e.g. I.vi, p. 29.
[4] *The Marriage of Heaven and Hell*, in *Poetry and Prose of William Blake*, ed. Geoffrey Keynes, 1956, p. 184. Seventeenth century analogues,

But the desire utterly to submerge the ego in the object is too extreme to be common. Nostalgia for the object has expressed itself more often, and more persistently, in weaker forms. It is strange how many modern writers betray real anxiety in their efforts to give a rich, felt 'substance' to the things they describe. The greenness of grass, the wetness of rain, all the abrasiveness and viscosity of the world, have become the explicit object of the author's energy as they never were before the nineteenth century. And yet Shakespeare's Cleopatra remains more real than anyone in Lawrence Durrell; the forests of *A Midsummer Night's Dream* or of *Comus*, with all their enchantment, are more substantial than the forests of Hardy. One begins to suspect that there is something self-defeating in the emphasis of the moderns. Perhaps they protest too much. Indeed the very shrillness of the reaction invites a sort of literary psychoanalysis. Perhaps, in short, the romantic and post-romantic stress on 'impact' is *compensatory*. The quality (and it would seem to be the quality underlying all other qualities) on which they most insist is in fact disastrously lacking. It is a theme to which we shall have to return before we have finished. Even the overmastering 'thisness' of Sartre's chestnut roots in *La Nausée* is somehow inwardly weak; it smells of mentality.

But the word 'thisness' should make us pause; it recalls the poetry of Hopkins and thus reminds us that the thing we have diagnosed as a disease could also be a source of poetic power. And indeed if we are to be just to the phenomenon of object-nostalgia it is imperative that we attend for a while to the work of Hopkins. His ostensible philosophical interests, being firmly grounded in the Middle Ages, would appear to have small connexion with the philosophical tradition of British empiricism on which everything has thus far depended, but this is all to the good. I have made very general claims for 'romantic empiricism', tracing its influence at every level—even the most instinctual—of literary expression. In the circumstances the most obviously unlikely specimen is the most potentially useful to my argument. If we can discern the same

though very rare, are available; e.g. Vaughan's strangely Wordsworthian line, 'Yet stones are deep in admiration', from 'The Bird', in *The Works of Henry Vaughan*, ed. L. C. Martin, 2nd edn., 1957, p. 496.

characters in Hopkins, the Jesuit priest, then they are indeed deeply inscribed.

IX

Hopkins's poetry is rooted in a kind of generous greed. He is hungry for vividness, colour, texture, substance, and his intelligence seizes them in the consciousness that by such voracity no man is deprived; the riches of the world are 'all mine, yet common to my every peer'.[1] Moreover, this feast has its host, one who is, as hosts should be, unobtrusive and yet omnipresent, and the character of the host further complicates the paradox of generosity:

> Give beauty back, beauty, beauty, beauty back to God,
>   beauty's self and beauty's giver.
> See; not a hair is, not an eyelash, not the least lash
>   lost; every hair
> Is, hair of the head, numbered.[2]

Host: hostage: the Host: God is the giver and the gift; he squanders himself in the world and yet every penny is counted; our reception of his gift must be of that special kind which is also a restoration; and if we hunger and thirst thus we shall be satisfied beyond all expectation: 'You must Want like a God that you may be Satisfied like God.'[3] Thus, in cooler language, for Hopkins a sense of phenomenal splendour is connected with God. Sometimes God seems to interpenetrate his creation:

> The world is charged with the grandeur of God.[4]

Yet at other times he seems to grow less accessible even as we watch; he is no longer in but under the world, we perceive him only in a special tension:

> . . . tho' he is under the world's splendour and wonder,
>   His mystery must be instressed, stressed;
> For I greet him the days I meet him, and bless when I
>   understand.[5]

---

[1] 'To Oxford' (i), in *Poems of Gerard Manley Hopkins*, the 4th edn. by W. H. Gardner and N. H. MacKenzie, 1967, p. 21.

[2] 'The Leaden Echo and the Golden Echo', *Poems*, p. 92.

[3] Thomas Traherne, *Centuries*, i.44, in *Centuries, Poems and Thanksgivings*, ed. H. M. Margoliouth, 1958, vol. I, p. 22.

[4] 'God's Grandeur', *Poems*, p. 66.

[5] *The Wreck of the Deutschland*, *Poems*, p. 53.

Further, though God is the source of this torrent of colour, this Heraclitean fire in which we burn, he is himself immutable:

> Whatever is fickle, freckled (who knows how?)
> With swift, slow; sweet, sour; adazzle, dim;
> He fathers forth whose beauty is past change:
> Praise him.[1]

There were even times when the glory was visible and yet God himself seemed to have gone away:

> We see the glories of the earth
> But not the hand that wrought them all:
> Night to a myriad worlds gives birth,
> Yet like a lighted empty hall
> Where stands no host at door or hearth
> Vacant creation's lamps appal.[2]

But this is rare in the poetry. Normally the quest for the 'abrupt self' which 'so thrusts on, so throngs the ear'[3] is a form of worship, and even of intercourse with the Creator. God sustains the universe, and when a man drops from it into death, he catches him up again in the strength of his resurrection; we are told so in 'That Nature is a Heraclitean Fire and of the Comfort of the Resurrection' (*Poems*, pp. 111–112).

There is an extremism in Hopkins's religious language, but it alone will scarcely account for the impact of his verse. Christianity is after all traditionally audacious in its conceptual structure. But the audacity of this poetry is something new. In fact, Hopkins *perceives violently*, and it is this, more than anything else, that distinguishes his poetry from every other poet's.

Critics and commentators have been quick to connect this feature of Hopkins's poetry with the philosophical problem of individuation—the problem posed in the question: 'What is it which makes a thing an individual thing?' It is quite natural to attempt this connexion; after all, there are various signs that Hopkins tried it himself. But while the historical link between the poet and the works of Duns Scotus is undoubted, the precise logical relations between the poetic conduct of the

---

[1] 'Pied Beauty', *Poems*, p. 70.   [2] 'Nondum', *Poems*, p. 32.
[3] 'Henry Purcell', *Poems*, p. 80.

one and the theological tenets of the other are much more elusive. This much at least we have to build on; Hopkins, who had formed the notions of 'inscape' and 'instress' some time before, felt a shock of recognition when he read Scotus.

But we must be careful. There are very few signs in Hopkins's writings of any spontaneous interest in the logical and metaphysical problem of individuation, except where, as in the case of the individuality of persons, salvation was at stake. While the well-known moral scrupulosity which led him to add penances of his own to the impositions of his confessor could extort from him laborious disquisitions on self-hood and responsibility, he possessed no equal philosophical scrupulousness to carry him through questions which are logically more fundamental, if personally less momentous. It is ironical that writers on Hopkins have used as evidence for his philosophical temper a feature which, carefully construed, tells a different story. Let us imagine Hopkins confronted by two objects: say, a beach-ball and a moth. Obviously, he would ignore the first and scrutinise the second; yet both are, equally, individuals. 'See how no object is too minute, too strange for his attention', runs the General Voice, 'How plainly this declares his interest in individuation!' But, logically, freckled things, things counter, original, spare, strange are no more individuals than large, uniform objects. They are just more unusual, or more striking. Though nothing is too minute for his attention, many things are too big, or too simple. Anyone approaching the metaphysical problem of individuation must begin by ridding himself of any such partiality for the variegated. Hopkins shows the perennial artist's refusal to work at a level prior to that of experience; instead he works within experience, and an apparently metaphysical thesis shrinks (or grows) to a synthetic, empirical observation, true of some things but not all.

> Each mortal thing does one thing and the same:
>> Deals out that being indoors each one dwells;
>> Selves—goes itself; *myself* it speaks and spells,
> Crying *What I do is me: for that I came.*[1]

The poem tells us which they are: kingfishers, dragonflies, the sounds made by stones dropping in wells, Only in some things

[1] 'As kingfishers catch fire', *Poems*, p. 90.

the voice is louder, the accent shriller. The religious use of the insight demands a metaphysical generality, but this is denied by a sensibility which remains irremediably selective.

The problem of individuation as it confronted the mediaeval mind carries little immediate appeal for the modern. It is a legacy from Aristotle. In his *De Anima* the soul is defined as the form of the body, and in his general theory 'form' is identified with 'definition'. Averroes, in an argument which severely exercised the wits of Aquinas, reasoned that if the human soul is the same as the human definition mankind has but one soul. This was sufficiently counter-intuitive to provoke a widespread reaction; some rational basis had to be found first for human individuality and then for individuality in general. The Aristotelian terms, of course, continued to be used. Accordingly they asked, 'What is it that makes the individual; is it form or matter, or something else?' Although the question is unfamiliar, one can guess with some confidence what the instinctive response of the post-empiricist mind would be–namely that it is 'this matter' which makes the individual. A mediaeval Schoolman would be likely to reject such an answer. His objection would fall into two parts; first he would point out that in the words 'this matter' it is 'this' rather than 'matter' which bears the weight of individuation; secondly he would suspect that the modern had no adequate conception of what matter is. Today we think of matter as tangible, solid, as bits of stuff rather than as the pure antithesis of form. We must go back to the Aristotelian tradition to learn again that First Matter is simply that of which things are formed, and nothing more. Matter is thus only conceptually and not practically separable from form. One cannot isolate matter. An objector might say: 'That chair is made of wood; the matter: Wood, is in the form: Chair. I will grind the chair into shavings, show them to you, and then you will see the matter without the form.' Certainly this would show the material of the chair, after a fashion (which is as much as to say, in a certain form). It would not, however, show us First Matter. For, as I have hinted, it is still in the form of something, namely wood-shavings. Even mud and sand, which one thinks of as mere 'stuff,' are strictly speaking in the form of grains *etc*. Thus we begin to see that matter as such is by definition undifferentiated and incapable of differentiating. It might be objected that to the makers of the scientific revolution matter was scarcely more accessible and that I exaggerate the difference between the Aristotelian and the seventeenth-century mind. Certainly, the technical conception of matter which dominated seventeenth-century science was intangible, inaudible, invisible and so on,[1] but it was so, not by definition but by that epistemological accident which confined us to our own ideas; moreover, it was felt by almost everyone but Berkeley to be the fundamental, hard reality. But to Aristotle matter is not hard but soft; as such it is mere potentiality which cannot grow into being without the imposition of form. And of course to the seventeenth century matter was nothing if not measurable.

There are signs in Hopkins's writings that he was attracted by the notion that it was the formal principle which conferred thinghood; and this would seem to imply that by some idiosyncrasy of temperament he was more attuned to certain very ancient modes of thought than to the empirical tradition into which he had been born. But it is not difficult to show that this independence of the empiricist tradition is more apparent than real. In 'Binsey Poplars'[2] he laments the 'unselving' of the scene by the breaking up of the trees, that is, by the destruction of their proper form. He criticises a painting by Millais on the ground that it wants 'instress', and offers only a 'casual install of woodland'.[3] In his Spiritual Writings (1881–2) he says[4] that broken or fragmentary things have only an artificially independent being because they have no true self. In all of these examples, thinghood, or even reality, is fully present only in that which has a determinate shape. We sense that there exists for Hopkins some sort of imprecise equivalence between the concepts of mud, fragments, mere stuff on the one hand and on the other absence of personality, even of reality. Particularly interesting from this point of view is a youthful essay[5] in which he discusses being and not being and rather

---

[1] See above, pp. 22–23.

[2] *Poems*, no. 43, p. 78.

[3] *Journals and Papers of Gerard Manley Hopkins*, ed. H. House and G. Storey, 1959, p. 244.

[4] *The Sermons and Devotional Writings of Gerard Manley Hopkins*, ed. C. Devlin, 1959, p. 146.

[5] *Journals and Papers*, pp. 127–30.

oddly[1] observes that according to Parmenides men sprang
from slime. He did not forget the notion, for it reappears in
'The Sea and the Skylark'.[2] One is tempted to say that the
Aristotelian doctrine of movement from formless potentiality
to concrete actuality is here given mythical expression. If that
is so, we must add at once that Aristotle himself was never
mythical in that way. This is the point at which we can begin
to see that Hopkins's rejection of the empiricist tradition is
superficial only. The truth is that his language remains, from
the metaphysician's point of view, illegitimately sensuous.
Even Plato confesses that Forms might be conceded to hair and
dirt.[3] Strictly speaking, slime is no less informed than a tree.
Hopkins's identification of that which is shapely and strongly
defined with the informed material thing, the concrete, is
exactly parallel to his mistaking the distinctive for the
individual. And this is essentially the mistake of a man confined
within experience, a man unapt for metaphysics. His empirical
intelligence can do nothing with such radical generalities. His
sensibility makes him into a positivist in spite of himself, for
it insists that words derive their force and meaning from a
contrasting context; it says in effect 'I can understand the
word "formed" when it means "like a vase and unlike treacle";
I can make nothing of it if it applies to any and every thing'.
The completely general terms of Form and First Matter do not
admit of any comparison of particular objects in terms of
'formed-ness'. All concrete objects have their forms and there
is no more to be said. The poetic sensibility, incorrigibly
comparative, will always transmute such doctrines.

Nevertheless, when Hopkins encountered the philosophy of
Scotus he evidently experienced something which was, at the
same time, a sweet shock to his understanding and a kind of
recognition. He wrote in his Journal for the year 1872:

> At this time I had first begun to get hold of the copy of
> Scotus on the Sentences in the Baddely library and was
> flush with a new stroke of enthusiasm. It may come to
> nothing or it may be a mercy from God. But just then

[1] Oddly, because Parmenides, as far as I can discover, said no such thing.
[2] *Poems*, no. 35, p. 68.
[3] *Parmenides*, 130 c-d.

when I took in any inscape of the sky or sea I thought of Scotus.[1]

If Hopkins was at bottom the loam-footed empiric I have described, what food for his spirit can he ever have found in the crabbed Latin of the Subtle Doctor?

Scotus held that neither the Aristotelian 'form' nor the Aristotelian 'matter' can individuate. Each can give us a 'such' but neither will yield a 'this' (incidentally, Aristotle himself likewise rejects either term, form in *Metaphysics* Z 8, 1034a5, and matter in *Metaphysics* Z 3, 1029a20). It might be suggested that an object can be individuated by giving a precise spatio-temporal location; a sufficiently fine-grained specification of his latitude and longitude at a given time will distinguish Dromio I from Dromio II. But in fact such an individuation can be accomplished only at the cost of presupposing another individual, such as the Terrestrial Globe, as a point of reference. Scotus rejects 'position' in his *Opus Oxoniense*, II, dist. iii, q. 2, n. 2. The question is thus retorted back upon the mind. Matter, since it is in itself 'purely undifferentiated and indeterminate' is 'not a diversifying but a unifying principle'[2] and since form, as that which is common to members of the same species, was designed to account for the existence in our conceptual scheme of universals it can hardly be expected to account for individuals too. The factor which Scotus offered was, as is well known, the famous *haecceitas*, or, literally translated, 'thisness'. The term itself appears nowhere in the *Opus Oxoniense* but the concept is there plainly enough. Thus far, Scotus is pure metaphysician. But press a little on this conception and a secondary Scotus begins to appear. It is in this secondary person, I suggest, that Hopkins found a congenial spirit.

One is tempted to interpret the Scotist doctrine as a simple atomistic dismissal of the question: 'The mind knows individuals neither by their form nor by their matter, but in themselves', but the careful reader of Scotus will sense that such a view is less than just to the marked strenuousness with which Scotus presents his notion, and the notion's own appearance of bearing a mysteriously positive force.

[1] *Journals and Papers*, p. 221.
[2] C. R. S. Harris, *Duns Scotus*, 1927, vol. II, p. 92.

The principal relevant figure here is Scotus's predecessor, Henry of Ghent. Henry, like Scotus, rejected both form and matter as individuators, but in their place he set up an utterly negative principle: the individual is neither a multiple nor a fraction; it is an individual in so far as it is nothing but itself. Scotus's *haecceitas* was conceived as an explicit rebuttal of this view. For him the individual exists, not just by some failure to integrate itself into the scheme of universals but by a certain power of its own: '. . . necesse est per aliquod positivum intrinsecum huic lapidi, tanquam per rationem propriam, repugnare sibi dividi in partes subjectivas: et illud positivum erit quod dicitur esse per se causa individuationis'.[1]

Now, strenuous affirmation is one thing, philosophical demonstration is another. It is very easy to sympathise with C. R. S. Harris when he seems to conclude that the difference between Henry and Scotus is here merely verbal: that where Henry said 'is not divided' Scotus happened to say 'resists division'. Yet Scotus's self-dissociating 'positivum' is very emphatic. In a place where no metaphysical distinction can be made it seems obstinately to warn us that a difference of another kind must be made. It may be that it is here that we shall discover what in Scotus moved Hopkins so strongly.

I suspect, in fact, that the distinction which Scotus has in mind is neither logical nor ontological but has to do with the felt impact of the world on the mind. The resistance he refers to is a resistance *felt* and *encountered* by the knower; something which calls out to the intellect, the architect of interlocking concepts 'Halt here, for I am mere Thing'. Suddenly one senses that the empiricism of which Locke, Berkeley and Hume are the most celebrated exemplars was a national characteristic long before their time. Of course there are names, such as Roger Bacon or William of Occam, which leap to mind in such a connexion. But it is more interesting to discover radical scepticism in more unlikely places—that is, not in Occam, but in Occam's teacher, Scotus, not in the young reductionist but

---

[1] It must be through something positive, intrinsic to this stone that it resists, as through a reason of its own, division into subordinate parts; and that positive element will be what we call the cause *per se* of individuation. *Opus Oxoniense*, II, dist. iii, q. 2, n. 4, in *Commentaria Oxoniensia*, ed. P. Marianus Fernandez Garcia, vol. II, Florence, 1914, p. 236.

in the old hair-splitting scholastic. Of course an anti-rationalist tendency in the Franciscan-Scotist school is clearly discernible long before Occam appeared. In all sobriety, strange anticipations of later philosophy can be found in the main fabric of Scotus's thought. He is more than half a fideist and in his theology faith comes to function somewhat as sentiment does in Hume. Meanwhile his famous voluntarism anticipates existentialism. But we are here concerned, not with the metaphysical achievement of Scotus but rather with a curious aberration from metaphysics. The Scotist *haecceitas*, in so far as it differs from the negative principle of Henry of Ghent, is itself dissociable from the scholastic problem of individuation. To this problem Henry and Scotus have indeed but one answer between them. 'Individuals are known in themselves.' In so far as he contradicts Henry, Scotus is telling us, not about logical discrimination but rather about the way knowing feels. He thus almost touches hands with English Johnson who kicked the stone to refute Berkeley. Hopkins, though he will never be the poet of individuation, will always be one of our greatest poets of the distinctive passion of reality. Likewise Scotus was for Hopkins not the logician of individuation but

> Of realty the rarest-veinèd unraveller; a not
> Rivalled insight, be rival Italy or Greece.[1]

We are dealing here not with an (anti-) philosophical position held by the poet but with a fundamental cast of mind, the kind of thing that is betrayed not only in the argument of a poem but also in its diction. John Wain has observed[2] that Hopkins shared with William Morris a strong preference for the Anglo-Saxon elements of the English language, even to the point of a forcible substitution of terms. Today we tend to dismiss this literary fashion with a derisive reference to formations like Morris's 'push-wain' for 'perambulator.' But we have only to think of the felt difference between, say, 'latent' and 'lurking', and imagine ourselves explaining the difference to a cultivated Frenchman, to realise that we are confronted once more by what I have called the passion of reality. Hopkins carried this

[1] 'Duns Scotus's Oxford', *Poems*, p. 79.
[2] 'Gerard Manley Hopkins, an Idiom of Desperation', *Proc. Brit. Acad.*, XLV (1959), pp. 173–97.

practice into his most abstruse speculations, took a peculiar pleasure in searching out those places where the greatest abstraction was required and there intruding a sudden sense of the concrete. Fr Devlin, expounding Scotism, uses astringently abstract terms like 'nature' and 'degree', while Hopkins indulges himself with much more sensuous words, like 'inscape' and 'pitch'. That it is an indulgence I have little doubt, though most modern readers, being children of the same tradition, will instinctively side with Hopkins. Note that Hopkins is not simply being 'down to earth'; he is not insisting that we discover the cash value of an abstraction by investigating its source in experience. He takes a shorter, and an easier, route. He simply extracts the concrete metaphor, deriving from that stage in the history of a word when its abstract signification was not yet fully achieved, and offers it, crude, for our inspection. Putting back the semantic clock in this way is not in itself philosophically fruitful. The truth is that Hopkins's saxonisms are often abstractions masquerading as concrete expressions. Take this sentence: 'Now a bare self, to which no nature has yet been added, which is not yet clothed in or overlaid with a nature, is indeed nothing, a zero in the score or account of existence.'[1] We grow suspicious of the plethora of synonyms, and feel that Hopkins, poet-like, is enjoying the play of figures instead of being exasperated at their inadequacy like a true metaphysician. The experiential tang of his language is out of place here, even misleading. When the density of actual experience is absent from his subject matter, he must smuggle it in by the back door of an earthy, Saxon vocabulary.

We begin to understand why Hopkins was so strongly attracted by the 'pre-philosophical' writings of the Ionian and Eleatic thinkers. Bruno Snell has shown[2] how the celebrated 'oppositions' of Heraclitus are not stated in an abstract way at all, but that the connexion between opposites is rather deduced from the realm of personal experience; words which describe the behaviour of things—words invented before abstract thought was common—tend to describe those things in terms of the individual's reactions to them. Thus Heraclitus had himself observed that his body varied between warm and

---

[1] *The Sermons and Devotional Writings*, p. 146.
[2] 'Die Sprache Heraclits', *Hermes*, LXI (1926), p. 356.

cold, and so on, and from this he derived not a logical principle but a generalisation about the way things behave; at the same time he would regard the objects of his observation as living subjects in some sense like himself, having the power to modify themselves.[1] The crucial difference is of course that Heraclitus and Hopkins are moving in contrary directions. Where Heraclitus is labouring to make abstraction possible, is slowly disengaging the human mind from the features Snell describes, Hopkins is retreating into the womb of the intellect. The romantic regression to the primitive here affects the very process of reason. In a letter to R. W. Dixon, written on September 26th, 1881,[2] Hopkins accuses these thinkers of taking account of natural suggestion only, and neglecting the supernatural. In fact, however, it is here that the strange conformity of Hopkins's intelligence to a pre-abstract age is most evident. For no hard-headed nineteenth-century physicist could have written the letter Hopkins wrote. He would have been as perplexed as we at the quasi-mystical content of pre-Socratic physics. Heraclitus and Hopkins, journeying from the opposite poles of concrete and abstract, have met, and indeed passed on. Where we find an oddly moonstruck primitive physicist, Hopkins saw a sadly earthy theologian. It might be objected that to pass from physics to theology is really to move not against but in the direction of the abstract. But this is not so. The realm of the Spirit is the realm of the Defeated Abstraction.

The quasi-divine status accorded to logical formulae by Heraclitus springs from the same cause as does his curiously sensuous language. If 'the warm' and 'the cold' are viewed experientially, the formula for their co-existence, 'strife', is viewed in a parallel way. Heraclitus's 'war, the father of all things'[3] is only a little less divinised than Parmenides' 'Necessity'.[4] That which obstinately retains the flavour of the concrete and yet is nowhere to be seen at once assumes the intermediate status of spirit. In these circumstances physics can

[1] See G. S. Kirk *Heraclitus, the Cosmic Fragments*, 1954, p. 151.

[2] *The Correspondence of Gerard Manley Hopkins and Richard Watson Dixon*, ed. C. C. Abbott, 1935, p. 61.

[3] Fr. 53 [44] in H. Diels, *Fragmente der Vorsokratiker*, 6th edn. Berlin, 1951, vol. I, p. 162.

[4] *Ibid.*, p. 237.

easily take on the appearance of mystical theology. It is no accident that with the development of the mind's capacity for abstraction the very concept of spirit becomes dispensable. It was never really anything but a crutch.

We may add one more improbable comparison, though it should be in a way predictable from what has already been said: the Heraclitean character of intrusive experience can be traced in Scotus. When Scotus defines *haecceitas* as not matter nor form nor the concretion of both, but as the *ultima realitas entis*,[1] it looks as if *realitas* is conceived as having an active force, related to the divine creation. The experiential language from which the Greek philosophic genius slowly freed itself remained endemic in the empirical British. Obtrusive in the seventeenth and eighteenth centuries, half-latent in the fourteenth, it was always present. Those who rejoice in this national character may reflect that it makes it quite impossible not only to believe the philosophy of Hegel but also to reject it. Experience can make no pronouncement, either unfavourable or favourable, on its own status.

Fr Peters's confident identification[2] of the Scotist *haecceitas* and Hopkins's 'inscape' has been sufficiently refuted[3] by Fr Devlin, who, as we ought to have expected, found many more connexions in the field of epistemology and psychology. Scotus, unlike his Nominalistic successors, was interested not only in concepts considered as non-personal functions—'the concept of gravity'—but in the actual *having* of concepts, in mental events—getting the hang of a scholium in Newton. In this constant reduction of logical questions to psychological contents Scotus is indeed more empirical—certainly closer to Locke—than is Occam.

Hopkins always loved watching and making better than thinking. Even the elucidation of general ideas from the confused data of experience was, to him, something to be watched. It might be objected that I have taken just one

[1] 'The ultimate reality (realisation) of being', *Opus Oxoniense*, dist. iii, q. 2, n. 15.

[2] *Gerard Manley Hopkins*, 1947, p. 23.

[3] In his commentary (1959) on the *Sermons and Devotional Writings*. See also his article, 'Hopkins and Duns Scotus', *New Verse*, XIV (1935), pp. 12–17 and his two articles called 'The Image and the Word', *The Month*, CLXXXIX (1950), pp. 114–27, 191–202.

tendency of his mind and pretended that it was the whole;
after all, Hopkins himself wrote in an undergraduate essay on
'The Origin of our Moral Ideas': 'In art we strive to realise not
only unity, permanence of law, likeness, but also, with it,
difference, variety, contrast: it is rhyme we like, not echo, and
not unison but harmony.'[1] But I have already suggested that
the sort of Empiricism I have in mind operates below the level
of the overt philosophical 'position', though it will modify,
from below, the real character of that position. So here the
discrepancy Hopkins has in mind is felt rather than analysed,
aesthetic rather than logical.

In the *species specialissima* of Scotus, in the intimate touch
of the real, Hopkins found something very intimate to his
genius. The Latin term (in Scotus as in Hopkins we find the
same regression to the etymological ancestor!) has recovered
its pristine meaning, 'sight', or rather, taking the superlative
into account, 'glimpse'. It thus denotes something more
primitive, psychologically, than our awareness of the individual.
And so it carried for Hopkins an appeal even stronger than that
of the *haecceitas*. To proceed from the *species specialissima* to
the individuation of public objects, and thence to the construction of a body of knowledge was not for Hopkins. The bent of
his mind lay in the opposite direction. This has one very
curious consequence.

The poetry of Hopkins is so enamoured of the *glimpse*, that
it loses its capacity—not just to resolve the problem of individuation (that is already conceded) but even to *individuate*. For if
we ask what we are given in his poetry, it is not this known
tree or that stone. Rather, he tells us of this brief perception,
that almost instantaneous vision. 'The Windhover' describes,
not so much a particular bird as a moment in perception. Thus,
it may be that there was something self-defeating in Hopkins's
desperate striving after 'things'; in his hunger he leaned too
far, and instead of grasping the rounded form of the real, he
lost himself in it.

> He leans to it, Harry bends, look.[2]

Here we have all the shock and density of the thing as perceived,
but Harry himself is half-lost. By an extraordinary irony, to

[1] *Journals*, p. 83.　　[2] 'Harry Ploughman', *Poems*, no. 71, p. 104.

restrict him to an instantaneous existence is to turn him into something very like an archetype.

Hopkins was interested, not in philology, but in the semantic developments of particular roots, not in formality but in shapely objects, not individuality but in arrestingly distinctive individuals. Whether he knew it or not, he was deeply opposed to the rationalism of a Plato, who scorned those who mistake 'the things of morality' for morality itself. It is indeed doubtful whether Hopkins would even have understood the Platonic gibe. It is no accident that his progressive dissection of the surrounding world, first into things, and last into percepts is a sort of echo of a philosophical work in which he never took the slightest interest—the *Treatise* of David Hume. But the intellectual tradition was there and it is easy to show how it worked. We have seen how Hume provided a ready basis for Romantic theory. As an undergraduate Hopkins was taught by Walter Pater, who is a perfect specimen of the romantic, post-Humian epistemology of aesthetic scepticism. For Pater, indeed, sentiment (that was Hume's word: perhaps we should now say, sensibility) was all (and the world well lost). Indeed reading Pater is very like reading a sort of commonplace book on that isolation of the mind which forms the subject of this book:

> At first sight experience seems to bury us under a flood of external objects, pressing upon us with a sharp and importunate reality, calling us out of ourselves in a thousand forms of action. But when reflexion begins to act upon those objects they are dissipated under its influence; the cohesive force seems suspended like a trick of magic; each object is loosed into a group of impressions— colour, odour, texture—in the mind of the observer. And if we continue to dwell in thought on this world, not of objects in the solidity with which language invests them, but of impressions unstable, flickering, inconsistent, which burn and are extinguished with our consciousness of them, it contracts still further; the whole scope of observation is dwarfed to the narrow chamber of the individual mind . . . Every one of those impressions is the impression of the individual in his isolation, each mind keeping as a solitary prisoner its own dream of a world. Analysis goes a step

further still, and assures us that those impressions of the individual mind to which, for each one of us, experience dwindles down, are in perpetual flight . . . To such a tremulous wisp constantly reforming itself on the stream; to a single sharp impression, with a sense in it, a relic more or less fleeting, of such moments gone by, what is real in our life fines itself down. It is with this movement, with the passage and dissolution of impressions, images, sensations, that analysis leaves off . . .

Not the fruit of experience, but experience itself, is the end . . .

To burn always with this hard, gemlike flame, to maintain this ecstasy, is success in life . . . While all melts under our feet, we may well catch at any exquisite passion, or any contribution to knowledge that seems by a lifted horizon to set the spirit free for a moment . . . With all this sense of the splendour of our experience and of its awful brevity, gathering all we are into one desperate effort to see and touch, we shall hardly have time to make theories about the things we see and touch.[1]

It is likely that Pater's breaking down of the world into discrete moments of perception was a crucial influence on Hopkins. But if it had not been Pater it would have been (and perhaps was) someone else. And to be sure Hopkins was defended by his religion from the worst consequences of this retreat from the object. For him God was not only ontologically anterior to the public world but also to consciousness itself. By a strange alliance, his religious devotion and his radical empiricism supported one another:

> Selves—goes itself; *myself* it speaks and spells;
> Crying *What I do is me: for that I came*.[2]

When we read these lines we must think not only of the scholastic Scotus (though he, too, was engrossed in the ceaseless noise of experience) but also dull John Locke: '. . . it is easy to discover what is so much inquired after, the *principium individuationis*; and that, it is plain, is existence itself; which

---

[1] *The Renaissance*, 6th edn., 1901, pp. 234-7 (written in 1868).
[2] *Poems*, no. 57, p. 90.

F

determines a being of any sort to a particular time and place, incommunicable to two beings of the same kind.'[1]

Perhaps because of his belief in a sustaining God the objects of Hopkins's verse have a vivid reality which is not merely 'compensatory'. It would have been easy to have fitted his evident greatness into the general thesis of this chapter in much the same way as I did Wordsworth; that is, I might have argued that the power of Hopkins is all interior, that he gives the stresses of an isolated spirit rather than public realities. But such an account would be wrong. Certainly the stresses of spirit are there but they hang between the single Creator and a manifold creation. Although I think Wordsworth a greater poet than Hopkins I can never escape the sense that Wordsworth's poetry moves in a kind of dream, while the poetry of Hopkins is wide awake. The formula which everyone remembers for Wordsworth's verse is 'emotion recollected in tranquillity'. The proper formula for the poetry of Hopkins is *Sentio et excrucior*.

[1] *Essay* 11.xxvii.4, vol. I, pp. 441–2.

CHAPTER 4

La Nausée

I

The literature of the nineteenth century offers many versions of the imprisoned soul, but to explore them all would be a sadly repetitive business. It is, as Aristotle says, 'Any man's work'. Instead, we must hasten on to the next point at which a radical development in philosophy is registered in the work of novelists and poets. It is easy to lay one's finger on the next major movement in philosophy: it is, of course, German idealism. But the point at which idealist epistemology importantly modifies the literary sensibility proves strangely elusive. Even the English romantics were far more deeply affected by Hume than by Kant (just as Kant was more deeply affected by Hume than by Kant). If this were a book about literature and ethics a very different (and much fuller) account of German philosophy would be forced upon us. But, as it is, the next crisis in our story is provoked by a lesser philosophy: existentialism. Admittedly, in the poetry of T. S. Eliot some echoes of idealism can be caught by the attentive ear—and in due course we shall listen to them. But meanwhile Jean-Paul Sartre bestrides the path.

It may seem perverse to picture Sartre even momentarily as an obstacle to intellectual progress. He is, after all, commonly thought of as an avant-garde thinker, the voice of youth, the scourge of complacency. And all this may be true of Sartre the politician. But in purely philosophical terms it is very far from the truth. He is a terminal figure, filled with all the vacuous energy, the fear of silence, which commonly mark old age.

But he also wrote a very interesting novel: *La Nausée*, which presents with singular force that epistemological imprisonment of the soul which is the subject of this book. But in *L'Être et le Néant* (which is supposed to contain a formal exposition of the philosophy implied in the novel) Sartre rejects all forms of subjective idealism. Let us begin, then, with this seeming contradiction.

First, Sartre thought that he could dispense with, or by-pass the phenomenology of Husserl. Husserl, being a phenomeno-logist, believed it was necessary to restrict his philosophy to the immediate contents of consciousness as they flow, and to bracket off all presuppositions, whether of the plain man or the philosopher, about the proper ordering of these contents. This bracketing-off is called the *epoché*. Having performed his *epoché* Husserl was, predictably, assailed by an anxiety to secure the objectivity of the public universe and was forced by his chosen method to look within consciousness itself for a guarantee of the independent existence of its objects. Predict-ably, he failed. Sartre proposed an outright rejection of the *epoché*; instead (he urged) let us take seriously the primacy of things as existing in their own right. Consciousness, so far from being a sort of magic lantern, becomes for Sartre an entity essentially constituted by its relation to objects. In itself it is nothing (or, more mysteriously, a nothing). It draws its sole claim to reality or substance from its relation to things. Conscious man, or the *pour-soi* ('the for-itself'), is thus seen as a sort of ontological parasite upon the massive primacy of the *en-soi*, the brute 'existence-in-itself' of the real.

The gradual deliquescence of this thesis (which we cannot here trace in detail) is very curious. The broad lines of it are simple enough: the for-itself becomes gradually more 'thingy', the in-itself less. The nothingness which is consciousness turns out to have certain very positive characteristics. For example, it seems at times as if consciousness is called a nothing because it is essentially a capacity for 'projecting' that something is not the case, or considering that something might not be the case. In this *L'Être et le Néant* is the proper sequel to Sartre's two books on the imagination, in which enormous stress is laid on man's ability, by imagining, to take up an attitude to some-thing which does not exist. The imagination is seen as perhaps the most fundamental and characteristic movement of the human consciousness, and as providing the necessary condition of an existentialist choice (for in the constipated ontology of the in-itself there is plainly no room for that pre-rational vertigo which is existentialist freedom). But to say that consciousness is not the name of a substance but must on the contrary be resolved into talk about people in various sorts of relation with the world–to say this is one thing; it is quite another to say that consciousness consists in entertaining unrealised possibilities. The break with Husserl is most effectively made in the first of these alternatives but it seems doubtful whether Sartre ever distinctly commits himself to it. Certainly it is the second which rapidly engrosses him, thus allowing Husserlian idealism to seep back into his philosophy.

Again, Sartre claims that his philosophy is distinguished from idealism in that consciousness is not regarded as constituting, or even circumscribing, reality, but on the contrary the mind not only takes all its colour from, but is transcended by the indefinite plenitude of reality. Once more we have a hopeful beginning; one can scarcely, it would seem, claim Sartre for a latter-day idealist when he forms his basic thesis by inverting idealism. Certainly; in the circumstances it is possible to claim only that Sartre is a *covert* idealist. But this, when we watch him at work, proves only too easy. The assertion of the transcendence of the in-itself is in fact the beginning of its dissolution. For example, the fundamental assertion of the primacy of *things* soon resolves itself into the different thesis, at once more modest and more disquietingly portentous, that *reality* is primary. 'Reality', 'existence', the 'in-itself' remain other than consciousness, but at the same time they begin to show themselves as other than the world of ordinary objects. For it turns out that without the conscious mind there are no tables, chairs or bottles; only undifferentiated Being. The differentiation is the work of the mind (no mean task for a Nothing to perform) and from here it is a short step to see Being, for all its awesome, unfathomable mysteriousness, as no more than the brute material of the informing mind. And then we have only to remember the trick played by Philonous upon Hylas,[1] whereby such brute matter, never the object but only the proposed condition of perception, could be exposed as a groundless and dispensable metaphysical hypothesis. This surgery completed we have before us a singularly pure form of idealism.

At other times Sartre seems to be working with a rather more

[1] See above, pp. 32–33.

mysterious conception of negation, according to which Nothing is a sort of felt emptiness, having its own peculiar sort of vividness. Thus in the first chapter of *L'Être et le Néant* Sartre describes[1] himself as visiting a café, and finding that his friend Pierre is not there. The absence of Pierre is then favourably compared with the merely 'abstract' absences of Wellington and Valéry. The reader needs a little of Hume's backgammon — or, say, a cup of coffee — before he is relaxed enough to recognise, beneath the extraordinary involution of Sartre's account, the simple truth: he *misses* Pierre more than he misses Valéry or Wellington. Obviously we have to do here with a phenomenon familiar to students of introspection. A man of active imagination can produce, in response to almost any word at all, a vague composite image which, if he is philosophically uncritical, he is prone to regard as the real meaning of the term. Thus, we can imagine 'metropolitan' (a glittering, roaring image) or 'hope' (supply your own). On these lines it is not difficult to produce some introspectible content to attach to the word 'nothing'. I have discussed elsewhere[2] the influence, largely pernicious, on metaphysics of this so-called generalising imagination.

The pleasures of such pseudo-metaphysical imaginings are insidious. In particular, it is easy to think that they corroborate Sartre's Theory. The notion that man is the point at which nothingness enters the universe can seem strangely convincing to a person staring at a hot, sunlit landscape, struggling to find by introspection a mental reality as hard and bright as the scene he surveys, and discovering instead only a frustrating obscurity. The fields before him blaze, but there is no light within. He can then tell himself that he has experienced the nothingness of which Sartre speaks. Indeed, as we have suggested, the experience can have its own paradoxical sort of vividness. This, he is willing to say, is what consciousness itself is. One is tempted to invoke, as Sartre himself loves to, the Cartesian apparatus, and to suggest that in certain lights the nothingness of which he speaks is not so much the essence as a spurious product of the post-reflective *cogito*.

In fact, *L'Être et le Néant* generates more difficulties than it

----

[1] *L'Être et le Néant*, I.i.2, Paris, Gallimard, p. 45; in Hazel E. Barnes's translation, *Being and Nothingness*, 1957, p. 10.

[2] *Two Concepts of Allegory*, 1967.

resolves. One turns to it hoping for a clarification of *La Nausée*
and ends by using *La Nausée* as a gloss on *L'Être et le Néant*.
Certainly the novel is more interesting, more cogent, more
univocal. In particular, it differs from the treatise in making
fewer gestures in the direction of publicity before settling on an
ostentatiously subjective view of the world. For example,
L'Être et le Néant places a good deal of stress on the thesis that
objects are not created by consciousness and in this way delays
its final capitulation for some time. But in *La Nausée* the
fundamentally viscous, unmanageable nature of reality is
swiftly set in antithesis to the mendacious clarity of ordinary
language. In *L'Être et le Néant* Sartre urges that the 'thinginess'
of things becomes more apparent, not when they are contemplated but when they are acted on. But those moments in *La
Nausée* when the hero confronts the real are essentially moments
of contemplation. To be sure, one is tempted to resolve this
discrepancy by saying that two sorts of 'thinginess' are at issue:
the sort we encounter by doing is the sort expressed by ordinary
language: 'table', 'pillar-box' and so on. It is action, not contemplation, which has yielded the great range of ordinary
objects. On the other hand the reality encountered by Roquentin
as he gazes at a tram-seat or a chestnut tree-root is (in Sartre's
own language) transphenomenal, the black flux upon which our
'objective schemata' are perilously cast. This is at least partly
correct. But it leaves the crucial question—what is *really* real?—
unanswered. *La Nausée* leaves us in little doubt that our
ordinary language is a self-protective screen, sustained only by a
gigantic conspiracy of bad faith. Furthermore, there is a special
difficulty in describing Roquentin's experiences and encounters
with the transphenomenal. To begin with, it would appear to
be a consequence of mere etymology that the transphenomenal
is, precisely, that which we do not encounter. Yet the difference
between Roquentin and his fellow men is supposed to lie not in
the fact that he alone looks *through* objects but in the fact that
he alone looks *at* them. Thus, in a way, he is the only one to
concern himself with the genuine *phenomenon*, and, if so, we
must say that it is precisely the phenomenon which turns out,
on inspection, to be formless, fluid, viscous, nauseating.

It seems wisest to concede that Sartre himself is confused. At
one place in *La Nausée* we read, 'Things are entirely what they

appear to be and *behind them* . . . there is nothing'.[1] But later this gives place to a near-pathological mistrust of ordinary appearances:

> A priest walks slowly along, reading his breviary. Now and then he raises his head and looks at the sea approvingly . . . Delicate colours, delicate perfumes, springtime souls. 'What lovely weather, the sea is green . . .'
>
> I turn my back on them. I lean both hands on the balustrade. The real sea is cold and black, full of animals; it crawls underneath this thin green film which is designed to deceive people. The sylphs all round me have been taken in: they see nothing but the thin film, that is what proves the existence of God. I see underneath! The varnishes melt, the shining little velvety skins, God's little peach-skins explode everywhere under my gaze, they split and yawn open.[2]

In *L'Être et le Néant* the term 'transcendent' as applied to the in-itself proves so vague as to be unmanageable. But if it is possible to discern a tendency in the proliferating ambiguities, it is one by now familiar: from the ostentatiously down-to-earth to the high-flown metaphysical. The in-itself is transcended in that it overflows appearance, overflows all my efforts to grasp or contain it. Very well. What is meant here by 'overflow'? One might answer as follows; real existents, unlike the objects of mathematics, can never be exhaustively described. We say that a straight line is the shortest distance between two points and the subject is cleared up. But when I transfer my attention from geometry to the child's tennis racket before me, I discover that I can continue indefinitely to describe this humble thing. The unfathomable richness of being in the simplest existent is what constitutes its transcendence, and underlines its independence of my consciousness. This conception of transcendence was obviously forged to combat the idealist. But it is not obvious how we are to reconcile it with Satre's observation that the in-itself differs from the for-itself in that the first has a determinate essence while the second has not. We are told that the fundamental tenet of existentialism is that existence precedes

---

[1] *La Nausée*, English title, *Nausea* (trans. Robert Baldock), Penguin: Harmondsworth, 1935, p. 140. [2] *Ibid.*, pp. 178–9.

essence; that is, that our attempts to categorise existents will always fall short. Often this thesis is tacitly limited to the existent for-itself. But to emphasise the transcendence of the in-itself is to extend the principle into the objective universe. It seems that the in-itself is *massif* ('solid') and 'viscous' at the same time. In *L'Être et le Néant* there are signs that Satre felt a certain discomfort over this issue. The examples of determinate essences which he gives tend to be, as Mary Warnock has noted,[1] artefacts rather than ordinary objects. In *La Nausée* he apparently commits himself to the view that to ascribe a determinate essence to *any* existent is to falsify it.

Nevertheless, apart from the fact that it sits uneasily with other parts of Sartre's philosophy, the notion seems sound enough. One might object that it will never be possible to prove from experience that reality goes beyond experience, to which an intelligent answer would be that the argument is not from experience (in the phenomenological sense) but from experiment; that is, we learn inductively from repeated trial and failure that real objects are inexhaustible; their inexhaustibleness forms no part of any single experience, but is rather inferred after we have put together, and reflected on a whole series of experiences. However, there are signs that this answer would not appeal to Sartre. Its rationalism, its trust in induction would seem to him abstract, anti-empirical and fundamentally unconvincing. Instead, he takes the steeper road and suggests that transcendence is directly experienced, whether it be the transcendence of other people or of objects. We watch a man reading in a park and we experience his ontological independence as a kind of crack in the surrounding massivity; his preoccupation is a phenomenon expressible in images such as that of water running away down a hole.[2] The notion of 'hole' is supposed to differentiate Sartre's transcendence from Husserl's, which has already been seen to lead its author back into the idealism from which he fled. Thus, Sartre suggests that we do not *perceive* the man's otherness. Rather we become aware of the incompleteness of our perceptions. The evasion is patently sophistical. Just as in the sphere of physical perception we perceive a hole or a cave

---

[1] *The Philosophy of Sartre*, 1965, p. 62.
[2] *L'Être et le Néant*, III.i.4, p. 313; in Hazel Barnes's translation, p. 256.

in exactly the same way as we perceive a post or a notice-board, so in our awareness of other people we become aware of their preoccupation in exactly the same way as we become aware of their interest. We notice it. Sometimes we even feel it vividly. The vigour of Sartre's imagery (which often betrays his philosophy) suggests that Sartre certainly did so. Thus to say that we learn the transcendence of others not from immediate awareness but from a felt intermission of that awareness turns out to be a desperate intellectual subterfuge. The very fact that the intermission is felt shows that it cannot be an intermission of consciousness as such, but only a modification of the *character* of consciousness. But that consciousness should be varied in character is scarcely surprising. Thus Sartre's attempt[1] to disengage himself from the company of Husserl fails, and he follows his master back into the prison-house.

After all, this sort of experienced transcendence should not now be too much for the reader, who has already cut his teeth on such conceptions as the palpable absence of Pierre in the café. And although this particular example of the man in the park deals with the encounter (or rather the failure to encounter) of two consciousnesses, and the hole is precisely a hole made in the in-itself by an alien for-itself, we shall find when we turn to Sartre's exploration[2] of the primarily viscous nature of the in-itself, that the same image – that of a hole – eventually engrosses him there too. He moves insensibly from the primordial image of slime to the yet more primordial image of a sticky, slimy hole; that which merely fails to provide tangible resistance to the athletic mind becomes that which actually caves in before us. We may thus begin to suspect that Sartre is subject to some sort of drive towards the postulation of nothingness, a postulation made less, not more, credible by an accompanying eagerness to invest the proposed negation with a quality of felt vividness by offering it as an object of experience. Thus while subjective consciousness becomes increasingly active and vivid, objective reality is presented under an escalating series of symbols, the progress of the escalation being marked by a gradual softening: 'things': 'the *massif*': 'the viscous'; 'the hole'. Thus the new

[1] See *L'Être et le Néant*, III.i.3, pp. 288 ff., in Hazel Barnes's translation pp. 233 ff.
[2] *Ibid.*, IV.ii.3, pp. 695–706; in Hazel Barnes's translation, pp. 604–14.

'philosophy of things' has turned into a metaphysic according to which a nothingness meets a hole. Popular legend provides us with a ribald emblem for this intellectual progress which Sartre's own Freudian excursion on 'le trou' forbids us to repress. In *L'Être et le Néant* Sartre resembles nothing so much as the fabled Wagga Wagga Bird. From this derives, by a cosmogony more barbarous than any in Hesiod, the world of language, objects and action. One is free to reflect that the common-sense philosophy of England was once subject to a similar solvent at the hands of David Hume, and that the job was carried out with more modesty, more simplicity and incalculably more intellectual power on the earlier occasion.

II

The claims of *L'Être et le Néant* to be considered as the key to *La Nausée* are therefore very dubious. The wards are faulty and in any case the lock may have been changed. For *La Nausée* appeared in 1938 while *L'Être et le Néant* was not published until 1943. In discussing the novel I shall ascribe opinions sometimes to its hero, Roquentin, sometimes to Sartre himself. The reader should not imagine that much hangs upon this difference. The view of *La Nausée* as an intricate system of intentionally absurd self-reference is chimerical. There is no sign in it of that distance, at once instinctive and controlled, between author and fictional narrator which runs through a book like Dostoevsky's *Notes from Underground*.

The novel is strange, but not paralysingly so. Its narrator and central figure, Antoine Roquentin, contrary to the manifest intention of the author, emerges as a rather romantic figure: tall, ugly, a traveller in exotic places, with memories of Tangier and Marrakesh, a man who has fought with armed Moroccans and brought off a spectacular feat of academic espionage.[1] To be sure, Roquentin never mentions such episodes unless to shrug them off, but the more he minimises them the more the adolescent reader (and *La Nausée* goes down very well with the intelligent adolescent) glows with admiration. The rhetoric is identical with Bulldog Drummond's – 'Just a scratch.' Of course

---

[1] The theft of the Moscow holdings of de Rollebon's correspondence, *La Nausée*, p. 138.

Sartre would scarcely welcome this analysis. With the top of his
head he plainly assents to Roquentin's sturdy refusal to admit
any real significance or pattern in his life. The particular brand
of visceral metaphysic with which Roquentin surrounds his
disclaimers is unmistakably Sartrian; self-parody is too much to
hope for. Life in itself is a meaningless flux, says Roquentin, and
'adventures' belong in books, though they may enjoy a spurious
existence in self-deceiving reminiscence.

Roquentin has just enough money not to need to work. His
status as a disinterested spectator of reality is thus economically
secured at the outset. He is, however, at least for part of the
book, a little more than 'tout juste un individu'.[1] For example,
he is an historian, writing the life of an eighteenth century
political adventurer called the Marquis de Rollebon. Sartre's
book is in the form of a casual diary kept by Roquentin, and is
at once recognisable as belonging to the Romantic tradition in
virtue of its evident distaste (ostensibly at least) for the sequen-
tial, the developing, the discursive, and its predilection for an
atomised experience, separated out into chunks or moments of
perception. One moment may be especially important but never
because of what it leads to or discloses at the level of ordinary
plot, only because it tastes stronger than the others. The only
important characteristics of any moment of perception (leaving
aside the philosophic *use* of such moments) will be those intrinsic
to it. The informed reader will easily supply analogues–
haecceitates or epiphanies–from other writers in the same tradition, beginning with Wordsworth. We even find persisting in
Sartre the Wordsworthian 'nostalgia for thinghood': 'The being
of human reality is suffering because it rises in being as perpetually haunted by a totality which it is without being able to be it,
precisely because it could not attain the in-itself without losing
the for-itself.'[2] If a phrase is needed to describe this strand in
romanticism, 'quest for the intrinsic' will do well enough. Thus
Roquentin's diary consists of a string of perceptual occasions,
noticing a doorknob, a man's braces, a piece of newspaper, a
chestnut tree-root; and along with these an exiguous plot.

---

[1] The phrase comes from a speech of Yudenzweck, in Act III of Ferdi-
nand Céline's *L'Eglise*; in his *Oevres*, Paris, 1966, p. 447. It is used as the
epigraph of *La Nausée*.

[2] *L'Être et la Néant*, I.ii.3, p. 134; Barnes, p. 90.

Roquentin grows disillusioned with his historical researches, is repelled by bourgeois complacency, as expressed in the portraits of Bouville Art Gallery, and by humanitarianism in an eccentric acquaintance; becomes sceptical about any attempt to find structure in reality, meets an old girl friend and finds that she has passed through an analogous process in her relations with the world; becomes apprised of the intolerable otherness of reality; resolves to write a work of fiction.

Roquentin's moments of perception are distinguished from their romantic analogues by their jaundiced flavour. Hence, indeed, the title of the book. It is indeed very easy to dismiss them (as many critics have) as pathological delusions. Certainly, it is not immediately clear why the perception of an object removed from the normal categories of utility, function and so on should be so dreadful. To make us understand that he perceived another man's hand in an entirely new light, Roquentin-Sartre says[1] it was like a maggot. Why not, say, warm leather? A tram-seat, divorced from function and origin, becomes a bleeding belly.[2] Why not a fair hot wench in flame-coloured taffeta? For Roquentin, the discovery that reality is other than his expectations, other than the expectations induced by language, indeed essentially inexhaustible—is a dreadful one. It may be said that his reaction is philosophical, since the mind naturally desires to contain, transcend, dominate reality. But does it? Some minds do, no doubt, but others do not. One thinks of Simone de Beauvoir's anecdote of Sartre, throwing out a definition of London, while she, the stern Existentialist Conscience, persistently cast it back at him, insisting that London was, because real, indefinitely rich and therefore informulable.[3] Sartre, it seems, became angry, and we diagnose his anger as that of the disappointed Platonist. But the Platonism is more a matter of temperament than of philosophy. Certainly a mind can differ from Sartre's and still be, quite recognisably, a mind. Conversely, it might be asked, is the following passage self-evidently illustrative of mind as such, or of mind ceasing to be mind?

> I couldn't stand it any more. I couldn't stand things being so close any more. I push open a gate, I go through, airy

[1] *La Nausée*, p. 14.   [2] *Ibid.*, p. 80.
[3] *The Prime of Life* (*La Force de l'Âge*), trans. Peter Green, 1962, p. 119.

existences leap about and perch on the treetops. Now I recognize myself, I know where I am: I am in the municipal park. I flop on to a bench between the great black trunks, between the black, knotty hands reaching out towards the sky. A tree is scratching the earth under my feet with a black nail. I should so like to let myself go, to forget, to sleep. But I can't, I'm suffocating: existence is penetrating me all over, through the eyes, through the nose, through the mouth . . .[1]

R. D. Laing in a book on mental disorders describes a schizophrenic who 'feels *persecuted by reality*' (his italics), 'longs to transcend the world' and has 'a constant dread of being overwhelmed'.[2] There is a certain irony here: the author of *The Divided Self* supposed himself to be an existentialist and a follower of Sartre, yet faced with a perception closely similar to that used by Sartre as the basis of an intuitive metaphysic he construes it, not philosophically but clinically, as paranoic schizophrenia. Laing's later irrationalism[3] scarcely commends itself as a way of resolving this difficulty.

Fortunately, however, there is more to Roquentin than this. Sartre is fully aware that his narrator will be classified as sick and forestalls the dismissive critic by a rhetoric of anticipation. Roquentin in fact begins by referring to a cessation of his special awareness as showing that he is 'cured'.[4] The diary proper opens with the phrase 'It came as an illness does'.[5] Later he speaks of 'a really bad attack'.[6] But soon after he makes it clear that having seen the merits of a clinical diagnosis he rejects them. Roquentin stands upright and affirms the truth of what he has seen. '. . . the veil is torn away, I have understood, I have *seen*.'[7] Try as he might, Sartre is unable at such moments to exclude from his style a note of Gallic orotundity.

In fact the attempt to describe things in themselves, seen in their full indifference to our normal categorisations, has a real claim upon our interest. Moreover, not all Roquentin's essays in this direction are characterised by such extreme disgust. At times another, and a better sort of rhetoric seems to be at work.

---

[1] *La Nausée*, p. 181.   [2] *The Divided Self*, 1960, p. 84.
[3] See the preface added to the Penguin edition of *The Divided Self*, 1965.
[4] *La Nausée*, p. 11.
[5] *Ibid.*, p. 13.   [6] *Ibid.*, p. 176.   [7] *Ibid.*, p. 181.

'Just now, when I was on the point of coming into my room, I stopped short because I felt in my hand a cold object which attracted my attention by means of a sort of personality. I opened my hand and looked: I was simply holding the door-knob'.[1] The tone of this is subdued, but the effect is powerful. The reader's intelligence is at once baffled and stimulated. Roquentin has already reached the point where he can actually be *using* an object in the ordinary way—not staring at it—and yet can find himself suddenly transfixed by a glimpse of its independent identity. Opening a door is a continuous half-instinctive action which is normally carried out with perception half-shuttered and one's attention fixed on a practical purpose. But this easy, purposive flow of things is for Roquentin momentarily arrested, and shivered into its constitutent atoms. A single cold chunk of it is left in his hand. He is, so to speak, for an instant left alone with the doorknob. All other projects, expectations, queries drain out of him and he is absorbed by the doorknob—its properties of coldness and massiness momentarily hypnotise his arm. Most important of all, the reader finds this far harder to classify than the apparently pathological quasi-hallucinations. And since the whole book is an attempt to duck under the net of categories, to have done this much is an achievement.

But perhaps we can learn more about the difficulties which face Sartre if we consider a mixed example; Roquentin is describing a man sitting opposite him in a tram:

> His terracotta face with its blue eyes. The whole of the right side of his body has collapsed, the right arm is stuck to the body, the right side is scarcely alive, it lives laboriously, avariciously, as if it were paralysed. But on the whole of the left side, there is a little parasitic existence which proliferates, a chancre: the arm started trembling and then it rose and the hand at the end was stiff. And then the hand too started trembling and, when it reached the height of the skull, a finger stretched out and started scratching the scalp with the nail. A sort of voluptuous grimace came and inhabited the right side of the mouth and the left side remained dead.[2]

[1] *Ibid.*, p. 13. [2] *Ibid.*, p. 181.

It will be seen that what is difficult is to find language which will convey with sufficient force the terrifying uniqueness of the perception without suggesting that there is anything objectively abnormal about the *object* of the perception. The technique was well defined by the Russian formalist Shklovsky as 'making it strange' (one of the marks of 'making it strange' is the refusal to recognise objects, the attempt to describe them as if they were being seen for the first time).[1]

But all is not easy. This passage is in real danger: it could easily be read as a description of a partly paralysed man, a man who would alarm anyone by his appearance. But if Sartre is to succeed the reader must be made to see that *this* sort of perception is perfectly undiscriminating in its choice of objects. The man on the tram is frightening, not because he is markedly different from other men but because he has been seen as a pure existent. The opening references to colours, terracotta and blue, are successful. They brutally restrict us to the phenomenal and succeed in surprising the reader without turning the subject into a commonplace curiosity. Similarly; a little later, the order of words: 'A finger stretched out' (not 'He stretched out a finger') is effective for the same reason. On the other hand, the reference to trembling is much less certain in its effect. Perhaps it is the sort of trembling that appears, so to speak, only under the microscope of an especially intense observation; or else the man was trembling violently. As long as the reader is uncertain, the special significance of the words is muffled. The language of pathological delusion can deflect us in a very similar way. As long as we suspect that Roquentin may be hallucinating, and that the objects of his hallucination are such things as maggots and centipedes, we shall find nothing to wonder at in his nausea. The special order of metaphysical disgust which springs not from an object's prickliness or sliminess but from its mere existence (which means any object whatsoever could produce it) eludes him. Anxious to impress his reader with the horrifying independence of existence, Sartre naturally describes his specimens in terms of things which the reader already accepts

[1] See Victor Erlich, *Russian Formalism*, 2nd edn., The Hague, 1965, p. 177. The ideas of Sartre seem not to be connected directly with those of the Formalists, though both were influenced by Husserl; see Erlich, *op. cit.*, pp. 61–2.

as disgusting. How else is nausea or shock to be conveyed? To tell the reader that Roquentin perceived a tram-seat as itself will effect nothing; to tell him that it looked like a skinned animal will only cause him to say: 'Lord, a tram-seat that looked like that *would* be frightening'—and once more miss the point. As we have seen, the best way with this problem is also the hardest: to describe the object in a way which shocks while yet satisfying the standards of objective normalcy. The best example of this rhetoric I know comes not from *La Nausée* but from a remark I once heard: 'Have you ever noticed that, when people eat, they tuck food into a slightly crumpled hole in their faces?' Dryden, with a very different motive, brought it off in a phrase ultimately derived from Plato—'to that unfeather'd, two-legg'd thing, a Son.'[1] The disgust it expresses is fathomless, yet the best son in the world has no feathers, and no more legs. The philosophical tradition to which Sartre belongs supplies us with another phrase to describe this technique. It is, very clearly, rhetoric of the *epoché*; that is, rhetoric which succeeds in imparting a special, experiental force to the object by isolating it, by bracketing off all the normal presuppositions and opinions concerning it. If we discover the Husserlian *epoché* in the intimate texture of Sartre's style (at its more successful moments) a certain doubt arises as to whether it was ever really banished from his thought.

Sartre could not in fact venture outside the *epoché* without a (quite unnecessary) feeling of guilt at his own supposed abstraction. The notion that it is the inner field which is the abstraction, less immediately known than tables and chairs, never fully penetrated his Cartesian mind. Hence, as we have seen, his attempts to reject the *epoché* because of the licence it affords idealism are themselves founded on a phenomenology which differs from Husserl's only by being more devious. Assimilation, at all costs, of the general to the experiential is the keynote of *La Nausée*. To exist is to be conscious or else to be the object of a consciousness. 'Monsieur de Rollebon was my partner: he needed me in order to be and I needed him in order not to feel my being'.[2] The simplicity which would say, 'M de Rollebon *used* to exist' has been excluded by the *epoché* and a dummy conception

---

[1] *Absalom and Achitophel* I. 170. The attribution of the phrase to Plato rests on Diogenes Laertius, *Lives*, VI.40.   [2] *La Nausée*, pp. 142–3.

of phenomenology has been set in its place. Because our awareness of others is a fluctuating thing, existence, reduced to that
awareness, becomes a predicate admitting different degrees of
intensity. The objective part vanishes and is replaced by its
phenomenological equivalent, which is memory; and memory
which is no longer related to a real past is no longer true memory
so that even that was too strong a term:

> Never have I felt as strongly as today that I was devoid
> of secret dimensions, limited to my body, to the airy
> thoughts which float up from it like bubbles. I build my
> memories with my present. I am rejected, abandoned in
> the present. I try in vain to rejoin the past: I cannot escape
> from myself.[1]

It is interesting to pause here and look back at the way an
eighteenth-century writer used this idea. Thomas Amory wrote
in his *Life of John Buncle*, 'The wife we lose by death is no more
than a sad and empty object, formed by the imagination, and
to be still devoted to her, is to be in love with an idea.'[2] The
precise degree of Amory's simplicity is a mystery which seems
to deepen with time, but it is hard not to see at least the
shadow of conscious humour in this passage. And, if we are
right, this means that Amory can see what Sartre cannot, a
certain over-all absurdity in the idea. And of course when
Sterne sets his pen to the same notion, we find real intellectual
fire, not Sartre so much as Wittgenstein in comic dress: '. . . for
consider, brother *Toby*,–when we *are*–death is *not;*–and when
death *is*–we are *not*. My uncle *Toby* laid down his pipe to consider the proposition.'[3]

Perhaps the most naive example of Sartre's reduction of the
concept of existence occurs in the strained suggestion that you
relieve a fly of *existence* by killing it[4] (though I imagine that the
strain is less evident in French than in English). But the most
important is Roquentin's transformation of the Cartesian
cogito:

> I *exist*. It is I. The body lives all by itself, once it has
> started. But when it comes to thought, it is I who continue,

---

[1] *Ibid.*, p. 53.
[2] *Op cit.*, vol. III, in E. A. Baker's edn., 1904, p. 180.
[3] *Tristram Shandy*, V.iii, p. 356.   [4] *La Nausée*, p. 150.

I who unwind it. I exist. I think I exist. Oh, how long and
serpentine this feeling of existence is–and I unwind it
slowly . . . If only I could prevent myself from thinking! I
try, I succeed: it seems as if my head is filling with smoke
. . . And now it starts again: 'Smoke . . . Mustn't think . . .
I don't want to think . . . I think that I don't want to think.
I mustn't think that I don't want to think. Because it is
still a thought.' Will there never be an end to it?

My thought is *me*: that is why I can't stop. I exist by
what I think . . .[1]

This is hardly to be surpassed as a piece of introspective fiction:
the mind falling into vacuous regresses as it struggles either to
observe or forget itself: thinking about thinking. But is this
quite just? It might be said that the difference between Descartes
and Sartre lies precisely in the fact that Descartes really *thought*
about thinking while Sartre chose a method which prevented
him from doing so. Descartes moves; he reviews and compares
the possible contents of his mind, isolates the idea of God,
proves his real existence, derives thence a guarantee of the
justness of his other ideas as representatives of external nature,
and so on. For Descartes, unlike Roquentin, still has three
tenses to work in; past, present and future. Retrospection is as
open to him as introspection. But Roquentin is confined to the
present moment, and must extract from it, and it alone, the
essence of the mind. But the individual moment is inert. The
result is the sort of intellectual constipation here feelingly
described. Dulled and blinkered, the mind can only ruminate,
sniff and salivate.

It may be objected that our strictures on this passage can be
dispelled by a reading of Sartre's essay *La Transcendance de
l'Ego*. This, unlike *L'Être et le Néant*, does not post-date *La
Nausée*. It first appeared in *Recherches Philosophiques*, VI,
1936-7. In this essay Sartre attacked Husserl for postulating a
transcendental ego, that is, an ego which stands behind consciousness and, so to speak, operates it. Believers in such an ego,
says Sartre, have difficulty in explaining exactly how it is
related to the external world. The difficulty is like that which
Cartesians faced in the seventeenth century: how was the soul,

[1] *Ibid.*, p. 145.

a non-extended substance, to act on extended objects? Its solution involved the notorious recourse to 'animal spirits', partaking of the nature of both mind and body and thus able to mediate between them. The Husserlian equivalent of animal spirits is his *hylê*, a word which in Greek philosophy means 'matter'. In Husserl's phenomenology *hylê* is roughly what used to be called the *sensum*, and it serves as matter to the active consciousness, as clay to the potter. It needs no great perspicacity to see in Husserl's *hylê* the *idea* of Locke, itself mental and yet mediating the physical to the watching mind. But Husserl differs from Locke in the idealist activity he ascribes to the ego, an ascription in no way forced on him by the need to end the isolation of the ego, but springing from other philosophical sources. Sartre suggests that this unhappy state of affairs can be cleared up if we refuse the first step. There is no need, he says, to postulate a transcendental ego at all. The ego is really not the agent but the object (or product, it is not entirely clear which) of consciousness. It is an object *for* consciousness, and is in the world, like other objects. With this philosophic surgery, it would seem, our difficulties are at an end. If there is no transcendental ego, there is no longer any need to postulate a mediating substance; the so-called 'contents' of consciousness were never anything more than a desperate subterfuge, the necessity of which has now lapsed. Images, sensa, ideas now become, like the ego, like the world, objects *for* consciousness.

It is not easy to share Sartre's sanguine view of this redaction. Like Bishop Berkeley he is for turning ideas into things, and, like the Bishop's, his ideas obstinately retain their mental smell. For Sartre still holds to the Husserlian notion of intentionality, according to which every state of consciousness will be consciousness *of* an object and yet must not be identified with an object. The imagining of a tree is not the same thing as the tree imagined. To retain this conception and yet to reject the notion of conscious contents leaves the concept of consciousness itself in a sorry condition. Sartre, unabashed by this, assumes his Delphic style. Our inability to discover the nature of consciousness becomes accountable, he thinks, when we recognise that consciousness has no character at all: it is, precisely, a nothing. It is of course no accident that the phrase, 'a nothing', is *linguistically* odd. If to say that consciousness is a nothing does not mean that there is no such thing as consciousness then the phrase must really be a (quite remarkably) misleading way of saying that consciousness is a something, of a very negative kind! Quite clearly Sartre means the latter: his 'nothing' blows towards the object like a dark wind.

This is philosophy at its most culpably verbal. The terms may be re-shuffled almost at will. Sartre's dark consciousness, reaching towards objects (and how is a nothing to be joined to a something without some mediating substance, partaking of the nature of both?) can be called, without violence, an ego. In *La Nausée* it is called 'moi', which doubtless sounds earthier, less abstract than 'ego', or even 'je', but is in like case philosophically.

Similarly, his attempt to reallocate conscious contents to the world at large remains a mere gesture. The Cartesian model still rules him. In practical terms consciousness is for Sartre like the postulated eye the viewpoint of which is obeyed in a perspective picture. Though this eye forms no part of the picture's contents, the ordered subjectivity of the whole ensures our realisation that all is watched by *this*, standing *here*, and nowhere else.

The constant confinement within the individual perspective of the *epoché* thus undermines Sartre's every attempt to get rid of the watching 'I'. And when, as in the last passage from *La Nausée*, we find that this *néant* or 'nothingness' can actually, in a cramped sort of way, scrutinise itself, Sartre's rejection of mental contents ceases to carry conviction. It is no accident that when he writes with his usual vigour of this emptying into the world of contents previously thought of as 'inward' we feel, as mere literary critics, that the opposite has happened: that public objects have begun, as in Wordsworth, to smell of consciousness.

Take the passage (it might also be Paul Jennings parodying Sartre) where Roquentin is disgusted by the barman's braces, and then by his shirt:

> His blue cotton shirt stands out cheerfully against a chocolate-coloured wall. That too brings on the Nausea. Or rather it *is* the Nausea. The Nausea isn't inside me: I can feel it over *there* on the wall, on the braces, everywhere

around me. It is one with the café, it is I who am inside
it.[1]

In analysing this passage one is tempted to mimic, if not the style
of Sartre, at least his mode of thought: 'in banishing the Nausea
to the café wall, Roquentin has not freed it from interiority;
rather it carries its interiority with it, and envelops the room;
the café cannot carry the Nausea away; instead, the Nausea
fetches it' (it is fatally easy to fall into this manner: to set up an
anti-Sartre to catch a Sartre; to counter Sartre on the absent
Pierre[2] with some such nonsense as 'But do you not feel the
absence of Valéry to be more unfathomable, more palpably
nihilate than that of Pierre, who is, in comparison, almost
here?').

The usefulness of such mimicry lies in its power to provide
practical illustrations of the incurable fluidity of such concepts.
The really interesting thing about the passage on the barman
(and again the literary point is precursor to the philosophical)
is that Sartre's sophistical attempt to resolve the situation by
turning it inside out—by placing the consciousness inside its
objects instead of outside—has only resulted in the familiar
model of the imprisoned mind. The *literary* impact of the passage
tells us that Roquentin is shut in, enclosed in a room stained
with the mental vomit of his subjective nausea. The philosophical analysis, which shows how a consciousness separated
from its contents becomes a disguised Cartesian ego—indeed, a
néant is a kind of ghost—helps to articulate the reasons for our
intuitive response.

And indeed, to revert for a moment to the pathological
parallel, still disturbingly close, the language of schizophrenics
can, it seems, take one route as easily as another: the schizophrenic can describe the world as a phantasm of his own mind,
or like this girl see his own identity as absorbed into the
environment:

> I was about twelve, and had to walk to my father's shop
> through a large park, which was a long, dreary walk. I
> suppose, too, that I was rather scared. I didn't like it,
> especially when it was getting dark. I started to play a
> game to help to pass the time. You know how as a child

---

[1] *La Nausée*, p. 35.　　[2] See above, p. 166.

you count the stones or stand on the crosses on the pave-
ment—well I hit on this way of passing the time. *It struck me
that if I stared long enough at the environment that I would
blend with it and disappear just as if the place was empty and
I had disappeared. It is as if you get yourself to feel you
don't know who you are or where you are.* To blend into the
scenery so to speak. Then you are scared of it because it
begins to come on without encouragement. I would just be
walking along and felt that I had blended with the landscape. Then I would get frightened and repeat my name
over and over again to bring me back to life, so to speak.[1]

III

The metaphysical heart of *La Nausée* is, by common consent,
the episode in the park where Roquentin stares at the root of a
chestnut tree. It is the most powerful and elaborate set piece in
the book, and formally (for *La Nausée* has form) it functions as
a long delayed declaration of love might have in an older novel.
It is, unhappily, too long to quote in full and too intricate to
discuss by mere allusion. Here, then, is a selective quotation,
and the reader is advised that if he is to guard himself against
possible distortion in the selection his best remedy is the text
itself:

> Never, until these last few days, had I suspected what it
> meant to 'exist' . . . If anybody had asked me what exist-
> ence was, I should have replied in good faith that it was
> nothing, just an empty form, which added itself to external
> things, without changing anything in their nature. And
> then, all of a sudden, there it was, as clear as day; existence
> had suddenly unveiled itself. It had lost its harmless appear-
> ance as an abstract category: it was the very stuff of
> things, that root was steeped in existence. Or rather the
> root, the park gates, the bench, the sparse grass on the
> lawn, all that had vanished; the diversity of things, their
> individuality, was only an appearance, a veneer. This
> veneer had melted, leaving soft, monstrous masses, in
> disorder—naked, with a frightening obscene nakedness . . .
>
> The chestnut tree pressed itself against my eyes. Green

[1] Case history cited in R. D. Laing, *The Divided Self*, p. 118; italics
R. D. Laing's.

rust covered it half way up; the bark, black and blistered,
looked like boiled leather . . .

. . . without formulating anything clearly, I understood
that I had found the key to Existence, the key to my
Nausea, to my own life. In fact, all that I was able to grasp
afterwards comes down to this fundamental absurdity.
Absurdity: another word; I am struggling against words;
over there, I touched the thing . . . A circle is not absurd,
it is clearly explicable by the rotation of a segment of a
straight line around one of its extremities. But a circle does
not exist either. That root, on the other hand, existed in
so far that I could not explain it. Knotty, inert, nameless,
it fascinated me, filled my eyes, repeatedly brought me
back to its own existence. It was no use my repeating: 'It
is a root'—that didn't work any more. I saw clearly that
you could not pass from its function as a root, as a suction-
pump, *to that*, to that hard, compact, sea-lion skin, to that
oily, horny, stubborn look. The function explained nothing;
it enabled you to understand in general what a root was,
but not *that one* at all . . . when I took my foot away, I saw
that the bark was still black.

Black? I felt the word subside, empty itself of its meaning
with an extraordinary speed. Black? The root *was not* black,
it was not the black there was on that piece of wood . . . I
didn't see that black in a simple way: sight is an abstract
invention, a cleaned-up, simplified idea, a human idea. That
black, a weak, amorphous presence, far surpassed sight,
smell and taste. But that richness became confusion and
finally ceased to be anything at all because it was too
much . . .

The essential thing is contingency. I mean that, by
definition, existence is not necessity. To exist is simply *to
be there*; what exists appears, lets itself be *encountered*, but
you can never *deduce* it . . .

Existence everywhere, to infinity, superfluous, always
and everywhere; existence—which is never limited by
anything but existence . . .

Did I dream it up, that huge presence? It was there,
installed on the park, tumbled into the trees, all soft,
gumming everything up, all thick, a jelly. And I was

inside with the whole of the park? . . . I was suffocating at the bottom of that huge boredom. Then, all of a sudden, the park emptied as if through a big hole . . .[1]

We can say that we have here a fairly precise pre-echo of the progress of *L'Être et le Néant*: we pass from things to jelly and thence to a hole. And yet the entire passage is a description of a particular experience. It is strictly phenomenological from beginning to end. Which recalls us to our unanswered question: did *La Transcendance de l'Ego* ever really free Sartre from the domination of Husserl?

It did not. The subservience could scarcely be more complete. Not only is the *epochê* observed but the Husserlian moral is drawn; the mind, like a potter, shapes the soft masses of reality into objects and only reluctantly confesses that what first confronted it was not vessels but clay. Indeed Husserl's term *hylê* is accidentally useful if at this point it reminds us of the 'matter' of Aristotle. We have seen too many of Sartre's ponderous gestures of self-dissociation from tradition to be much inhibited by them now. The terms have changed but we have visited this philosophical *locus* before. Hopkins on the distinctiveness of individuals led us to Duns Scotus and Scotus to Henry of Ghent and Henry to Aristotle. Aristotelian matter, we saw, was incapable of individuating or differentiating, being itself formless and undifferentiated.[2] For Hopkins's slime was that which preceded individuality. It is no accident that in Roquentin's vision 'the diversity of things' and their 'individuality' vanishes.

It would seem that Sartre's mind is deeply imbued with an originally Greek conception of the world as constituted by form and matter. But here we must pause to point out a real distinction. Whereas the older thinkers (Plato strongly, Aristotle weakly) tended to ascribe reality to the operation of the formal principle, Sartre, even though it costs him the world of individual objects, opts for the material. In this, it might be said, he is an honest son of the Scientific Revolution, since the great thinkers of the seventeenth century made the same transference of allegiance. If this is indeed the basis of Sartre's preference, one can only wonder at the unthriftiness of a mind which accepts

[1] *La Nausée*, pp. 182–93.   [2] See above, pp. 150–1.

the scientific modification of metaphysics without also accepting that revised concept of matter which alone made the modification possible.

The psychologically interesting thing about Sartre is that the ancient apparatus of the European mind has sunk so deeply into him that it can condition even his experience, and that to a point approaching hallucination. Some might say, however, that it is not so much interesting as incredible. After all, the distortions and deliquescences 'reported' by Roquentin might in fact be no more than a subtle rhetoric, a technique for 'making it strange'. The art of Seurat provides a useful comparison here. His picture, *Le Bec du Hoc, Grandcamp* (in the Tate Gallery), is plainly an attempt to convey the 'merely visual': an immense rock, sandy, turfy and mottled, hanging in the watcher's field of vision, before a prosaic yet subtly obtrusive sea. Here, we are tempted to say, is the eye's truth, innocent of preconception. But is it what we see when we look at the Bec itself? Hardly. However scrupulously we divest our minds of concept or category as we stare, the object obviously keeps its merely visual smoothness of definition and clarity. It seems clear that Seurat is conveying the special quality of preconceptual seeing (a curious and artificial condition) by a sort of imaginative equivalent—the fuzzing of contour and outline which occurs when vision is temporarily impaired; 'Seeing-without-knowing' is presented as 'not-quite-seeing'—a different thing altogether, yet one which can stand as a sort of instinctual metaphor for the other. In the same way, it might be said, Sartre's talk of dislimning is no more than a kind of visual metaphor for an epistemological process which would otherwise be incommunicable.

But I doubt if Sartre would welcome this account. To transform the one truth of nature (for Roquentin) into a figurative technique for communicating some other truth is a real disservice. And whereas Seurat uses a fuzzing technique to convey a shape, a light and an atmosphere, for Sartre the decomposition of things is itself the object of the description. He writes too urgently of the deliquescence and too negligently of the ordinary public object, so that we can no longer believe that the first is merely a means of enhancing or purging our perception of the second. We are to take it that Roquentin saw what he describes.

Certainly, it is counter-intuitive, at least to me, for I am tempera-
mentally closer to Hopkins than to Sartre, in that if I were to
shut myself up with a biscuit tin for three hours to contemplate
its biscuit-tin-ness, the object would tend to grow harder and
more angular rather than to melt. In the sub-philosophical
symbolism with which we are dealing, this would be interpreted
as showing that the individuality of the biscuit tin would be,
for me, the crucial and ultimate datum of the experience. But
for Sartre (Roquentin and he are, in this, one) to see an object
in itself is to see it independently of the schemata of language
and thought. Now by the Aristotelian model it is ultimately
through form or shape that objects are integrated into language,
become thinkable (for it is the shape of that wood which pro-
claims its function, and its function declares its definition, which
is 'seat'). Therefore, for an object to be disjoined from this web
of concepts, it must actually become shapeless. It must melt.
The strong Aristotelian chain between mind and matter must be
snapped at this weakest point: where it joins the formless.
Nothing shows more clearly than this the limitation of Sartre's
mind. So assiduously has he confined himself to the savouring
of experience that he is no longer capable of distinguishing a
symbol from the philosophical generality it is designed to
express. For Aristotle, as we have seen, actual slime is as
concrete as an egg-whisk; matter-as-such is unimaginable
because pre-experiential. But Sartre, staring gloomily at spilled
treacle, is half-able to convince himself that he is *seeing* the
prime *hylê* of all things.

Thus our link with Scotus is even closer than we thought. It
was by a spurious release of the felt quality of experience into a
realm properly pre-empirical that Scotus broke away from
Henry of Ghent. Henry had said that an individual was an
individual only by a negative principle: in so far as it was
nothing else. Scotus, if my interpretation is correct, had retorted
with the felt impact made on his awareness by a stone. Similarly
Roquentin rejects the negative conception of 'existence' in the
second sentence of the long quotation above and replaces it
with a metaphysically inept palpation.

It is perhaps worth asking: why does Sartre so mistrust
language? In a way, the answer is obvious. We all know how it is
possible to escape from reality by 'verbalising' it. Sometimes

the psychological mechanism involved in this is manifest. Suppose a man is jilted by his mistress; he says 'She has left me' and at once the pain is less. Presumably the 'verbalising' here works by permitting the man to prove that he can keep his head above water. As long as he can express his situation in words he can show himself and others that he is not afraid to admit what has happened and, more subtly, that he is still in intellectual control of what has passed beyond his practical power. At other times the petrifying power of words is less easily accounted for. If a friend says to me 'How beautiful this view is' the view becomes less beautiful by just five words. But here too we can guess at the reasons: there are certain things which we feel should be left in an innocent condition of spontaneity, love must not be forced nor must beauty be hunted down. The situation in which the friend offends with his 'How beautiful!' is really the obverse of the jilted lover's. There verbal control was welcomed because desiderated; here, on the other hand, is a feature of experience which must, we feel, be left alone. But in either case the diminishing power of words lies in the sense of intellectual control that they give. They carry with them the unsaid corollary: 'I am not over-whelmed or passive; I am able to analyse and appraise.' To be sure, other explanations are possible, and will be in certain cases more convincing. Words can themselves become an object of attention, and if we are preoccupied with the way we say some-thing we may forget for a while the things, terrible, glorious or boring that we are talking about. What is indisputable is that this is the *sort* of explanation that is appropriate; that is, we are dealing with a particular and local psychological phenomenon and therefore a particular and local psychological explanation is relevant. Nothing that we have said so far justifies the belief that language is *inherently* a sort of systematic mendacity. Rather we have been concerned with quite obviously unusual moments, moments when language is not her normal self. Therefore the general claim—that language as such falsifies, needs more for its validation than an appeal to experiences like these. And indeed, the experiential evidence offered by Sartre is in any case not quite of this kind. He shows us his hero honestly striving to apply the word 'root' to a root, and failing. This is obviously something other than what is ordinarily called 'verbalising'. Why then is *'that'* in the park not a root? Why is it a lie to call it so?

It is ironic that Sartre should always lead up to his epiphanies with tracts of ordinary, narrative French. He takes care to milk the cow before he drives her off his land. Thus ordinary language is used to appraise the reader of the fact that Roquentin is riding a tram before expressions like 'tram-seat' are rejected with contempt. Similarly it is made quite clear in commonplace language that Roquentin is looking at the root of a chestnut tree before the *fortissimo* note is assumed to tell us that 'root' is no use. This is a situation which lends itself to caricature (to be delivered in the manner of Morecambe and Wise):

> *Sartre:* Roquentin went into the park and stared at the chestnut tree-root–
>
> *Reader:* A chestnut tree-root.
>
> *Sartre:* Right.
>
> *Reader:* Right.
>
> *Sartre:* And it was black, and wet and pachydermatous; it melted and rotted against his eyeballs; words became puny and fell back, sick. It was not a root–
>
> *Reader:* Not a root?
>
> *Sartre:* Please don't interrupt. It was not a root–
>
> *Reader:* What was it then, his foot?
>
> *Sartre:* Clearly you have not understood anything. Didn't I *tell* you it was a root?

Presumably an entire novel might have been written at the pitch of Roquentin's encounter with the (as it were) root. But it would not have been intelligible. Both Sartre and Roquentin still care enough for the individuated surface of phenomena to be anxious that the reader should not think that Roquentin was in church when he was in the park, or in a slaughterhouse (which would, incidentally, make the chosen symbolism unworkable at this point) when he was on the tram. It is not enough to say that ordinary language is proper to ordinary life; violent, self-lacerating language to the special disclosures of reality. The information purveyed in the first sort of language remains in a humble fashion, essential to the understanding of the second. There is a level at which we need to know, throughout all the bombinating darkness of the Disclosure, that it is a root that

Roquentin is staring at. And it is language, ordinary language, which alone can tell us.

I have already called Sartre a disappointed Platonist. And indeed the 'mathematicals' of Plato–circles, metra and so on–recur in *La Nausée* as objects of a sort of nostalgia. One wishes to say that these are attractive to the mind because they conform to their definitions, whereas trees, benches, animals do not. But is even this true? In fact the phrase 'conform to' is ambiguous. According to one sense an object conforms to its definition if nothing about it contradicts what is said in the definition: this we may call negative conformity. But according to another sense, an object conforms to its definition only if it contains no features not mentioned in the definition: positive conformity. It seems clear that for ordinary purposes of living and talking, negative conformity is enough. We need only to demarcate the object; because the object is itself publicly available there is no need to exhaust it verbally. Positive conformity would be tedious, otiose and impossible.

One suspects, however, that it is positive conformity that Sartre, absurdly, expects. We may imagine the child Sartre growing up on a far-off planet where only two sorts of animals are to be found: men and cats. The philosophers of that planet define the cat as 'four-footed animal', and, since there are no other four-footed animals, this serves. Sartre's reaction is predictable: 'How false to call *that* a "four-footed animal"–that fluid, dark, spring-footed, cool-nosed, disappearing-under-doors thing-presence . . .' and so on. Sartre confounds the ideals of sufficient definition and exhaustive description. Ordinary use of language is impossible without some sort of success in definition (or demarcation); on the other hand a truly exhaustive description is perhaps never attained at all. For practical purposes we require from language its services as a guide; it conducts us to the object, but seldom (outside the mysterious identifications of poetry) seeks to enact it. It is ironic that Sartre's own method in *La Nausée*–to manœuvre us into position with ordinary words before stunning us with Existence–should so firmly corroborate this, to him, alien view.

Here the deepest irony of *La Nausée* begins to emerge. Sartre implicitly accuses the rest of the world of a kind of bad faith since it tries to pretend that its language is a truthful representation of reality. Since Sartre understands 'truthful representation' in our sense of positive conformity, he naturally concludes that, as the Cretan said, all men are liars. But the charge will not stick, since no-one really assumes that his language conforms positively with real objects. Our pretensions are much more modest. They cannot therefore be condemned for failing to achieve that which they never attempted. But what of Sartre himself? I said that no-one assumes that language should attain positive conformity, but there is a possible exception to this rule, and that is the author of *La Nausée*. As the accusing voice grows shriller, we slowly realise where the guilt lies.

We began by asking: why does Sartre mistrust language? Having arrived at a possible answer to this question, we must now ask another: why, then, is Sartre so loquacious?

The episode of the chestnut tree-root is really very verbal, indeed a kind of orgy of words. And these words really are striving to exhaust, if not the object as such, then certainly one presentation of it. 'One cannot pass', says Sartre-Roquentin, 'from its function as a root, as a suction-pump, to *that*', and we expect the words to efface themselves, leaving only the ostensive gesture of the pronoun; but, characteristically, the sentence flows on: 'to that hard, compact, sea-lion skin' and so on–may we say?–*ad nauseam*. Sartre cannot bear to let a thing be. He must clobber it and chain it with words. This is true of the author of *La Nausée* no less than of the young man in London, described by Simone de Beauvoir. To be sure, his strategy was simpler then; he offered, it seems easily falsified epigrams; now he offers elaborately self-refuting verbal expressions of the inexpressibility of things. It is of course a mere facet of the central inconsistency of existentialism, which is its systematic denial of the possibility of system. 'The essential thing is contingency,'[1] says Sartre. But contingency belongs not with essence at all but with the unthinkable category of existence which is always prior. To those of us who believe that *anything* can be an object of thought and that anything (but not everything) can be said, there is here no cause for alarm. But existentialist thinkers appear to assume that the world is inexorably partitioned; there are objects of thought, and then, separate

[1] *La Nausée*, p. 188.

from them, there are subjects, and, then, existence, the *hylê* of the objects. But the mind will not submit to this ruling. Anything can become an object of thought–even a subject. Thus anything can have an essence–even existence.

Thus Sartre is left in what is, logically, a pretty bad spot. One is reminded of Grelling's celebrated Heterological Paradox,[1] whereby some words, like 'rope', which were not instances of themselves were for that reason called 'heterological', while others, like 'word' or 'English', which *are* instances of themselves were therefore called homological. The question was then asked: 'Is the word "heterological" heterological?' and the answer was, 'If it is, it isn't, and if it isn't, it is.' So with Sartre here. If the writing in the chestnut tree passage succeeds, it fails, and, if it fails, it succeeds. Let us spell this out more slowly. Taking the first half of our paradox first; this means: if Sartre has really shown us in this piece of writing that the tree-root is beyond language–if he has really made this clear and intelligible to us– then he has, pragmatically, refuted himself, since the thesis directly implies that language can do no such thing. If on the other hand (and here we come to the second part of our paradox) Sartre has entirely failed to express the mystery of the tree-root, then his thesis is safe, though presumably it remains uncommunicated. It follows that no man can say that *La Nausée* succeeds in its main philosophic impulse.

Of course Sartre's paradox is more easily resolved than Russell's; our distinction between the positive and negative conformity of things to their definitions will do this well enough. The language of negative conformity is competent to condemn the language of positive conformity. By using that language which does not pretend to say everything, which offers only a modest, flexible, loose-textured set of guide-lines, we *can* express the impossibility of the *other* language of positive conformity, according to which everything in the object must be exactly conveyed. Of course this is a good deal less radical, less surprising than Sartre's first thesis. True theses are often thus.

---

[1] For a brief discussion of Grelling's paradox see W. and M. Kneale, *The Development of Logic*, 1962, p. 656. The paradox is one of a group which caused Russell to construct his Theory of Logical Types. See A. N. Whitehead and Bertrand Russell, *Principia Mathematica*, the 1960 reprint of the 2nd edn. of 1927, vol. I, pp. 37–8.

Once we realise that language contains not only words like *circle* and *straight* but also words like *mysterious, problematic, half-known* and *absurd*, we must give up the radical thesis. On the last of these words Sartre himself paused for a moment,[1] and then roared on. Moreover, when once the full implications of this linguistic variety are grasped, we shall revise our expectations even of such words as *red, root* or *chair*. In fact, we shall cease to expect the word to be a sort of *ersatz* thing, and to compare the imitation unfavourably, in point of richness or substance, with the original. Would that the author of *Laputa* had lived long enough to review *La Nausée*.

If we ask: what is the connexion between this curious theory of the incommensurability of language and reality on the one hand and Sartre's Husserlian epistemology on the other, the answer must be that Sartre offers the story about language as a manifest truth tending to confirm the accuracy of his epistemology. It seems to be implied that the fictions of language are closely allied to the fictions of cognition which seduce us into a belief in objects. If this is indeed an alliance and not an identity, a certain representative accuracy might be conceded to language: it correctly expresses that system of cognitive illusions in which most of us live. Both systems, the system of language and the system of objects, are, we are told, at odds with experience, if experience be once minutely attended to. But to speak in this way is to impart an inappropriate and perhaps undesired tidiness to Sartre's thought.

Some people will say that within the story of *La Nausée* a solution is offered. Roquentin at the end of the book proposes to write a work of fiction. Some critics see in this episode an allusion to *La Nausée* itself.[2] If they were right, and *La Nausée* were the sort of book that Erasmus's *Praise of Folly* is sometimes supposed to be, this would scarcely extricate Sartre from his logical difficulties. In fact it seems quite clear that Roquentin has in mind a very different kind of book, a kind which only throws into yet stronger relief the guilt of *La Nausée*:

> Couldn't I try . . . Naturally, it wouldn't be a question of a tune . . . But couldn't I in another medium? . . . It would

---

[1] *La Nausée*, p. 185.

[2] For example, Anthony Manser, *Sartre: a Philosophic Study*, 1966, p. 3.

G

have to be a book: I don't know how to do anything else.
But not a history book: history talks about what has
existed–an existent can never justify the existence of
another existent. My mistake was to try to resuscitate
Monsieur de Rollebon. Another kind of book. I don't quite
know which kind–but you would have to guess, behind
the printed words, behind the pages, something which
didn't exist, which was above existence. The sort of story,
for example, which could never happen, an adventure. It
would have to be beautiful and hard as steel and make
people ashamed of their existence.[1]

The symbolism of the novel makes it quite clear that this book
will not be *La Nausée,* and indeed such force as it possesses
as a 'solution' depends upon its not being. To begin with, the
projected work is offered as analogous to the jazz song 'Some
of these days'. This song is liked by Roquentin, not because of
its truth, or its honest acceptance of the flux of reality but
because it offers a refuge from that flux. What Roquentin
likes is the sense of inner necessity, the feeling that the words
exist in a kind of Empyrean in which all the unsatisfying
incompleteness of reference to real objects (*Bedeutung*) has
been cut away, leaving only the perfect coincidence of word
and meaning (*Sinn*). There is nothing unilluminated, unshaped,
no loose ends. Essence is all, existence nothing. The disappointed Platonist has found a place to lay his head: 'Another
few seconds and the Negress will sing. It seems inevitable, the
necessity of this music is so strong: nothing can interrupt it,
nothing which comes from this time in which the world is
slumped.'[2] A little later he associates the song with circles and
metals, symbols of the realm of essence (we remember the
allusion to this platinum metre they keep near Paris–to
Sartre's absurdly licentious imagination, a Platonic form,
trapped and guarded). So too Roquentin's project is compared
with steel. Later in the book the song is explicitly contrasted
with existence[3] (and at the same time Roquentin tells us that
it is not as a link with the negro performers that he values it).
So, too, Roquentin's book is to be 'above existence'.[4]

[1] *La Nausée,* p. 252.
[2] *Ibid.,* p. 37.   [3] *Ibid.,* p. 149.   [4] *Ibid.,* p. 252.

It seems clear that some sort of ostentatiously artificial work is intended. This would offer an escape in the following way. Language which tries to tell the truth will always lie, and mendacity is the prime sin in the existentialist canon. To face the viscous in unblinking silence is, on the other hand, more than man can bear. Thus the least culpable way of flinching from it is to do so without any pretence of truth-telling; to build against the black tide of existence tiny castles of artifice, introverted, making no claim to colonise, only to exclude. In this way at least we do not lie.

It will be seen that we have here a view of the writer very different from that offered in *Qu'est-ce que la Littérature?* where we are told that the function of the writer is to call a spade a spade.[1] Equally certainly it differs from that exemplified in *La Nausée* itself. The drive of the book is towards understanding reality as Sartre conceives it. It is, precisely, an attempt to colonise existence, to do with language that which language, *ex hypothesi*, cannot do.

IV

I have tried to show that Sartre's metaphysical imagination remains, in *La Nausée*, circumscribed by the individual consciousness. The subjective awareness, as Sartre partly knew, will not yield metaphysical conclusions, for metaphysics aims at the utmost generality. Metaphysics discusses not experiences but experience. But a man who restricts himself too long to the subjective view will tend to lose any vivid sense of the difference between particular and general. There are signs that this began to happen to Sartre.

His ideas commonly become metaphysical by degrees. A sort of gradual stylistic inflation leads to a greater and greater scope of reference. An idea proper to a particular empirical situation takes hold of him and gradually he enlarges it until– *voilà*–it is metaphysical. The want of philosophical argument is supplied by a sense that here philosophy is vivid and experiential, which it may have been at the (non-metaphysical) beginning of the process but can scarcely be at the end. Thus in *La Nausée* the epistemological *epoché* is preceded by one that

[1] 'D'appeler un chat un chat', in *Situations*, II, Gallimard, Paris, 1948, p. 304; trans. Bernard Frechtman as 'What is Literature?' 1950, p. 210.

is merely social, Roquentin is economically bracketed off from his fellow Frenchmen before his mind is bracketed off from its own preconceptions. This prefigures one of the main irrational escalations of the book—that from the bad faith of the bourgeois —the 'salauds'[1] of Bouville Art Gallery—to the bad faith of language itself. This is worth calling irrational because the later stage, so far from being a deepening of the initial insight, is in fact incompatible with it. If Bad Faith is general the bourgeois are no more guilty than the proletariat, and the adverse political judgments based on this insight lapse: all parties alike are users of language, believers in objects. Yet one is uncertain whether Sartre is fully aware that his thesis has changed crucially. The use of corroborating examples in *L'Être et le Néant* tends to confirm this suspicion. These are empirical in exactly the wrong way. For example Sartre will seek to show the universality of mendacity by brilliant novelistic descriptions—of the girl who modifies her own consciousness in order to exclude the fact that an erotic advance is being made,[2] of the waiter who *plays the part*—with superb finesse—of a waiter.[3] These are, so to speak, star cases, but star cases are the exact opposite of what he needs, since their very strikingness implies the existence of other cases less strong than themselves.

There are two ways of using concrete examples to support a general philosophic thesis: one is to take that which is manifestly commonplace—which everyone will agree to be general—and these examples, actually, will not read like passages from a novel. It is no accident that the examples given by real philosophers, such as Aristotle or Hume, seem much duller than those in *L'Être et le Néant*. But another and more exciting way is open: to take the *invidious* example; to lavish one's novelistic skill on the example which no-one would have expected to confirm the theory and yet can be shown to do so. To support the thesis of universal rôle-playing, let us use, not a waiter (for anyone could believe that at once) but, say, a tired housewife taking the shopping home. If Sartre had been able to show that the tired housewife was really playing the part of a tired

---

[1] *La Nausée*, p. 138.

[2] *L'Être et le Néant*, p. 94; in Hazel Barnes's translation, p. 55.

[3] *Ibid.*, pp. 98 ff.; in Hazel Barnes's translation, p. 59.

housewife we might have begun to believe that rôle-playing really is universal. In terms of pure argument, his example would have lifted a far greater weight. As it is, he merely continues to hunt joyously for the most vivid example, without sensing that, now that his thesis has become general, the whole function of the illustration has changed.

In general this chapter has been concerned with a later stage of the existence-precedes-essence escalation than that usually discussed. According to the popular ethical philosophy of existentialist freedom, the existence which is indefinable is properly that of persons; things retain their essences. The extension in *La Nausée* of this principle of indefinability from the for-itself to the in-itself is just such another 'mere enlargement', symptomatically accompanied by an increasing stridency of style. The phenomenon is easily parallelled. In the short story *L'Enfance d'un Chef* the slow tacit consent of a human soul to a Fascist mode of consciousness is brilliantly articulated, yet Sartre there, in one purple patch, suddenly extends the principle of role-adoption even beyond persons—to a carafe of water.[1]

The truth is that Sartre writes by a subjectivist *method* and, like a kind of curse, his method prevents him from understanding his own best insights. Take, for example, his notion that a man forms his idea of himself not from immediate inner awareness but from the reactions, and in particular the looks, of other people. This, in that it switches epistemological primacy from the inner to the public world, looks promising. But observe how the idea is handled in *La Nausée:*

> Now when I say 'I', it seems hollow to me. I can no longer manage to feel myself. I am so forgotten. The only real thing left in me is some existence which can feel itself existing. I give a long, voluptuous yawn. Nobody. Antoine Roquentin exists for Nobody. That amuses me. And exactly what is Antoine Roquentin? An abstraction. A pale little memory of myself wavers in my consciousness. Antoine Roquentin . . . And the I pales, pales and finally goes out.[2]

[1] In *Le Mur*, Gallimard, Paris, 1939, p. 152; in Lloyd Alexander's translation, 'The Childhood of a Leader', in *Intimacy*, 1949, p. 134.
[2] *Ibid.*, p. 241.

Plainly, for Sartre, being-reacted-to-by-others is simply the name of yet another mental state. In the end the question whether we have a situation of recognition-by-the-other is settled, not by investigating the other but, like all the other questions, by introspection. Roquentin looks for the reaction of others in his own consciousness. Thus Sartre has not assimilated his own fugitive doctrine of the primacy of public situations. If a man really finds his identity in the way others relate to him, he will write in the public style of a Tolstoy or a Scott—he will write about the other people, what they said and did, and also about what *he* said and did, and from this public commerce his own identity will emerge. If all personal relations are withdrawn from him, his self-description will simply peter out, simultaneously with the description of the others. This simultaneity is conspicuously absent from the above passage from *La Nausée* and its absence gives the whole game away. Antoine Roquentin is still there, huddled inside, savouring the solitude as formerly he savoured his own responses to society. Soon, we predict, he will be extracting a vivid emotion from the palpable nullity, the darkness which follows the extinction of the 'Je'! Who, after all, is doing the talking here? A self constituted by relation with others would before now have been silent. But this self is as vigilant and loquacious as ever. Grammatically, it could easily use 'Je' ('I'). Why then is *it* not, philosophically, an 'I'? In the circumstances we grow suspicious of the metaphysical authority of the experience described. Have we here another example of inflation? Anny has gone away, and Roquentin feels blank and empty. Was it necessary to say anything more?

This chapter began with the assertion that Sartre was no true modern. We can now see that he belongs in many ways in the eighteenth century. Psychologism is endemic in his writing. Human characteristics are always to be resolved into that which here and now confronts the sensitive mind. Mental objects are known first; our knowledge of the rest, after all the metaphysical posturing, remains indistinct. The Copernican revolution of twentieth-century philosophy, whereby things in the public world are placed first as more obvious objects of knowledge than mental images, so that, for example, the notion of a disposition, publicly checkable, succeeds repeatedly in accounting for what could not be explained in terms of the introspective field—all this seems scarcely to have touched the outermost surface of his thought.

Is it then a mere accident of chronology that makes Hume so great and Sartre so awful? In fact, Hume and Sartre are separated by more than time. For example, Roquentin is given a doubt about induction which superficially resembles the celebrated scepticism of Hume, but while Hume plays remorselessly on the intellectual nerve, asking blandly 'What else have you got, beyond habitual concurrence?' Sartre retails a set of nightmare visions, tongues turning into centipedes[1] and the like. As we reject this as obviously pathological we forget what strength the intellectual argument, in another's hands, once possessed. To those who say how much more vivid and frightening Sartre's version is one is tempted to say, inverting the sentiments of the philosopher in *Rasselas*,[2] 'Sir, you speak like one that has never known the torment of intellectual fear.'

Hume by reasoning dethroned reason. He left his reader with perceptions only, of greater or less vivacity; Sartre, on the other hand, is so far a disciple of Hume as to work always *within* the field of perceptions, which is as much as to say that he is not the disciple but the slave. Sartre uses feeling to dethrone reason and at the same time—by mere inconsistency—to support rationalist generalities. Since feeling is in any case incompetent to do either of these things the metaphysical anguish of Sartre leaves us unmoved. Hume devoted his powers to showing that nothing could be said about what lay beyond the field of consciousness; the field itself was common property and its piece-meal exploration no work for a philosopher. Thus Hume's philosophy leaves us with a sense of profound paradox: if reason has done this to reason then the mind is at a standstill; reason to do this must be valid, but what it has done is to deny validity. In comparison the paradoxes offered by Sartre are factitious, and cave in at a touch.

[1] *La Nausée*, p. 226.
[2] xix, 1927, p. 86.

CHAPTER 5

T. S. Eliot

I

'Classicist in literature, royalist in politics, and anglo-catholic in religion.' So Eliot in the preface to *For Lancelot Andrewes*.[1] I suppose that, after the initial bewilderment, it is the royalism that first provokes a faltering dissent, or at least enquiry. What, in 1928, are the *royalists* working for? Then the other doubts begin to take shape: a '*classicist* in literature'? Which poem of Eliot's is classical, as Milton, Gray and Shelley are classical? But then perhaps he only means the Harvard classicism of Irving Babbitt, the well-loved teacher . . . Yet, even if this be so, did Eliot ever in fact apply the precepts of his master? Is it not Babbitt's interest in Buddhism rather than in 'Aristotle, Longinus and Dionysus of Halicarnassus'[2] that marked the verse of Eliot? What then of the anglo-catholicism?

Here the doubts are abruptly silenced, only to reappear a little later in an attenuated form. For we cannot doubt the sincerity of Eliot's Christianity; yet here he has not called himself a Christian; nor yet an Anglican; instead, he has trailed the polemical term before us. We sense something flaunting, quizzical, even, in a manner, provocative; in a word, we smoke the actor.

> How unpleasant to meet Mr. Eliot!
> With his features of clerical cut,
> And his brow so grim.
> And his mouth so prim
> And his conversation, so nicely
> Restricted to What Precisely
> And If and Perhaps and But.[3]

[1] 1928, p. ix.
[2] 'A Commentary', *The Criterion*, XIII (1933–4), p. 116.
[3] 'Five-Finger Exercises', V ('Lines for Cuscuscaraway and Mirza Murad Ali Beg'), *Collected Poems 1909–62*, 1963, p. 151.

Eliot's self-descriptions are marked by a curious mingling of the self-immolation of the *dévot* with the half-narcissistic self-mockery of the expert comedian. Walton tells us that when John Donne came to die, he did it very well, 'for he had studied it long'[1] and the modern reader is puzzled. The twentieth-century poet is scarcely more perspicuous. On the other hand he is not, *pace* Mr. Kenner, invisible. We have already drawn two tentative conclusions; that Eliot's Christianity is real, and that it is overlaid by a tendency to assume postures dictated by a rhetoric of paradox. We need not withdraw them before we must.

An onion is, in a way, all skin, a mere series of layers without a heterogeneous centre, and this fact has furnished poets with a symbol for the insubstantial; yet most sensible men know when to stop peeling their onions; it should be so with the criticism of Eliot. The outermost skin of his literary personality is, perhaps, merely social, arising from his special position as an American penetrating Europe.

It is after all no accident that a sense of effort pervades the deeply European poetry of Eliot. He is no more an Englishman than Milton was a Greek. For this—whether or not it agrees with the principles of 'Tradition and the Individual Talent'—we should be grateful, since it is in large measure the source of his peculiar excellence. Now the Europeanising of the American at once suggests the obsessive preoccupation of Henry James, and indeed there is a certain analogy between the two writers. Both write in a manner which enemies call 'precious' and friends 'delicately suspended.' Both are suckers for refinement. The European upper classes exasperated but, still more, fascinated James; it was not that they were more virtuous, or more intelligent, or better educated than he; not even that they were richer; instead they forced upon him a fresh category of value, a category perilously close to cynical snobbery: they knew how to behave, where knowledge had nothing to do with ethics or wit but rather with the accumulated tissue formed by centuries of continuous civilisation. He found that tradition—not the good in tradition but tradition itself—had the power to abash him. He was never deceived; his eyes remained vigilantly

[1] Izaak Walton, *Lives*, 1927, p. 81.

open and he never lost the sense that Europe was either corrupt
in itself or corruptive of strangers and yet, with all these
defences, he suffered himself to be bound in the net of manners.
All this is applicable, with only a little adjustment, to Eliot.
Who else calls himself 'the present writer'?

I imagine that, since Osbert Lancaster changed his archetypal
American from the loud-mouthed Texan to the bespectacled
scholar, the social basis of this phenomenon has virtually
disappeared. Yet in 1960 an American told me that every time
he opened his mouth among Englishmen his voice sounded
barbarous in his own ears. Conversely, it can still happen that
the occasional Englishman, marooned among American journ-
alists, can be distressed by the twittering pedantry of his own
accents. It is therefore at least possible that the tendency of
both James and Eliot to write what is really a caricature of
polite English may be traced to a surprisingly mundane source:
the barbarian genius strenuously mastering the *courtesye* of his
intellectual inferiors. No doubt this account is a simplification.
The complex experience of Harvard probably included a pre-
echo of the experience of Europe. The style itself remains.
Eliot's poem with the Jamesian title, 'Portrait of a Lady', is
partly mockery and partly obsequious aping of high manners.
In the lines:

> —And so the conversation slips
> Among velleities and carefully caught regrets . . .[1]

the word 'velleities' sets up a little fever of pleasurable refinement in the reader.

This sedulous style can be treacherous. I suspect that the
anti-semitism which notoriously recurs in the poetry of Eliot
(than whom few men were less anti-semitic) is in substance
almost entirely rhetorical—that is, the product of an almost
purely stylistic interest in a certain sort of club-room knowing-
ness. Nevertheless, a constant preoccupation with the linguistic
habits of an ancient culture cannot but have a certain effect
on the mind. Hence we find in Eliot what we may call a rhetoric
of ideas, existing in a kind of limbo between pure experiments
of style and seriously held doctrine (and here we come to the
second layer of his personality).

[1] *Collected Poems*, p. 18.

When Eliot began to write the romantic tradition was at an end. The Georgian poets had failed to revive it. Plainly, something new was required, in poetry as in the other arts. Eliot knew as well as anyone that the times demanded a poetic revolution. The burden of revolt fell on Eliot, the secret lover of tradition. It was only very gradually (so great was the damage done to poetic diction) that Eliot was able to disengage this love from a defensive irony. For a man in this position, a Christian posture had much to offer. For Christianity in the 1920s was unfashionable enough to break the stylistic spell of the Georgians and rich enough in remote, traditional material to satisfy Eliot's temperament. Thus we find Christian writers of the time employing what may be called the stratagem of the paradoxical-orthodox. G. K. Chesterton was one of the first to use it. His book, *Orthodoxy*, opens with a fable,[1] to which he reverts elsewhere, about a man who disembarks on what he takes to be a strange shore, and discovers only by degrees that he is on the South Coast of England; this, being interpreted, means that Chesterton thought he was following the lead of pure intelligence into the trackless waste but found instead that it brought him in the end to the Christian principles he had learned from mother and nurse. It is no accident that Eliot later became friendly with various Christians lineally descended (idealogically speaking) from Chesterton: Charles Williams, C. S. Lewis, J. R. Tolkien, Anne Ridler. Of these the most articulate, C. S. Lewis, made the greatest use of the paradoxical-orthodox. In some ways Lewis's autobiography. *Surprised by Joy*, is a rewriting, more highly educated, less epigrammatic, of Chesterton's *Orthodoxy*. In the dedicatory epistle prefixed to Lewis's *Preface to Paradise Lost* we have a pleasingly crude and therefore very clear example of the technique at work (Lewis is describing Charles Williams's lectures on Milton):

> There we elders heard (among other things) what we had long despaired of hearing—a lecture on *Comus* which placed its importance where the poet placed it—and watched 'the yonge fresshe folkes, he or she', who filled the benches listening first with incredulity, then with

[1] 1939, p. 12.

toleration, and finally with delight, to something so new
and strange in their experience as the praise of chastity.[1]

That is: 'You'll think me terribly odd, but I actually think
that chastity is a good thing.' Open paradox calls out to submerged orthodoxy and they join hands. In the same book
Lewis suggests that the ranks of the new-old Christians are
closing, with Eliot inside, their greatest prize and champion:

> If I make Mr Eliot's words the peg on which to hang a
> discussion . . . it must not, therefore, be assumed that this
> is, for me, more than a convenience, still less that I wish to
> attack him qua Mr Eliot. Why should I? I agree with him
> about matters of such moment that all literary questions
> are, in comparison, trivial.[2]

And Eliot himself observed in 1931, whether joyfully or rue-
fully, 'The orthodox faith of England is at last relieved from
its burden of respectability.'[3]

All this is so much fancy footwork, and it would be unjust to
Eliot to ascribe a higher status to it. I am tempted to place in
the same category quite a lot of his more bizarre pronouncements 'from somewhere to the right of Jenghiz Khan'. This, the
Eliot of the Second Skin, is the lean and slippered pantaloon
banging on an antique drum who pirouettes through the first
chapter of Northrop Frye's book:[4] the Eliot who blandly
suggests that 'the great majority of human beings should go on
living in the place in which they were born',[5] who considers
that the value of Welsh and Scottish nationalism lies in its
power to preserve *racial* character,[6] who exalts the Virginian
conservative above the New Englander on the ground that his
soil is more opulent and his race purer.[7] Frye rightly observes[8]
that all this, if taken literally, is inessential to Eliot's true
doctrine. He wryly concludes[9] his account of Eliot's fantastic
polemic (which tended of itself to lapse into sanity and

---

[1] *Op. cit.*, 1942, p. v.　　[2] *Ibid.*, p. 9.

[3] 'Thoughts after Lambeth', in *Selected Essays*, 1951, pp. 368–9. Cf. *The
Idea of a Christian Society*, 1939, pp. 50–1.

[4] *T. S. Eliot*, in the Writers and Critics Series, 1963, pp. 7–24.

[5] *Notes Towards the Definition of Culture*, 1948, p. 52.

[6] *Ibid.*, p. 57.

[7] *After Strange Gods*, 1934, p. 16.

[8] *T. S. Eliot*, p. 10.　　[9] *Ibid.*, p. 23.

platitude in later years) with a line from 'Little Gidding':
'These things have served their purpose; let them be.'

Thus far I follow Frye, but not much further. In fact I
suspect him of being the kind of irrationally hard man who
peels onions until nothing is left. If I understand him, he wants
the reader to conclude from his reductive account of Eliot's
controversial stance that the rest is only myth and fiction.
Some of us are not so easily discouraged; there is a kind of
dogma there if we can but get at it.

Perhaps the best way is to look at Eliot's essays on Arnold
and Bradley. Here the analysis is more minute, the loves and
distastes more immediate, and all in all we encounter a certain
pungency which warns us that soon, perhaps, the peeling
process may stop. Eliot attacked Arnold for making religion a
matter of feeling, thus preparing the way for a Paterian reduction of all things to the aesthetic plane; only a man whose
religion had undergone a profound impoverishment could ever
have made a religion out of poetry in the way Arnold did:
'The way up and the way down are one and the same.' It seems
that Eliot's hatred of the romantics for substituting subjective
vision for public tradition here finds theological point. He reacts
with a considerable appearance of magisterial censure. Arnold
is severely reprimanded for indiscipline; further, his powers of
reasoning are not great:[1] 'The effect of Arnold's religious
campaign is to divorce religion from thought.'[2]

At this point Eliot enters the arena, and criticism proper can
begin. Let us start by conceding that Eliot is obviously right to
suggest that the religion of *Literature and Dogma* is im-
poverished. I fancy that the author of 'The Scholar Gypsy'
and 'Dover Beach' knew this as well as Eliot, but felt that
anything else would be less than honest; 'His gift knew what
he was.'[3] In *Literature and Dogma* there is, of course, a note of
forced optimism, and let us agree at once that it should never
have entered. This concession made, it remains to consider
Arnold's argument as such. Against this argument Bradley, in
his *Ethical Studies*,[4] directed his artillery, and Eliot eagerly

[1] 'Arnold and Pater', in *Selected Essays*, p. 432.   [2] *Ibid.*, p. 434.
[3] W. H. Auden, 'Matthew Arnold', *Another Time*, n.d., p. 58. Not in
Collected Shorter Poems.
[4] 1876, pp. 282–284.

applauds what he conceives to be the utter destruction of the
enemy. Arnold wished to strike out of religion all that he could
not verify. He wished to establish a position from which he
could define ostensively why he believed what he believed. As
we watch the progress of his enterprise we may be struck by
the contrast with such a twentieth-century figure as Graham
Greene who also, it would seem, proceeds by throwing everything he has got at his religion until what is left can rightly
receive devotion. For while Arnold's progress left him with a
mysterious moral phenomenon, in Greene morals is almost the
first thing to go ('I know what's right', says Ida Arnold) and
what is left is magic, the feet of the priest showing under the
soutane, as he comes nearer and nearer, bearing the Body and
Blood. There is little doubt that Greene's position is the more
fashionable but I am not sure that Arnold's does not have the
better intellectual credentials. The special terrors of ritual are in
Greene always laid in the reader's lap, a simple datum. The
source of their coercive power is never laid bare–and indeed
it is idle to complain that Greene has failed where no-one else
has succeeded. These things are, at the literary level as at the
devotional, *de fide*.

We can only conclude, then, that the process of 'knocking
away to see what is left standing' is not in Greene an enterprise
of the analytic intelligence, but is rather a rhetorical strategy:
the suspense and the anagnorisis are of the literary rather than
the philosophical kind. There is one brilliant exception to this
rule. In *The End of the Affair* an unbelieving girl whose lover
is trapped in a burning house finds herself praying: 'Lord, if
you'll save his life, I'll give him up'; the lover is saved
miraculously and she is left with the question whether she is
under any obligation to keep a promise made thus, under
pressure, to an invisible and unverifiable being. Everything is
thrown at this obligation, at once so coercive and, to the
positivist, absurd, but in this novel the process is not merely
rhetorical. But it is worth noticing that *The End of the Affair*
is closer to Arnold (miracles apart) than is any other of Greene's
books, in that the whole revolves round the felt force of a
mysteriously prepersonal *moral* imperative.

But Arnold was able, to his partial satisfaction, to ground
his religious security on two things which, taken in conjunction,

are at least remarkable. The first is a matter of plain fact: there is observable in human action, at all periods of history and in all places, an impulse, operating below the level of the ego, towards righteousness; it seems empirically sound to say that although X in 1940 did this and Y in 1620 did that, both their actions express a tendency which neither individual, knowingly, instigated; there is something common to both their actions which seems to be *in* the agents rather than of them. Look further and the field of this force, which has its own empirical unity, is indefinitely extended. This, in a rough and ready way, makes sense. No-one is claiming that the movement of history is beneficent or that all moral action is unconscious; only that moral behaviour, viewed in the long term, suggests a suprapersonal pattern. The humanity of Pliny the Younger and the kindness of Sir Walter Scott are, though not identical, parts of the same, larger thing. Arnold called it the eternal not-ourselves that makes for righteousness. The second thing Arnold found was that the Bible, carefully read, tells us the same thing. All our language of a transcendent god-head, all the eschatological apparatus of Heaven and Hell, is no more than a later mythological accretion (Arnold's 'Aberglaube') upon an original doctrine of immanent, morally active deity; this ancient doctrine is re-discovered in the New Testament: 'The Kingdom of Heaven is within you.' And it was found again, Arnold would have been delighted to own, in the Cambridge Platonists.[1]

Bradley's criticism, which Eliot calls 'final',[2] was in fact a very coarse-grained piece of work. Arnold, like Shaftesbury before him (though Butler is the man he cites) moves insensibly from a strong emphasis on the necessity of disinterested conduct to a recognition of the beauty of virtue, which recognition he too eagerly seizes (for his primary thesis is now in danger) as a sanction and an inducement: '. . . joy and peace, missed on every other line, were to be reached on this.'[3] This, as we have seen,[4] has shown itself before in the history of

---

[1] For Arnold's knowledge of, in particular, John Smith, see 'A Psychological Parallel', in *Last Essays on Church and Religion*, Popular Edition, 1903, esp. p. 19.   [2] 'Francis Herbert Bradley', *Selected Essays*, p. 451.

[3] *Literature and Dogma*, Popular Edition, 1909, VIII.i, p. 128.

[4] See above, pp. 77 ff.

English Platonism. And there is little doubt that, as a pattern
of thought, it is very vulnerable. Arnold the Hellenist never
attains to the Hellenic conception of happiness according to
which Socrates is happier (more blessed, more enviable) than
the contented pig. But he does at least write with a vivid
awareness of the difficulties which attend his position. He
knows that the English are often accused of 'proneness to an
unworthy eudaemonism'[1] and quotes[2] St Augustine to reassure
us that the special hedonism he is commending is not confined
to Britain. This at least ought to appeal to Eliot, in whose
criticism terms like 'cranky', 'provincial' and 'central' carry a
tartling weight. Arnold takes a grim pleasure[3] in Bishop
Wilson's paradox: 'If it were not for the practical difficulties
attending it, *virtue would hardly be distinguishable from a kind
of sensuality*'. To turn from Arnold's tense writing at this
point to the gibes of Bradley is a curious experience: '. . . they
will not find [God] in an hypostatised copy-book heading,
which is not much more adorable than "honesty is the best
policy", or "Handsome is as handsome does" . . .'[4] This is level
with Bishop Berkeley's rejoinder to the cynic Mandeville:
hooped petticoats, Mandeville had said[5] in the full bravura of
his economic paradox, did more for human happiness than the
Reformation. Mr de Mandeville is absurd, the Bishop witlessly
replied, he actually says that hooped petticoats did more for
human happiness than the Reformation![6] To be sure, I have
detached this particular Bradleian snort from a sentence which
carries real point: Bradley is saying that the God with which
Arnold is left at the end of *Literature and Dogma* is not a God
whom we can worship or pray to; we need, he says, a great
deal more than this. 'Need, perhaps, but what have we got?'
Arnold might well have answered. An honest thinker will not
cut his religion according to the figure of his hopes. Arnold, I
suspect, knew well enough what he had done.

[1] *Literature and Dogma*, Popular Edition, 1909, III.iii, p. 74.
[2] *Ibid.*, I.iv, p. 35.
[3] *Ibid.*, I.iv, p. 34.
[4] See *Ethical Studies*, p. 284 n.; quoted by Eliot, *Selected Essays*, p. 451.
[5] *The Fable of the Bees, or Private Vices Publick Benefits*, Part I; in F. B.
Kaye's Edition, 1924, vol. I, p. 356.
[6] This is the force of the dialogue in *Alciphro*, II, Luce and Jessop, III,
p. 78.

And Bradley on the Arnoldian phrase 'the Eternal not-ourselves that makes for righteousness' is still worse than on Arnoldian happiness. The word 'Eternal' he takes to mean, 'whatever a generation sees happen, and believes both has happened and will happen'.[1] Now it is true that Arnold's 'eternal' falls short of the highest theological conception. But then it does not mean what Bradley says either. Arnold's reduction of the term is explicitly offered as a reduction, its meaning is modestly defined, and the interpretation is supported by a number of scriptural references: 'Let us put into their "Eternal" and "God" no more science than they did,' says Arnold; '—the enduring power, not ourselves, that makes for righteousness.'[2] Notice how careful Arnold is. He avoids even the term 'everlasting', which is presumably open to the charge of being unverifiable. Instead he says 'enduring' and Bradley's shot whizzes woundlessly past his ear. And on the most interesting phrase in Arnold's formula—'not ourselves'—Bradley has nothing to say. Instead he launches an unconvincing attack on the empirical status of Arnold's unitary stream or tendency of moral actions. The cat-call of 'metaphysician' comes ill from one who can end the chapter in which it occurs with a sentence like this: 'Here our morality is consummated in oneness with God, and everywhere we find that "immortal love", which builds itself for ever on contradiction, but in which the contradiction is eternally resolved.'

Eliot's treatment of Arnold leaves us with grounds for a serious suspicion. Arnold is accused of unreason and indiscipline, and to support these charges Eliot leans very heavily on Bradley, a broken reed. For himself, he intelligently notes the tendency to aestheticism, but of reasoned refutation we find not a word. Urbane deprecation is not argument; it is the luxury of those who stand on the side-lines. Arnold can say why he believes the little he believes. For Eliot's faith we suspect that an explanation, rather than a validating reason, is in order. And the way his prose combines considerable heat with a spurious assumption of rational detachment suggests that this explanation will have something to do with fear.

[1] *Ethical Studies*, p. 283; quoted in Eliot, *op. cit.*, p. 451.
[2] *Literature and Dogma*, I.v, p. 43.

II

Of course many readers have felt that there is a certain dis-crepancy between Eliot's theory and his poetic practice. The theorist preaches tradition, publicity and the extinction of personality and the poet gives us *The Waste Land, Ash Wednesday* and *Four Quartets*. The reader of the first of these is required to know, not only the Tarot pack of cards but Eliot's own misrememberings of the Tarot pack and associations therewith which Eliot himself blandly describes as quite arbitrary.[1] It has long been obvious that much of the surface obscurity of *The Waste Land* is a removable accident, rather than an essential part of the poem's 'proper pleasure'. The mysteriousness of Madame Merle in Henry James's *The Portrait of a Lady* is, so to speak, a public obscurity: one of the primary constituents of the novel as a work of art. The obscurity of 'Lycidas', on the other hand, is an accidental obscurity which commentary can legitimately remove. *The Waste Land* is in many ways a twentieth-century 'Lycidas', a labyrinth of allusions, half submerged by the flood of privacy (what in Milton was due to the degree of his learning in Eliot largely arises from mere idiosyncrasy). Eliot's notes to *The Waste Land* are only partly ironic, for they are desperately necessary if his poem is to be made visible to the reader. Both clarity and obscurity can in special circumstances be either a virtue or a vice in literature. But normally they are neither. Clarity is simply a condition of the poem's existence as a public work of art. And it is the ordinary situation which we find here. Eliot's notes clarify personal allusions in the poem. Larger com-mentaries clarify still more. The reading which follows a perusal of the commentaries is, in the case of this poem, richer and more powerful than one carried through in innocence. After all, were the Harvard men of Eliot's year (who all, it seems, read *From Ritual to Romance, The Golden Bough*, and the Sanskrit *Upanishads*) unfitted by their knowledge to be readers of Eliot's poem?

Nor is *The Waste Land* automatically incorporated into a suprapersonal tradition merely in virtue of its honorific litter of quotations. Eliot knew well enough, with the top of his head

---

[1] See Eliot's note on line 46 of *The Waste Land, Collected Poems*, p. 80.

at least, that it is possible to be part of a living tradition without once *quoting* a predecessor. In fact, if there is one thing which marks Eliot's independence from the tradition of Marvell it is his ineradicable itch–*citandi cacoethes*–for quoting snatches of verse by older poets. There is a wonderful moment in Castiglione's *Il Cortegiano* where humanism discovers its separation from the tradition of antiquity: 'If we will follow them of old time, we shall not follow them';[1] that is, if we write imitative poetry we shall not be like Homer, for the simple reason that his poetry was not, in that way at least, imitative.

Indeed with Eliot the irony is deeper still. The manifesto of 1919, 'Tradition and the Individual Talent' is a brilliant attack on romanticism, setting up in its place the value of tradition. But the tradition to which Eliot belongs is precisely that of romanticism. In time even exiles build cities. 'Tradition' is more generous than Eliot thought; it will admit the line of those who agree to write from inner illumination as readily as the line of those who work by less subjective methods. How else could Eliot–whose religious poetry runs, not on the majestic simplicities of communal devotion but on mystical experience in short supply–have got in at all? Of course Eliot belongs to a very late phase of romanticism, some will say so late as to be no longer romanticism. I have no quarrel with them so long as they concede a continuity–it was Eliot who taught us that true tradition is a developing and not a static thing–with the great movement of the nineteenth century. The continuity consists essentially in the emergence of the self-subsistent particular as the proper object of poetic art. This we have already discussed. English verse of the seventeenth and eighteenth centuries is full of *thought*–which may be frivolous or serious, but is, for all that, thought. In the poetry of the metaphysicals witty pseudo-argument alternates with reasoned cerebration. With the rise of romanticism all these structures begin to melt away, leaving us alone with our visionary moments, 'spots of time' whose nature is falsified if they are ever given a higher degree of organisation than that of a series.

[1] In Thomas Hoby's translation (1588), I; Everyman edn., 1928, p. 55.

We may note in passing that most of Eliot's epiphanies are situational rather than perceptual (that is, they convey felt moments of personal relationship rather than especially significant physical objects) which perhaps connects him more immediately with the Victorians than with Wordsworth or Keats. *The Waste Land* opens with vaguely heart-breaking fragments of overheard conversation, which seem like crises from some great unwritten novel, another *Zauberberg*. The Victorian who did this sort of thing (in a more leisurely fashion) was Browning. And Eliot's literary descent from Browning can be traced without difficulty. Eliot was interested in the poetic possibilities of successively assumed *personae*, and in this as in much else he explicitly followed Ezra Pound; in 'The Three Voices of Poetry' Eliot stressed that in Browning's 'Caliban upon Setebos' it is Browning we listen to, through Caliban, rather than Caliban himself. He goes on to observe that Pound, 'Browning's greatest disciple', used the term *persona* to describe this practice in his own work.[1] As Kristian Smidt notes Pound could have derived not just the technique but also the term from Browning, who called some of his poems *Dramatis Personae*. We have now only to link Pound to Eliot, which is easy, and the genealogy is complete.[2]

But this example is trivial and local. What lies behind it, namely imagism, is more important. Of course if imagism means that all discursive meaning is to be excluded from the poem, leaving nothing but the enigmatic simplicity of the resonant image, then there is hardly an imagist poem in the world. If on the other hand the term connotes a goal and a tendency rather than an accomplished fact then I think we must say that imagism, despite the degree of mythic design in *The Waste Land* and of musical design in *Four Quartets*, always remained congenial to Eliot. And although literary images are not the same thing as mental images, the analogy between the Humian flux of ideas and the literary programme of T. E. Hulme and Pound is too close to ignore.

Eliot was more philosophically sophisticated–more indeed of a philosopher–than either of his mentors and it is worth-

[1] In *On Poetry and Poets*, 1957, p. 95.
[2] This genetic connexion was first traced, I think, by Kristian Smidt, in his *Poetry and Belief in the Work of T. S. Eliot*, 1961, p. 92.

while to look at what many consider a futile accident in his intellectual career: his explicitly philosophical studies. In fact, these bring us closer to the poet than any of his other prose works. A phrase in 'Tradition and the Individual Talent' strongly suggests that Eliot was aware of a continuum between the problems of literature and those of metaphysics, and stopped himself from passing from one to another only by calling an abrupt halt: 'This essay proposes to halt at the frontier of metaphysics or mysticism, and confine itself to such practical conclusions as can be applied by the responsible person interested in poetry.'[1] But already in the essay he has more than once trembled on the edge. Take the following:

> The existing monuments form an ideal order among themselves, which is modified by the introduction of the new (the really new) work of art among them. The existing order is complete before the new work arrives; for order to persist after the supervention of novelty, the *whole* existing order must be, if ever so slightly, altered; and so the relations, proportions, values of each work of art toward the whole are readjusted . . . Whoever has approved this idea of order . . . will not find it preposterous that the past should be altered by the present as much as the present is directed by the past.[2]

This is a curious passage because in it propositions which make a certain sense when applied to literature are struggling to get into metaphysics, where they are altogether more vulnerable. It is no accident that this passage is remotely reminiscent of Sartre, whose Roquentin needed his Rollebon as much as Rollebon needed Roquentin.[3] Behind lie volumes of Gallic metaphysics, not least Bergson's. Bergson, again like Sartre, mistrusted the intellect, which, in a weirdly Platonic fashion, he conceived to be confined to the inorganic solid, unable to form 'a clear idea' (here a nod to Descartes) of anything other than 'the discontinuous'.[4] Since intellect represents 'becoming' as a series of states, intellect is a liar (the only intellect I have

[1] *Selected Essays*, pp. 21–2.
[2] *Ibid.*, p. 15.   [3] See above, p. 177.
[4] *Creative Evolution*, trans. Arthur Mitchell, the 1960 reprint of the edn. of 1911, p. 163.

come across which felt itself under a practical necessity to do this is the one which framed the definition of *time* in the Pocket Oxford Dictionary: 'the successive states of the universe regarded as a whole'). 'The intellect is characterised by a natural inability to comprehend life.'[1] But if the understanding cannot understand, what can? The answer seems to be intuition, uncritically wedded as it is to the shimmering flux of reality. The immediate point of contact between Eliot and Bergson lies in the Frenchman's notion of a *durée*. The *durée* enables the intellect to read off an organic wholeness into the flux of perception. In the words of Kristian Smidt, 'The *durée* is a moving present which accumulates all the past and holds preparedness for the future.'[2] In a passage[3] strongly reminiscent of Augustine[4] Bergson compares the *durée* with our apprehension of music, in which our hearing of a single note is conditioned both by what has happened, and by what is about to happen. Plainly, Bergson's *durée* has been produced in paralysing conformity to the requirements of the empiricist *epochê*. He has looked in the stream of immediate experience for something adequate to convey the serial nature of the world and has come up with our awareness of music as the best he can do; this, at least, succeeds in being multiple in its reference without losing its concrete immediacy.

The experience of music has, of course, real psychological interest. It seems to be true that our awareness of the first movement of a symphony is subtly modified by the completion of the second; and this can be epigrammatically but misleadingly expressed as the present modifying the past; in fact, of course, none of our responses is, so to speak, wiped out of the record of existence; we merely subject our tentative picture of the whole work to a continuous process of revision which ceases only with the last note of the work. It is only when we have moved into metaphysics, and bowed our necks to receive the yoke of the *epochê*, only, in short, when we have become so

---

[1] *Creative Evolution*, p. 174.

[2] *Poetry and Belief in the Work of T. S. Eliot*, p. 165.

[3] *Essai sur les données immédiates de la conscience*, Paris, 1889, p. 76.

[4] *De Vera Religione*, xxii. 42, in J.-P. Migne's *Patrologia Latina*, Paris, 1861, vol. XXXIV. See also my *Two Concepts of Allegory*, 1967, pp. 44–5 for a discussion of the relation between the Augustine passage and a passage in *Four Quartets*.

used to the blinkers of radical empiricism that we can no longer
distinguish memories from past events, that we can mistake this
process of involuntary revision for an actual modification of the
past by the present. The barbarous jibe of Bertrand Russell is
entirely in order: 'The whole of Bergson's theory of duration
and time rests throughout on the elementary confusion between
the present occurrence of a recollection and the past occurrence
which is recollected.'[1] It becomes evident that the rationalist
tag from Aristotle[2] which Eliot prefixed[3] to this section of the
essay is a mere gesture in the direction of a publicity of reason
to which his real philosophical affiliations are implicitly opposed.

It should be clear by now that it is the tendency of this book
to suggest that the number of philosophies, like the number of
jokes, is small. Some may doubt whether Eliot, the mannered
traditionalist, could ever have thought along the same track
as the iconoclast Sartre. In fact the example I have given is
not isolated. Eliot's doctoral thesis on F. H. Bradley, completed
in 1916, easily supplies further anticipations of *L'Être et le
Néant* or *La Nausée*. In particular, the psychologistic assimilation of existence to consciousness recurs ('finite centre', by the
way, is Bradleian for 'individual consciousness'):

> . . . it should appear that any object is real in so far as it is
> attended to . . . When I think of the golden mountain, I
> think of something which is to that extent real . . .[4]

> To say that the present king of France both exists and not
> exists is no more false than to say that my typewriter both
> exists and not exists inasmuch as it now exists for me who
> am looking at it, and not for Mr Russell who is looking at
> something else.[5]

> We have seen that there is no other object than that which
> appears, and its appearance as an object gives it, in an
> absolute sense, all that objectively it could possibly mean . . .
> And outside of the objectivity of objects appearing to
> finite centres, there is no objectivity at all . . .[6]

[1] *History of Western Philosophy*, p. 764.

[2] 'The mind is doubtless something more divine and less easily acted
upon'. *De Anima* (I.iv) 408b.

[3] *Selected Essays*, p. 21.

[4] *Knowledge and Experience in the Philosophy of F. H. Bradley*, 1964, p.
121.

[5] *Ibid.*, p. 127.   [6] *Ibid.*, p. 141.

Even Sartre's notion that our awareness of other minds is essentially an awareness of the incompleteness of presentation[1] is anticipated: 'The first objects with which we come into contact are *half-objects*, they are other finite centres, not attended to directly as objects, but as interpretations of recognised resistances and *felt* divergencies.[2] The italics are mine. It is interesting that the word 'somehow' which is the stylistic mark of philosophic bankruptcy, follows in the same paragraph, italicised (this time) by Eliot.

But all these passages are wantonly wrenched from their contexts. They are in fact variously fenced and armed against the imputation of solipsism, sometimes very ingeniously. Eliot is in many ways a subtler thinker than Sartre; he lacks only the Frenchman's staying power (by which nothing is meant but his power of writing on and on). For example, he transfixes the novelistic philosophising of Sartre with a single shaft, when he observes that a cardinal difficulty of epistemology lies in the way we are forced to use, in our descriptions of experience itself, terms and meanings 'which hold good only *within* experience'.[3]

First of all there can be little doubt that the element in Bradley which fascinated and frightened Eliot was the tendency to solipsism. It is no accident that Eliot chose to quote in his notes for *The Waste Land* this passage from *Appearance and Reality*:

> My external sensations are no less private to myself than are my thoughts or feelings. In either case my experience falls within my own circle, a circle closed on the outside; and, with all its elements alike, every sphere is opaque to the others which surround it . . . In brief, regarded as an existence which appears in a soul, the whole world for each is peculiar and private to that soul.[4]

This is the aspect of Bradley that most urgently occupies Eliot in his essays on Leibniz and Bradley.[5] For Eliot, Bradley is the prisoner of a solitary panpsychism:

[1] See above, p. 169.

[2] *Knowledge and Experience*, pp. 142–3.

[3] *Ibid.*, p. 19.

[4] F. H. Bradley, *Appearance and Reality*, 2nd edn., 1897, p. 346.

[5] 'The Development of Leibniz' Monadism', first published in *The Monist*, XXVI (October, 1916), pp. 534–56; reprinted as Appendix I in

. . . there is the view of Mr Bradley, for whom everything is in a way psychical, and for whom therefore the distinction between object and act is not identical with that between an internal and an external reality but is reducible to the problem of knowing one's own mind.[1]

It would seem that it was partly fear of this lonely situation that caused Eliot to grasp eagerly at the pre-personal theory of consciousness, which rids it of any smell of subjectivity:

> Thus we are led to the conclusion that the only independent reality is immediate experience or feeling. And we have seen that to think of feeling as subjective, as the mere adjective of a subject, is only a common prejudice. So far as it is feeling and nothing more, it is self-sufficient and demands no further supplementation. 'My' feeling is certainly in a sense mine. But this is because and in so far as I *am* the feeling. I do not in consequence know (in the sense of understand) . . .[2]

But if this is flight it is flight from bad towards worse. Eliot, with all the bite of his best poetry, sees this and surprises the reader by adding: 'And if anyone assert that immediate experience, at either the beginning or end of our journey is annihilation or utter night, I cordially agree.'[3] To be sure, the Stoic resignation may not be quite complete. There is a vague gesture in the direction of a saving Absolute, but Eliot could never bring himself to articulate the mechanics of a salvation so repugnant at once to intellect and to all good feeling. Later he was to choose a deliverance which satisfies the second though not the first. He never learned that this particular disease of the spirit is better cured by the World than by its Maker.

Clearly Eliot's account does nothing to refute panpsychism. The real tendency of his striving towards impersonalism can easily be mistaken. For him, the alternative to subjectivity is not objective reality, but 'primary-reality-which-is-neither-subject-nor-object'. Once we have located the source of Eliot's

---

Knowledge and Experience in the Philosophy of F. H. Bradley, pp. 177–97; 'Leibniz' Monads and Bradley's Finite Centres', *ibid.*, pp. 566–76; reprinted as Appendix II in *Knowledge and Experience*, pp. 198–207.

[1] *Knowledge and Experience*, p. 58.

[2] *Ibid.*, p. 58.   [3] *Ibid.*, p. 31.

constant suppression of the ego, we shall cease to confound it
with the recovery of extra-mental publicity.

It might be objected that this interpretation misses the point:
Eliot is here writing under the down-to-earth influence of
William James, that figure of luminous common sense who
dominated the Harvard of Eliot's day. I certainly have no wish
to deny the influence on Eliot of James, especially of his *Essays
in Radical Empiricism* which Eliot explicitly refers[1] to more
than once in his dissertation. He quotes these words: 'The
instant field of the present is . . . only virtually or potentially
either subject or object.'[2] A more famous phrase used by James
to express his belief in the derivative status of subject and
object is, 'Experience, I believe, has no such inner duplicity.'[3]
The substance of my reply should already be clear. According to
this 'down-to-earth' philosophy, knowing is an obscure relation
between two parcels of pure experience. Reading James one
begins to wonder why he continues to use the word 'experience'
at all. The question is an important one. At one point James
tries to answer another question: 'What is consciousness made
of?' His answer is that there are as many 'stuffs' as there are
'natures' in the things experienced.[4] His answer to this second
question suggests that he could have had no answer to the first.
James's position is in fact remarkably close to Berkeley's.
Berkeley was all for turning ideas into things, yet it was the
mental word, 'ideas' which continued to be used, and made him
an idealist. In James the word 'experience' continues to be used,
and imparts a smell of mentality long after all factors which
might have given it a specific meaning have been removed.
All this tells us much about the philosophic temper of James
and his time. 'Character,' said Aristotle, 'is revealed when a
person makes an unobvious decision.'[5] It is obvious that Shakespeare is better than Ford, and the critic who decides that this
is so has betrayed nothing of his distinctive critical temper. It
was not rationally obvious that the word 'experience' should be
kept, but James kept it and, by keeping it, betrayed much.
Santayana has a marvellous phrase to describe this philosophy:

[1] *Knowledge and Experience*, e.g., p. 29.
[2] *Essays in Radical Empiricism*, 1912, p. 23.
[3] *Ibid.*, p. 9.   [4] *Ibid.*, pp. 26-7.
[5] *Poetics*, 1450b.

he says that for James experience was 'the only fact, the flying fact of our being.'[1] It is, of course, a mental fact.

Once more the roads converge. What Eliot learned from the pragmatical psychologist James he could find with little difference in the idealist Bradley. Nor did Eliot's work on the phenomenology of Husserl and Meinong lead in any other direction. 'The natural wakeful life of our ego is a perceiving': the line from 'Triumphal March'[2] is a quotation from Husserl, eagerly grasped by Kristian Smidt as showing that Eliot belongs with the anti-Platonists, that is, with those who stress the reliability of the senses as the sure foundation of our commerce with the outer world. But we know from Sartre what happened to Husserl (and how it later happened to Sartre). Smidt quotes[3] 'Gerontion':

> I have lost my sight, smell, hearing, taste and touch:
> How should I use them for your closer contact?[4]

and observes, in blandly Aristotelian fashion, that Gerontion, lacking sense, lacks contact with others. *Verbatim*, the interpretation fits. But in fact the passage is more Husserlian than Aristotelian. Smidt would agree with this, but only because he does not know how they differ. The truth should be obvious to anyone who reads the poem.

Eliot begins his poem by establishing a personality and a context. As with Prufrock the personality is largely defined by negatives—this old man did *not* fight at Thermopylae. In a place of drought and decay he listens to a boy reading. But now the picture dissolves; the actual gives place to memory, dream and presentiment, the confined consciousness to the inwardly unconfined (in his thoughts one fettered like Prufrock to a local hell can be enlarged to wander, like Teiresias through the greater hell of history). Signs and wonders, Christ the tiger, pacing footsteps in the next room, Fraülein von Kulp. But now the picture changes again; the images are moralised and the inextricable confusion of virtue and vice is abstractly displayed before us. And then, as we near the end, our sense of the original

---

[1] 'A Brief History of my Opinions' (1930) in *The Philosophy of Santayana*: enlarged edn. by Irwin Edman, New York, 1953, p. 121.

[2] *Collected Poems*, p. 139.

[3] *Poetry and Belief in the Work of T. S. Eliot*, p. 118.

[4] *Ibid.*, p. 41.

context begins to revive. 'A thousand small deliberations' stimulated the jaded taste-buds of the mind. But death is near.

There are times when it is necessary to think very simply; Gerontion is not deaf or blind; he *has* all his senses, but they are failing to carry him beyond himself. The phenomenologists will only leave us with the moving present of James's or Sartre's consciousness. Look elsewhere in existentialism and we find the same message:

> The moment is the sole reality, it is reality in itself, in the life of the soul. The Moment that has been lived is the Last, the Warm-blooded, the Immediate, the Living, the Bodily-Present, the Totality of the Real, the only Concrete Thing . . .[1]

By this conception of reality as a moving field, the past naturally suffers. As Santayana said, in James's philosophy 'existence was a perpetual rebirth, a travelling light to which the past was lost . . .'[2] 'Ideas of the past are true,' says Eliot, 'not by correspondence with a real past, but by their coherence with each other and ultimately with the present moment'[3]–indeed, 'a way of knowing one's own mind'! Bradley himself is laboriously concerned to clarify the reality of Julius Caesar. The result of his deliberations is adequately summarised by Hugh Kenner:

> His ultimate answer to the question about Julius Caesar was that, Caesar's experience of himself being as inaccessible, and as irrelevant, as a geranium's experience of itself, the real Julius Caesar cannot be less than–for us–every impression, every sentiment, that attracts itself to that name, and every effect that can be attributed to it. In the same way J. Alfred Prufrock exists only while someone is reading or remembering the poem, and exists only *as* each particular reader experiences him.[4]

The qualifying 'for us' turns this into platitude and should be disregarded. This done, we can see that the literary analogy with Prufrock works and fails to work in exactly the same way

[1] Jaspers, *Psychology of World-Views*, 1919, quoted in Karl Popper, *The Open Society and its Enemies*, 5th edn., 1966, p. 317.

[2] *The Philosophy of Santayana*, p. 122.

[3] *Knowledge and Experience*, p. 54.

[4] *The Invisible Poet*, 1960, p. 53.

as the musical analogy in Bergson. Both are credible only to minds habituated to the *epoché*. Caesar is to Bradley as Rollebon was to Roquentin, an ontological parasite on his consciousness. Thus, whether Eliot's philosophical impersonalism derives from James or Bradley matters little. It may be thought that at least it ends the epistemological confinement with which we have been dealing. But this is not so; the confinement continues. It ceases to be felt as solitary only because the identity of the prisoner has been lost. And in this too–the shivering of the stable substance of the self into a stream of 'ideas'[1]–all our writers were forestalled by Hume. Once more it must be said: philosophies are fewer than we think. As I write these words I begin to think that there are only two, empiricism and rationalism, and that this book has had to do only with the first.

Many passages in Eliot's dissertation show how keen was his feeling that the mind's circumscription by its own sensations is a disabling, suffocating thing. For example, he argues[2] that when we recount the geological movements of pre-history we habitually overlook the development of mind. We do not describe how it really was, only how it would have appeared to us had we been present. This is of course a hoary chestnut of idealism, still liable to fall into our laps from the pages of, say, Owen Barfield. It is an unnecessary anxiety. The caveat, 'I describe the object as it would appear to a human mind' could be written into every pronouncement and need therefore be written into none. The sense of 'appearance' employed in it is in any case not that of which the opposite is 'reality'. Again we sense the assimilation of existence to consciousness. The surface of the moon did not *become* crunchy at the moment the astronauts landed, nor did the South Pole freeze up on the arrival of Amundsen. To be sure, these sarcasms seem more fittingly applied to Barfield than Eliot. But to Eliot we can say, '*Of course*, we wish to know how it would appear to us. What is the alternative? Would a description of the way it would have appeared to a fly be better? And what is the content of "really" unless some Barfieldian nonsense[3] to the effect that, strictly

[1] See esp. F. H. Bradley, *Appearance and Reality*, 2nd edn., 1897, pp. 80 and 256.

[2] *Knowledge and Experience*, p. 22.

[3] See Owen Barfield, *Saving the Appearances*, 1957, pp. 37 ff.

speaking, sparrows come into existence only when there are observers capable of conceptualising "sparrow" (before there was only a shadowy thickening of the ontological atmosphere, a bit of the prior material of perception bearing a special potentiality for being informed, when the right moment came, with the term "sparrow")?'

There is real irony in all such disquisitions on the necessity of remembering our limitations. The limitation in question is in fact so complete that its observance requires no effort on our part. Because the proviso 'as it would appear to human minds' writes itself into *every* human observation, Mr Barfield finds himself saying that something-which-would-have-appeared-to-a-human-mind-as-a-sort-of-misty-presence becomes something-which-would-appear-to-a-human-mind-as-a-sparrow. It is only thus that language can work.

Again, Eliot shows none of the determination which we find in Ryle, Wittgenstein and the young Sartre, to get rid of the inner object. He jealously preserves the objective status of memories, *qua* memories: '. . . the object of memory is memory itself . . . we must distinguish between the object of the memory and the object of our attention when we remember.'[1]

Again, when he sums up his chapter on 'the epistemologist's theory of knowledge' (what other is there?) he says, '. . . when we come to ask how we know this world, it appears that all we are sure of is certain data and forms of immediate experience, out of which the physical world is constructed—as a consequence of which the "objectivity" of the external world becomes otiose or meaningless.'[2]

No doubt we should remember that Eliot's shafts against radical empiricism are launched from the citadel of idealist metaphysics: he writes, it might be said, with the contempt of one inwardly secure. But the force of this reservation diminishes as we read. So little is said about the Absolute. The last part of the chapter on the epistemologist's theory of knowledge contains in addition a prospectus of the metaphysical Faith:

> . . . the object, to be an object, is always meant to be something more than its abstracted qualities, and to be directly

[1] *Knowledge and Experience*, p. 54.
[2] *Ibid.*, p. 111.

known cannot be directly experienced. But the object as
object cannot be self-supporting. Its objectivity is merely
externality, and nothing in reality can be merely external,
but must possess being 'for' itself. Yet to mean it as an
object means to mean it as more than object, as something
ultimately real. And in this way every object leads us far
beyond itself to an ultimate reality: this is the justification
for our metaphysics.[1]

Then Heaven help our metaphysics ('Precisely!' cries the ghost
of Eliot with mindless cunning and we despair of him). He is
concerned with the loss of ontological juiciness we feel when we
are told that a thing is a 'mere bundle of its properties.' He refers
to a passage in Bradley[2] on our inability to discover the unity
which makes sugar sugar, to discover anything beyond white-
ness, hardness, sweetness and so on. It is interesting in view of
Eliot's remarks elsewhere that Bradley's words betray far less
anxiety about this state of affairs than Eliot's. Eliot is unable to
accept the loss and makes it good by an ontologically compensatory metaphysic. One begins to feel about his metaphysics
what one occasionally feels about his Christianity; that at
bottom it is not explanatory, not even descriptive, but thera-
peutic.

But this, as I have hinted, is just what Eliot himself says about
Bradley. In his essay on Leibniz and Bradley the point of contact he finds between the two philosophers is their insistence on
the isolation of the soul; the Leibnizian monad is windowless
and the Bradleian finite centre is impenetrable.[3] The comparison
is interesting. One recalls that Leibniz himself once wrote that
it is not possible to demonstrate certainly that an external world
exists.[4] Eliot, though he does not use this quotation, presses on
this nerve. And he comments:

> Just as Leibniz's pluralism is ultimately based upon faith,
> so Bradley's universe, actual only in finite centres, is only
> by an act of faith unified. Upon inspection, it falls away

[1] *Ibid.*, p. 140.

[2] *Appearance and Reality*, 1897, p. 19.

[3] 'Leibniz's Monads and Bradley's Finite Centres', appended to *Knowledge and Experience*, p. 199.

[4] *New Essays concerning Human Understanding*, trans. A. G. Langley,
3rd edn., Lasalle (Illinois), 1949, Appendix XII.

into the isolated finite experiences out of which it is put together.[1]

Before the end of the essay, the distinction between Bradley and William James reaches vanishing point: 'The finite centre, so far as I can pretend to understand it, *is* immediate experience.'[2]

We can hear the same note, differently orchestrated, in the essay on Pascal:

> Pascal's disillusioned analysis of human bondage is some-times interpreted to mean that Pascal was really and finally an unbeliever, who, in his despair, was incapable of enduring reality and enjoying the heroic satisfaction of the free man's worship of nothing.[3]

Again, one is disconcerted to find the charge one was preparing against Eliot (certainly I should never have thought it of Pascal) hypothetically directed *by* Eliot at someone else. It is therefore interesting to note that in what follows Eliot never articulates a reasoned answer to the charge but instead begins to flounder. He says that Pascal's despair is objective, not subjective, which is scarcely to the point since it is not the pessimism but the Christian affirmation which is under fire. His observation that 'it was also a despair which was a necessary prelude to, and element in, the joy of faith'[4] is mere papier-maché. One feels that the derided author of 'A Free Man's Worship' could have made short work of it.

Again, in the defect of rational opposition, we are driven to a sort of psychoanalysis. An eager if incoherent attribution to others of a subject's own failures recurs in the case histories of Freud. It is called projection. Of course psychoanalysis is a notoriously slippery instrument. But with certain safeguards it remains usable. One of these (on which Alasdair MacIntyre, with more rigour than Freud, insists)[5] is the final necessity of a corroborative avowal from the patient. Eliot's avowal comes in *After Strange Gods* where he affirms that Marxism can never deliver man from the prison of the ego as Christianity can. Like

---

[1] 'Leibniz's Monads and Bradley's Finite Centres', *Knowledge and Experience*, p. 202.
[2] *Ibid.*, p. 205.
[3] 'The "Pensées" of Pascal' (1931), in *Selected Essays*, p. 412.
[4] *Ibid.*, p. 412.   [5] *The Unconscious*, 1958, p. 56.

the post-philosophical comforters of ancient Rome, he offers not truth but *ataraxia*, tranquillity, a salve for the burnt-out case.

'Human kind cannot bear very much reality'; the phrase recurs in Eliot's poetry.[1] The idea, though the phrase itself is absent, informs the opening section of *The Waste Land* and of course the ultimate reality to which it refers us is the reality of God. But what if this were only a brilliant rhetorical stratagem? The man who has fled to an easier clime is under a polemical necessity of representing that clime as harder than the one he left. Christianity is an optimistic religion. Dante rightly called his great Christian poem a comedy. Modern Christian writers dare not speak so lest they be found out. Instead, they give their books titles like 'Nought for your Comfort'. But Eliot outgrew this serviceable ingenuity as he did others. In *Four Quartets* the pretence is dropped; the joy and beauty, the allure of the all but inaccessible Christ, are honestly acknowledged. For the words in the Pascal essay are not an exact description of Eliot. I began by saying that his Christianity is sincere, and I do not retract. In one way this makes the situation all the sadder.

III

For Eliot never refuted the thing he feared. A sort of rebuttal is set out in his chapter called 'Solipsism', but it is friable stuff. After some conventional observations on the fantastical nature of this view–'solipsism has been one of the dramatic properties of most philosophical entertainers'[2]–five main reasons are given why solipsism is false. His first argument is the Sartrian one from the 'half-object': 'recognised resistances and felt divergences'.[3] This we have already discussed.[4] Next, he says that 'we feel obscurely an identity between the experience of other centres and our own. And it is this identity which gradually shapes itself into a public world.'[5] Can obscure feelings somehow melt through the circle which bounds the self while clearer feelings remain shut inside? Bradley could only shake his

[1] *Murder in the Cathedral, Collected Plays*, 1962, p. 43; *Four Quartets*, 'Burnt Norton', *Collected Poems*, p. 190.
[2] *Knowledge and Experience*, p. 141.
[3] *Ibid.*, pp. 142–3.
[4] See above, pp. 169 and 216.
[5] *Knowledge and Experience*, p. 143.

H

beautiful, weary head. Eliot's next argument runs as follows: although my mind is circumscribed by its own experience, I can trace its origin; this origin proves to be a common nature, recognisably the source of other finite centres.[1] It is not enough to parse a contradiction into a concessive and a main clause. If my mind is circumscribed I shall never be able to trace a common origin. I shall only find something which, in the inner theatre of my mind, masquerades as common, as the tables and chairs which also figure there masquerade as public. Eliot's fourth proposal[2] is that although immediate experience is private, ideal objectivity is not. This he answers himself in the essay on Leibniz and Bradley. The idealism is merely compensatory, reared by faith and founded upon nothing.

His fifth and last argument is his best: '. . . a doctrine of solipsism would have to show that myself and my states were immediately given, and the other selves inferred. But just because what is given is not myself but my world, the question is meaningless.'[3] But the psychologistic posture of the thesis taken as a whole prevents this argument from taking hold. The word 'my' betrays him. The world of objects, we have already been told, is a construction. Thus Eliot's phrase 'is given' can mean nothing but 'form part of consciousness', and the tendency of psychologism to solipsism lies precisely in the fact that it denies independent reality, not to the inferred, but to the given. What is given was already ours.

Thus Eliot's quotations[4] from H. A. Prichard and Theodor Lipps—to the effect that there is no need to construe our awareness of the outer world on the pattern of our awareness of our own feelings, and that a man who sees a thing is not seeing a sensation—prove less liberating than they promised to be. Bradley did not deny the difference between outer and inner. He merely pronounced the first no less private than the second. In the face of a metaphysic so radical, differentiation of contents into (pseudo) near and (pseudo) far is of little consequence. In his conclusion Eliot cites a remark of the formidable Professor Eucken of Jena: 'There are no private truths.' The force of the remark escapes him and, almost blandly, he inverts it: 'I do not recall the context, and am not concerned with the meaning

[1] *Knowledge and Experience*, p. 145.
[2] *Ibid.*, p. 147. [3] *Ibid.*, p. 150. [4] *Ibid.*, pp. 59 and 71.

which the phrase had there; but I should reverse the decision
and say: All significant truths are private truths.'[1]

But all the time he was writing poetry. And clearly the two
sides, the philosophical and the poetic, are in touch[2] (and not
just in the Bergsonian passages on time). Bradley's diagnosis of
the discontinuity of the personality—the personality being
resolved into the mere series of its contents—finds repeated
poetic expression:

> The thousand sordid images
> Of which your soul was constituted . . .[3]

> What we know of other people
> Is only our memory of the moments
> During which we knew them. And they have
> > changed since then.
> To pretend that they and we are the same
> Is a useful and convenient social convention
> Which must sometimes be broken. We must
> > also remember
> That at every meeting we are meeting a stranger.[4]

> Fare forward travellers! not escaping from the past
> Into different lives, or into any future;
> You are not the same people who left that station
> Or who will arrive at any terminus . . .
> Fare forward, you who think that you are voyaging;
> You are not those who saw the harbour
> Receding, or those who will disembark.[5]

Because these passages are poetry, the kind of contextual sense
which Bradley would scarcely have welcomed tends to intrude.
The first lines describe a woman; the whole description is
balanced by a subtly different description of a man, so that we
are free to construe it only as a bitter description of just one
type of psychology; perhaps in a better time and a better
place people's souls were not so constituted. Yet the subsequent

[1] *Ibid.*, p. 165.
[2] The conclusion of the essay on Leibniz and Bradley contains, in the
placing of the words 'of all imperfect things', a superb poetic effect.
[3] Preludes, III, *Collected Poems*, p. 24.
[4] *The Cocktail Party*, I.iii, in T. S. Eliot, *Collected Plays*, 1962, pp. 156–7.
[5] *Four Quartets*, 'The Dry Salvages', *Collected Poems*, p. 210.

description of the man also contains an element which refers us back to the philosophical situation:

His soul stretched tight across the skies . . .[1] This is parallel to Roquentin's feeling his nausea *on* the café wall, 'over there'.[2] It is, as we have seen, one of the tropes of solipsism.

The second passage is spoken by the Unidentified Guest in *The Cocktail Party*. Perhaps this is why it is almost pure Bradley, undiverted to a concrete, poetic specificity. The Unidentified Guest is a sage, and Bradley was the nearest thing Eliot knew to that. The passage casts some doubt on Smidt's observation[3] that Eliot's Anglicanism estranged him further from Bradley.

The last is the most subtle and the most powerful. Here the poetic context transforms, or even transfigures, the Bradleian material. In the seventeenth century Andrew Eliot set sail for America from East Coker (which gives the second of the Quartets its title). The Dry Salvages are the place of transit, of voyaging from old to new. The whole power of the poem turns on the tension between identity and chaos. Although the Andrew Eliot who set sail was not the Andrew Eliot who disembarked, the T. S. Eliot who is writing the poem (though not the same as the T. S. Eliot who studied at Harvard) is the same as all of them. 'In my beginning is my end . . . In my end is my beginning.'[4] Thus behind the Bradleian dissolution of self stands a religious conception of unity, spanning not just individual lives but generations. It is, however, precisely unity and not continuity. In Eliot's reaching out to his dead ancestor we find no recovery of common sense. Thus the paralysing scepticism of Bradley, instead of being dispelled by an ordinary human awareness of becoming, growth, development and change, is allowed to continue unaltered as the foreground to a starkly different religious faith. The metaphysical atmosphere is Platonic; no dialogue resolves the dualism; the separation between flux and permanence is complete.

Indeed, Eliot's poetry provides a vivid record of the kind of

---

[1] Preludes, IV, *Collected Poems*, p. 24.
[2] *La Nausée*, p. 37; Penguin, p. 35. See above, p. 181.
[3] *Poetry and Belief in the Work of T. S. Eliot*, p. 16.
[4] The first and last lines of 'East Coker', *Four Quartets*, *Collected Poems*, pp. 196 and 204.

terror which attends on Bradley's kind of empiricism. He used the imagist X-ray of his own literary *epoché*, and the result is desolation. As Smidt says, it ' "threw the nerves in patterns on a screen", but . . . obstinately refused to reveal more than hollow men'.[1]

Indeed we can even find the house of our frontispiece. Eliot too has been there:

> Tenants of the house,
> Thoughts of a dry brain in a dry season.[2]

Once more the poetic form tends to hold us to a specific meaning: 'in a dry season' suggests *in hoc saeculo* more strongly than the metaphysical *in saeculo*. But the metaphysical meaning is also there.

But such easily isolated points of contact are only signals, inducements to proceed further. Eliot was a master of language and there is a sense in which his poetic technique (not his rhetoric) engaged a more powerful intelligence than anything else he did. It is a curious thing that if we analyse his poetic development we shall be forced to think harder about privacy than we have so far had to.

Let us begin with a question: which is the more 'private' sort of poem, *The Waste Land* or *Four Quartets*? And let us hurry over the *pons asinorum* as quickly as we can. It might be said that *The Waste Land* is impersonal because in it many voices from many times and places speak to us, whereas most of *Four Quartets* is spoken in *propria persona*. Of course the word *persona* contains the germ of the proper answer; the voices in *The Waste Land* also emerge from *personae*, and indeed I might have said 'voice' not 'voices'; for, always, it is after all Eliot who speaks in *The Waste Land*. How Eliot learned from Laforgue the trick of *dédoublement* of personality, of splitting himself into a dozen phantoms, is an old story and need not be retold. We need only ask: which poem is the more private, that in which the poet speaks from within a succession of disguises, or that in which he speaks with candour? Is the stable 'I' of *Four Quartets* (as compared with the fluid 'I Teiresias' of *The Waste Land*) not the

---

[1] *Poetry and Belief in the Work of T. S. Eliot*, p. 126.
[2] 'Gerontion', *Collected Poems*, p. 41.

first mark of a frankly emergent personality? To be sure, *The Waste Land* (1922) is not so very far removed in time from the essay 'Tradition and the Individual Talent' (1919) and doubtless the poem's batteries of allusion are offered as, in some sort, a specimen of the doctrine as applied, a sort of young person's guide to the mind of Europe. Indeed it is perfectly correct to say that *The Waste Land* is impersonalist if by that we mean only that it belongs to the period in which Eliot wished to be impersonal (*Four Quartets* belongs to a later phase). But if we are at all interested in the soundness or unsoundness of theories, the success or failure of poems, we shall scarcely be content with this glib nomenclature. Two deep fissures threaten the stability of the mass: first, the web of allusion in *The Waste Land* does not automatically make that poem traditional, even as tradition is defined in the essay (as we have seen, the real tradition of the poem is awkwardly close to romanticism); secondly, the impersonalism of the essay is in any case scarcely equipped to resolve the problem of privacy, but is theosophical, *de fide*, compensatory.

But a salutary discomfort over the meaning of our terms grows as we contemplate such questions. Do we *really* want to apply the word 'private' to either *The Waste Land* or *Four Quartets*? Other words too begin to look more jagged, less fuzzily synonymous: 'subjective', 'obscure'; 'personal'. Thus *The Waste Land* was certainly more idiosyncratic in its range and mode of allusion than were the later poems. Words and images had a significance which only Eliot knew, or only Eliot until the notes were added to *The Waste Land*. But what sort of privacy is this, which can be dispelled by a footnote? The answer is: not the epistemological kind.

Cartesian privacy, which makes up half the subject of this book (the other half being literary and philosophical variations of it) is insuperable as long as you are you and I am I; I can *never* be sure that, when you look at a red pillar-box, the colour you see is anything like the colour I see when *I* look at a red pillar-box; if you send me a hastily scribbled note which reads, 'It is just like the colour of blood', I am not helped. For I have no means of knowing what blood looks like to *you*. Each person's entire empirical range is separate.

As compared with the necessary privacy of the Cartesian

consciousness, the privacy of *The Waste Land* is merely accidental; only, indeed, a kind of esotericism. But then, if our
only concept of privacy were the Cartesian one, we could never
ever have asked our original question, 'Which is the more
private?' Such metaphysical generalities do not admit compari-
sons of degree. To every fully developed post-Cartesian solipsist
(are there any nowadays?) this will be obvious. But, human
nature being what it is, there are various intermediate positions
which are psychologically if not rationally possible. For example,
there will be some who will say that Cartesian privacy, though
it does not belong to the colour of pillar-boxes, does nevertheless
characterise after-images, memories, aesthetic reactions: I
know what kind of car you drive but I shall never know what
Buxtehude means to you. Believers in this doctrine indeed do
not always see how it actually presupposes ordinary objectivism.
I cannot note the difference between your view of Buxtehude
and mine unless we are both listening to Buxtehude. If you
were hearing something which *I* would call 'Rachmaninov' the
point about differing tastes would simply vanish. For all I know
our tastes might be identical; your frowns and my smiles might
be equally appropriate, by identical criteria, to the differing
private displays which confront us. However, holders of this
view have the right to use 'private' as a comparative term.
Moreover, it is easy for them to feel that, as we can allude to our
private imagery though we can never show it to anyone, so
some poems may contain (by allusion) more essentially private
matter than some others do—poem A, for example, may contain
more remembered episodes crucial to the poet, named but not
described, than poem B. The proposition is not perhaps entirely
coherent, as we shall see if we ask '*Could* they then be described?'
But such questions must be postponed. For the moment we
must aquiesce in what is psychologically possible. And then we
may ask, which, in this sense, is the more private, *The Waste
Land* or *Four Quartets*? This time we shall get the answer, *Four
Quartets*. *The Waste Land* is full of idiosyncratic quotations, but
these, as we have seen, can be supplied by a simple, informative
commentary. *Four Quartets* is full of T. S. Eliot's memories,
dreams, presentiments, and it is suggested that such things are
in some way or in some degree inherently incommunicable. Let
us, then, examine *Four Quartets*.

But first we must look at a transitional poem; 'Ash Wednesday' lies between the major work of the young dog and the old possum:

> Because I do not hope to turn again
> Because I do not hope
> Because I do not hope to turn[1]

This *is* an image–turning in space, signifying unspecified expectations, surprise or the hope of surprise–but only just. There is no proliferation of detail, no luxuriating in the concrete. It is presumably as far removed as possible from the Homeric simile. It is probably true to say that the image is taken from the sphere of social relations and then generalised down to the bone. Specify it, eke it out with material accidents, and the effect is lost. In an early poem, Eliot wrote,

> I mount the steps and ring the bell, turning
> Wearily, as one would turn to nod good-bye to
> la Rochefoucauld . . .[2]

These lines provide a good comparison since they show with some exactness what Eliot expunged from his later technique. The ironic use to which the image is put in the early poem is not Dantean, but otherwise the lines belong with those passages in Dante which strenuously explicate the phenomenal–for example, the people in Hell who peered at Dante and Virgil as an old tailor peers at the eye of a needle.[3] The Dantean image is, I imagine, a pure example of its kind. It is there simply and solely to explain the way they looked. But in 'The Boston Evening Transcript' we have a double image. The man who turned to nod good-bye to la Rochefoucauld corresponds to the tailor in Dante, but the act of turning on a Boston doorstep is itself a sort of undeveloped image (of something as tremendous as the act itself is trivial) in a way in which the peering of Brunetto and his companions is not. And it is this half-buried image of the unnamed awakening which is, so to speak, disinterred in 'Ash Wednesday' and shaken free from its dusty

---

[1] *Collected Poems*, p. 95.

[2] 'The Boston Evening Transcript', *ibid.*, p. 30.

[3] *Inferno*, XV, 20–21. Eliot expresses a strong admiration of this simile in his essay on the *Inferno*, *Selected Essays*, pp. 243–4.

integument of adventitious detail. How can we express this change of emphasis?

In 'The Boston Evening Transcript' the poet was concerned to keep a look out in two directions: first, like a comic novelist, at the surface appearance of a faintly ridiculous posture; second, at the inner meaning of the movement. And now it has happened; the word 'inner' has entered. Why 'inner'? Presumably because we are now dealing with the kind of meaning which becomes evident only after a sort of introspection. We can reflect on the image of turning as we observe it in another: 'What is he going to do—what did his face look like?' or we can remember and imagine what it *feels like* to turn, oneself; to find oneself turning round in a crowded room, perhaps at the sound of what could have been one's name being called. This secondary egotistical use of the image is naturally much less prone to express itself in clear visual images. To use *them* is immediately to suggest the first, other-directed use. Indeed, the presence of such clarity in 'The Boston Evening Transcript' immediately imparts a sort of Narcissistic duality, a suggestion of the concealed looking-glass, to that poem (did he catch sight of himself in a window across the street . . .?). The egotistical image is largely kinaesthetic, and the kinaesthetic is the inarticulate.

I called this effect 'generalised'. There is a certain fitness in the word, but it must be used with care. The surrender of visual clarity is also the surrender of differentia, so that only a hair-line divides the opening of 'Ash Wednesday' from the abstract observation, 'because I do not hope to change'. But the division is there. The word 'turn' is enough to place us in a *situation*, which is kinaesthetically specific. It is an image, but it is doing what images rarely do. It is carrying us away from the public world. Eliot achieves the same result by syntactic methods; for example, by the reduplicated construction of 'I no longer strive to strive towards such things.'[1] What is striving? That is something we might observe in another. But 'striving to strive'? Professor Ryle will say, 'That too we can watch in another'; but the sense of strain is growing. It seems so much easier to take the short cut of self-examination; this way all is vivid, though not *visually* distinct.

[1] *Collected Poems*, p. 95.

In using the incantatory opening lines of 'Ash Wednesday' as a way into the special privacy of Eliot's later poetry, I am assuming, what seems to be obvious, that they are typical of a major change in his technique. I am aware that this is not the only technical innovation of the later phase.

In this withdrawal to inner regions we have, according to the view expressed above, a regression to that part of the world which is alone truly private in the Cartesian sense: the place of memories, aesthetic and spiritual apprehensions, the place of transit where dreams cross. Now Cartesian privacy is a synthetic *a priori*; it is not a remediable accident. Thus a withdrawal into such a realm, if it is really a withdrawal, ought to mean, from our point of view, a disappearance. In plain terms, the writer who refers to such a realm ought to be insuperably obscure, totally tedious.

In *Four Quartets*, Eliot, by the mere example of his technique, exposes the falsity of this view. Gone are the strenuous, half-ridiculous attempts to colonise the mind of Europe. Instead, like an expert in judo, he triumphs by a sudden yielding. The straining towards publicity suddenly changes into a free indulgence of privacy. *Four Quartets* is full of 'private' magic, spells, memories, stirrings, music, and it is at once the most popular and the most beautiful of all his poems. After pressing forward for so long, he falls back; *and he takes us with him*:

> Footfalls echo in the memory
> Down the passage which we did not take
> Towards the door we never opened
> Into the rose-garden. My words echo
> Thus, in your mind.
>   But to what purpose
> Disturbing the dust on a bowl of rose-leaves
> I do not know.
>   Other echoes
> Inhabit the garden. Shall we follow?
> Quick, said the bird, find them, find them,
> Round the corner. Through the first gate,
> Into our first world, shall we follow
> The deception of the thrush? Into our first world.
> There they were, dignified, invisible,

Moving without pressure, over the dead leaves,
In the autumn heat, through the vibrant air,
And the bird called, in response to
The unheard music hidden in the shrubbery,
And the unseen eyebeam crossed, for the roses
Had the look of flowers that are looked at.
There they were as our guests, accepted and accepting.
So we moved, and they, in a formal pattern,
Along the empty alley, into the box circle,
To look down into the drained pool.
Dry the pool, dry concrete, brown edged,
And the pool was filled with water out of sunlight,
And the lotos rose, quietly, quietly,
The surface glittered out of heart of light,
And they were behind us, reflected in the pool.
Then a cloud passed, and the pool was empty.
Go, said the bird, for the leaves were full of children,
Hidden excitedly, containing laughter.
Go, go go, said the bird: . . .[1]

Here as elsewhere in *Four Quartets* we are reminded of Keats's
'Ode to a Grecian Urn', with its demonstration that the inner
vision is sufficiently distinct as an object to separate itself from
the ordinary movement of growth and decay, to invite the mind
to entertain the idea of an instantaneous eternity; separate, but
not inaccessible. Eliot shows that Keats may have been right
when he said that, though heard melodies are sweet, the 'unheard
music' is ravishingly sweeter. 'My words echo Thus, in your
mind'; it is true. And the mind's picture has itself changed: no
longer a prison, but a secret garden; the 'tenants of the house'
are now children, hidden in leaves. Not that everything is happy,
or right. But life is here, and breath.

IV

We have watched writer after writer fleeing headlong from the
spectre of privacy. One after another, their flights seemed futile.
As in nightmare, or in Looking Glass Land, the more eagerly
you hasten towards your object the more surely it eludes you.
This, at the level of 'Tradition and the Individual Talent' and

---

[1] *Four Quartets*, 'Burnt Norton', *Collected Poems*, pp. 189–90.

the essays on Christianity and society appears to be true of
Eliot. His technical philosophy marks a vast improvement, in
that it articulates with greater honesty and greater imaginative
power, his intellectual abdication. This is the proper entrance
to the poetry which, in its darkness and its light, has something
more to offer than honesty, and that is *agency*. Eliot's language
is so brilliant that it forces the reflective reader to transfer his
attention from the dialectic to the pragmatic: to ask, not 'What
has he said?' but 'What has he done?' Stylistically and thema-
tically, Eliot hurled himself into privacy and thereby showed
that nothing is too private to be made public. Words can say
anything. But Eliot was never so much a fugitive as a half-
absurd, deluded hunter (and this is why he is the most instructive of our literary examples). He is like a man who, being
afraid of his shadow, resolved to kill it, and ran eastwards,
pursuing the insubstantial enemy who grew taller as he ran;
the man ran until he was almost exhausted, and then turned and
faced the sun, and found nothing before him but broad sunlight.
His epigraph from Heraclitus can now convince as the Aristotelian tag in 'Tradition and the Individual Talent' could not:
'Although there is a common meaning, most people live as if
they had a private insight.'

But if the practical lesson of Eliot's best verse is that nothing
is private, where does this leave our description of Sartre? Can
we any longer speak of withdrawal from the public world when
we have seen that no such withdrawal can ever be accomplished
or even begun? The materials of an answer are already before
us. 'Withdraw from the public world' can mean several things;
(*a*) enter a realm which is essentially incommunicable; (*b*)
gradually adhere (willingly or unwillingly) to the philosophy of
solipsism; (*c*) concentrate more and more closely on special
mental adventures which, though introspected rather than
watched, are nevertheless not essentially incommunicable. Thus
(*a*) is what never happens. Sartre is a mixture of (*b*) and (*c*),
and the fact that he is partly (*b*) entails that he secretly thinks
(erroneously) that he is (*a*) and at the same time that he does not
recognise the presence in his novel of (*c*), though it, unlike (*a*), is
really there. Of course Eliot too is a mixture of (*b*) and (*c*), but
in him the challenge implied by his ostentatiously stylish
commitment to inwardness, the shameless attainment of a vivid

communicativeness as he engages with his material, and perhaps
not least that histrionically expert self-consciousness of his
with which this chapter began—all these together alert us, open
our eyes; and thus (c) by becoming *artistically* self-aware proves
philosophically curative; (c) stands up, and stares down (b).

Perhaps, therefore, we should use the word 'inward' rather
than 'private' (though there is such a thing as a local and
remediable privacy) to express the difference between authors.
In Sartre we see a growing inwardness which fails to understand
itself; in Eliot an inwardness which virtually succeeds. Degrees
of inwardness are not, we now see, degrees of proximity to the
incommunicable. Eliot's dropping of the method of multiple
personae in favour of the stable 'I' of *Four Quartets* is not,
therefore, a journey from Essentially Private to Public, nor
vice versa; it is only a stage in the gradual clarification of an
inward perspective.

Thus we can say that Eliot's is a technical progress in the
direction of a more luminous inwardness. The most moving
line in 'The Journey of the Magi' to other readers besides me is
the one italicised:

Then at dawn we came down to a temperate valley,
Wet, below the snow line, smelling of vegetation,
With a running stream and a water-mill beating the darkness,
And three trees on the low sky.
And an old white horse galloped away in the meadow.
Then we came to a tavern with vine-leaves over the lintel,
Six hands at an open door dicing for pieces of silver . . .[1]

It is either a disingenuous or an unperceptive criticism which
says that this is ordinary, external world poetry. The simple
diction of 'The Journey of the Magi' has three functions; to
remind us, as Lancelot Andrewes wished to remind his flock, of
what the journey must really have been like; to part the curtains
before a theological mystery; to make that mystery intimate by
disclosing, at the same time, a country of the mind: an apprehension from within of all struggles towards a scarcely-hoped-for
good. As at the end of *The Waste Land* the approach is marked
by an oscillation between images of fear and felicity. We see

[1] *Collected Poems*, p. 109.

three crosses against the sky and a moment later we glimpse six hands dicing for silver. But the snow is melting and the grass is growing in the dark. That these things are good is part of a symbolism at once ancient and intelligible. And, as it happens, our intuition that the whole is informed by a sense of memory is confirmed from an external source. Eliot, writing elsewhere on the nature of memory, speaks of 'six ruffians seen through an open window playing cards at night at a small French railway junction where there was a water-mill.'[1] But these lines are over-determined by their reference to Calvary. We cannot say the same of the line italicised. Why should an old horse, galloping away in a field, be also, suddenly, so profoundly good as to bring tears to the back of the eyes? Eliot has risked a memory, or an inward image which has something of the poignancy of memory, and he finds his reader. The line is moving as the great lines in *The Prelude* are moving; because of a piercing, unrhetorical, undialectical intimacy.

But how appropriate is all this ecstatic imagery of exchanging the shadows for the sun—really—to *Four Quartets*? Why, if the philosophical critic is so overjoyed, is Eliot himself so sad? Of course my sanguine imagery had a specific reference: to the way Eliot's glowing verse vindicates the possible publicity of interior events. But since I have called his vindication 'conscious', the question remains: why is he not happier? Of course we could say that, although Eliot has recovered his grasp of reality, he has not regained his sense of continuity or order. Life has flowed back into the valley of dry bones, into the hollow men stuffed with sawdust, but they are not yet full, continuous human beings; nor is their world organized. But this is only part of the answer, and not an important part. It is really because his spiritual appetite is unappeasable. The world is not good enough for him, and so he hankers after a better. Almost from the first his poetry was marked by a hunger for God. *The Waste Land,* which in any case antedates Eliot's formal conversion to the Church of England, is only doubtfully Christian in direction. The myth of the Grail is ambiguous, composed, as Jessie Weston loved to point out, of material more ancient than Christianity, Christianised only by degrees. The voices of

[1] *The Use of Poetry and the Use of Criticism*, 1934, p. 148.

authority in the poem are not exclusively Christian but include prophets from well to the East of Jerusalem.

All these points can of course be answered; even if Jessie Weston would reduce the god of the Grail legends to an Eniautos Daimon, a Year Spirit according to the ill-starred theories of Gilbert Murray and Jane Harrison, Eliot obviously spiritualised the idea; in his poem the agricultural references compose a metaphor for, rather than the proper theatre of, divine action. Which is as much as to say, he Christianises it (Christ did little for the state of the crops in Palestine); again, though the religious references look promiscuous, it might be said that the principle on which they are selected owes more to ascetic Christianity than to any other single religion; again, there is an obscure forward impulse in the poem which suggests that, whereas Jessie Weston was interested in where the legend came from, Eliot is interested in where it is going–Christwards. But all this amounts to no more than an unresolved debate, which, like Stetson's corpse, revives annually in tutorials and classes. What is far more certain is that the poem expresses a real spiritual hunger: a hunger not for better living conditions, or better art, or improved personal relations (though it is a little strange to find at the end that the Thunder speaks with the voice of E. M. Forster[1]) but something else. And indeed the most natural way to express the difference between, say, Arnold's 'The Scholar Gypsy' and *The Waste Land*, is to note in the Victorian poem a craving to be religious and in the twentieth-century poem a hunger for God. 'Religious' is a word used by those who are not. Arnold (as we have seen from Eliot's skirmish with him) was a real empiricist. He therefore watches what Plato would call 'the things of religion' pass before him in profile on the stage of history and wishes he could join in. He wishes he could be like Glanvill's seventeenth-century scholar, but what Glanvill's scholar had he hardly knows ('what we have not'). Perhaps in his head Eliot thought it pusillanimous to shut up his appetite within the indistinct confines of his understanding. Thus we say: it is God he wants.

But at the time of *The Waste Land* it seemed as if he were

---

[1] *Datta . . . Dayadhvam . . .*, 'Give . . . sympathise . . .'; these are 'personal relations' values in an ancient Indian dress which must have delighted Forster.

doubly disinherited; God was beyond his grasp, and this time-fast world a mere constuct, which fell away to dust at a touch. The two halves seemed to fit, since Christianity has traditionally disparaged this mortal world. Which makes it somewhat ironic that, as Eliot's Christianity became stronger and more explicit, his grasp of this world became firmer, thereby increasing his sense of the pathos of its momentary wonders. Some will doubtless find in this a sign of the philosophic and moral health of Christianity. After all, Christianity is not only the religion of *contempus mundi* but of incarnation; and by God's incarnation nature is not discarded but redeemed. Why should not this be the real point of Eliot's conversion from Bradleian idealism to Christianity? In his essay on Lancelot Andrewes Eliot laid particular stress on the *Seventeen Sermons on the Nativity* (which could almost have been named *Seventeen Sermons on the Incarnation*). But he also wrote a poem founded on one of these sermons. And in 'The Journey of the Magi' nature is vivid to us only as long as we are on the road to Bethlehem; the effect of seeing the new-born God is an utter disorientation; a loss of familiarity and an impatient desire for death. Whatever is quickening Eliot's sense of the public world, it cannot be the Incarnation. One glimpse of the infant Christ is enough to crucify the soul with supernatural desire, and wither a world which had begun to turn green. Eliot's Christianity leaves him discontented. And, intellectually, it leaves him in a mess.

Look again at the passage quoted from 'Burnt Norton'. The beautiful images do not unambiguously show forth the divine splendour. They are so many Sirens against which we should stop our ears. Dream children calling, leaves, flowers, light in water and water in light, the beckoning thrush, these are a snare ('the deception of the thrush'). At last, just as they seem to be on the point of turning into something positive, the bird urgently warns us to flee:

> Go, go, go, said the bird: human kind
> Cannot bear very much reality.

To be sure the second of these lines turns the warning into a kind of invitation to whatever is strong in us; reality, after all, is here. But where? The light in the pool was momentary, the reflection vanished. Now the children are laughing in the tree but we have learned enough to sense that if we turn to look they will have gone. Whatever reality these things betoken, it is not the reality of sticks and stones.

The moment when the narrator looks into the pool can be compared with the moment in Guillaume de Lorris's mediaeval *Roman de la Rose* at which the lover's falling in love is allegorically expressed by the story of the well.[1] The lover sees the rose (which symbolises his lady) reflected in a crystal which lies at the bottom of the well. He sees it first there and already he loves it. Then he turns from the well and sees the rose itself. This is, at the very least, a remarkable piece of writing. Historically it marks a moment of revolution: that transposition of ideal love from a divine to a human context which makes the admirable blasphemy of Courtly Love. Falling in love begins with the luxurious exploration of an inward presentiment—and this moment is in a way morally perilous (we are told[2] that this is the crystal in which Narcissus caught sight of his own face and fell in love with it) but the affection then turns outwards into the sphere of the testable, the difficult, the unexpected, and becomes thereby real love (the lover's trials begin here).

In Eliot the moment of blessing when the lover turns and sees in reality what before he saw only in reflection is transformed to what is in comparison a more trivial spiritual melodrama; an evanescent love object which refuses to confirm the inward presentiment. The humanising tendency of the *Roman* is reversed. For Eliot's children, reflected behind him, *sotto in sù*, vanish when the cloud comes and the pool dries up. So too the recurrent hyacinth girl,[3] associated with rain and brown hair, is at best an ambiguous Beatrice to Eliot; in the *Waste Land* passage (where the inversion of Conrad's phrase to 'heart of light' also occurs) she drops out, leaving the desolate words from *Tristan und Isolde*:

> Oed' und leer das Meer.
> Waste and empty is the sea.

---

[1] In Chaucer's translation, 1553–1705; in *The Works of Geoffrey Chaucer*, ed. F. N. Robinson, 2nd edn., Boston, 1957, pp. 579–81.

[2] *Ibid.*, 601, p. 580.

[3] See 'La Figlia Che Piange', 'Dans le Restaurant', *The Waste Land*, 35–42; in *Collected Poems*, pp. 36, 53, 64.

There is something self-protective in this dalliance with Love Untestable, Love Unknowable, in this unwillingness to leave the momentary illumination of the inward presentiment for the enduring pains of exterior life and intercourse.

All this is only one more instance of the defeat in Eliot's universe of ordinary developing objects and persons, which stand in the vast rich area lying between the inner presentiment and the ulterior eternity. Always he deals with that which is 'more distant than the stars and nearer than the eye.'[1] Helen Gardner says[2] that whereas in the early poetry Eliot wrote of a world in shadow in the later he turns his attention to the shadow itself (and a shadow implies a light). It is a good image, but Eliot himself uses it differently:

> Between the idea
> And the reality . . .
> Falls the shadow.[3]

One has seen enough of his thought to suspect that idea and reality here denote the flux of presentation and the Absolute (though which is which, in an idealist, is always uncertain). It is a metaphysic which makes ordinary thought and intercourse impossible. It is scarcely surprising that in the later verse magic supplies the defect of reason. The style of *Four Quartets* with its circling echoes of sense and sound, its substitution of a music of ideas for a system belongs, as Smidt notes,[4] with the homonyms and onomatopoeas expounded by anthropologists who investigate primitive tabus. Even Helen Gardner observes[5] (she was thinking of 'Ash Wednesday') that it is as if the poet were not thinking what he was saying.

But this is the way the poem works. Always, the continuous, the growing or decaying of familiar things is subjected to a swift reduction followed by an unfounded inflation. Even in 'The Dry Salvages' which seems to offer a continuous human history, we find that the historical pattern is essentially suprapersonal, and that there is no continuous identity of individuals:

---

[1] 'Marina', *Collected Poems*, p. 115.

[2] *The Art of T. S. Eliot*, 1949, p. 99.

[3] 'The Hollow Man', *Collected Poems*, pp. 91–2.

[4] *Poetry and Belief in the Work of T. S. Eliot*, p. 106.

[5] *The Art of T. S. Eliot*, p. 102.

You are not the same people who left that station
Or who will arrive at any terminus.[1]

Again and again we are brought down to the moment, and the
moment is then offered as admitting us to eternity. I resent the
robbery and suspect the gift.

> What might have been and what has been
> Point to one end, which is always present.

These words conclude the first section of 'Burnt Norton'. In
the next section the opening invocation of pattern-in-flux,
conducted with a marvellous mannered grandeur of language, is
again revoked to 'the still point'; from this we move through
phases of growing yet unintelligible light to the Dantean
conclusion:

> Quick now, here, now, always–
> A condition of complete simplicity
> (Costing not less than everything)
> And all shall be well and
> All manner of thing shall be well
> When the tongues of flame are infolded
> Into the crowned knot of fire
> And the fire and the rose are one.[2]

And so the exhausted Eliot is dragged up into Heaven by
Mother Julian and Dante.

Surely the theology of St John of the Cross is very strangely
applied in this poem. The doctrine of God's closeness to man
in his Dark Night of Separation scarcely licenses the ambitious
poet to presume that his own despairs are his best security. The
nearness of God in the night is something which is properly seen
in grateful retrospect, from a vantage point of spiritual day, not
eagerly grasped in prospect. Yet such appears to be Eliot's way.
I have said that Eliot's religious verse depends not on the
communal practice of the visible Church but on inner experience.
It is a shock to discover that the experience itself is so thoroughly

[1] *Collected Poems*, p. 210.
[2] 'Little Gidding', *Four Quartets*, *ibid.*, pp. 222–3.

the experience of privation rather than of relation. Here there is only

> Desiccation of the world of sense,
> Evacuation of the world of fancy,
> Inoperancy of the world of spirit.[1]

It is true that in the second section of 'Burnt Norton' we are given something which sounds like a positive mystical experience. That Eliot implicitly characterises this as a temporary mode of consciousness does not matter so much as does his evident preference for privation as the better link with God. One wonders whether this is not at bottom a rhetorical preference. Paradox is seductive to some.

Eliot told us in another, seldom heeded poem that the Christmas children know can be lost in

> the piety of the convert
> Which may be tainted with a self-conceit
> Displeasing to God and disrespectful to the children.[2]

Here was another sort of Christianity; but we see no more of it.

We all go into the dark. And then—what Eliot really likes—the conjuring trick:

> I said to my soul, be still, and let the dark come upon you
> Which shall be the darkness of God.[3]

Negativity, privation, extinction, these are offered *per fidem* as a way to God by one who, for anything we can discover to the contrary, is still in this state—on the strength of a book he once read. And, indeed, if *The Waste Land* was dependent upon the writings of others for its spurious attempt at impersonality, *Four Quartets* is parasitic on its quotations in a more important, and more culpable fashion. Eliot supplies the dark night from his own experience; other authors (wonderfully orchestrated, we must confess) present, in well-chosen quotation, the positive insights without which the dark night remains nothing more than the darkness of T. S. Eliot.

It may be said that my complaint is misplaced. Christianity

---

[1] 'Burnt Norton', *Four Quartets, Collected Poems*, p. 193.
[2] 'The Cultivation of Christmas Trees', *ibid.*, p. 117.
[3] 'East Coker', *ibid., Collected Poems*, p. 200.

has never employed the word 'faith' as a term of abuse. I grant it, but with me it is so. But in any case my charge is more specific. In Eliot what offends is not faith but the peculiar combination of a covert reliance on faith with an ostentatious (and censorious) rationalism. Moreover, the personal faith on which he relies is strangely bloodless; it cries out, like Homer's ghosts, for the red sustaining draught which public orthodoxy can never in the end supply.

The fifth section of 'Burnt Norton' is in fact a curious mixture of Yeats and Sartre, hastily propped up by Aristotle, whose doctrine is no sooner mentioned than marred. Music and poetry, as in *La Nausée*, are extra-temporal. The Chinese jar has the impersonal, un-Christian eternity of the metal bird in 'Sailing to Byzantium'. And even poetry is located in words, which are almost as subject to decay as men. But then we are told (enter Aristotle) that love is itself unmoving, only the cause and end of movement. We recognise the eternal introvert so well characterised by A. O. Lovejoy in his *The Great Chain of Being*.[1] Plato's needy Love in the *Symposium*,[2] his 'unstinting' God in the *Timaeus*[3] are both more consonant with the Christian idea of love, whether in the creator or the creature. The Aristotelian God will never squander his radiance on the creature; we shall never find *him* in the momentary, heart-tearing experience. Eliot's is a world of historical patterns, meaningless flux, a cold eternity and a self-absorbed God. From which he relapses to the here and now. Even as we expatiate in the unlovely conception, Eliot tells us, by implication, that we could never have entertained it. Could we really have caught it as he suggests—

> in the aspect of time . . .
> Between un-being and being.
> Sudden in a shaft of sunlight
> Even while the dust moves . . .
> Quick, now, here, now, always.[4]

Aristotle's God? Here? Now? Hardly.

[1] 1936, p. 55. [2] 203 c. [3] 29 e.
[4] 'Burnt Norton', *Collected Poems*, p. 195.

CHAPTER 6

Conclusion

. . . no man is the lord of anything,
Though in and of him there be much consisting,
Till he communicate his parts to others;
Nor doth he of himself know them for aught
Till he behold them formed in th'applause
Where th'are extended; who, like an arch, reverb'rate
The voice again; or, like a gate of steel
Fronting the sun, receives and renders back
His figure and his heat.

SHAKESPEARE

I

The narrative of this book has been necessarily complex; but certain simplicities can be disengaged. We know now that there are two sorts of solipsism; that of reason and that of temperament. Hume appears to be a curiously pure example of the first. It was a train of argument and nothing else that drove him towards the thesis that no certainty existed behind ideas; a little leisure, and his habitual temper dispelled the notion. With Wordsworth it was perhaps the other way round; *his* reason told him that he inhabited a cosmos of Newtonian grandeur, ruled and pervaded by a loving God; but, left to himself, he had to grasp at the rough stonework of a wall to reassure himself of its reality. We have learned also that the solipsism we reach by argument is fundamentally unlike that which is given to some as part of their natural constitution. Rational solipsism expresses itself in an assertion: I know nothing but myself. Temperamental scepticism lacks this metaphysical generality; instead, we find records of particular feelings, and such records are by their very nature specific, non-metaphysical, significant only with reference to context and difference. The statement: 'I had a feeling that the world was unreal' describes a particular occasion and a particular feeling. That there are other occasions and other feelings is a necessary implication of the form of the

observation. Rational solipsism is a God's eye statement about
the universe as a whole; temperamental solipsism has the
universe for its context and tells only what it has seen. Rational
solipsism affects the synthetic *a priori*; temperamental solipsism
is modestly empirical, and deals, if the expression may be
allowed, only in *palpable* unrealities.

Consider this passage of seventeenth-century English prose:

> What cement should untie [unite] heaven and earth, light
> and darkness, natures of so divers a make, of such disagree-
> ing attributes, which have almost nothing, but *Being*, in
> common; This is a riddle, which must be left to the coming
> of *Elias*. How should a thought be united to a marble-
> statue, or a sun-beam to the lump of clay! The freezing
> of the words in the air in the northern climes, is as con-
> ceivable, as this strange union. That this active spark . . .
> should be confined to a Prison it can so easily pervade, is of
> less facill apprehension, then that the light should be pent
> up in a box of Crystall, and kept from accompanying its
> source to the lower world: And to hang weights on the
> wings of the winde seems far more intelligible.

This of course is not yet about solipsism but about the relation
of mind and body, but it does provide a subtle example of the
ways in which the language of feeling can mix illicitly with the
language of metaphysics. It comes from Joseph Glanvill's *The
Vanity of Dogmatizing* (1661)[1], a book with a curious subsequent
history. First Glanvill lightly revised the book and re-published
it in 1665 with the title *Scepsis Scientifica*. He then subjected
it to a far more thorough-going stylistic revision and abridge-
ment, in accordance with the ideals of the Royal Society, and
reissued it in 1676 as *Against Confidence in Philosophy* in his
Essays on Several Important Subjects in Philosophy and Religion.
This textual history affords an opportunity for almost clinical
comparison.[2] The crucial difference is, of course, between the

---

[1] P. 20. The texts of *The Vanity of Dogmatizing, Scepsis Scientifica* and
Against Confidence in Philosophy are available in photolithographic
reproduction, with an introduction by Stephen Medcalf, by the Harvester
Press, 1970.

[2] See Jackson Cope, *Joseph Glanvill, Anglican Apologist*, St Louis, 1956;
George Williamson, *The Senecan Amble*, 1951; R. F. Jones and others, *The
Seventeenth Century*, Stanford, 1951.

richly figurative language of the first and the almost eighteenth-century diction of the third.

In the passage quoted, Glanvill revels in the inconceivability of the relation between mind and body; indeed he is altogether too happy about it. This special delight is achieved by transposing a metaphysical difficulty into sensuously imaginative terms. Too many of his analogies involve merely physical incongruities. Naturally, the physical things he chooses are as disparate as can well be managed—light and dark, sunbeams and clay, weights and wind—but they are all of one category and therefore incapable of illustrating the truly categorical disjunction which seems to confront us here. It may be said that these are not analogies so much as metaphors. But even if they are metaphors they encourage subliminally the notion of a physical continuum, and begin to transform an *a priori* problem into an empirical difficulty.

In his *Essay against Confidence in Philosophy* Glanvill rewrote the passage quoted as follows:

> . . . what the *Cement* should be that unites *Heaven* and *Earth, Light* and *Darkness, viz.* Natures of so diverse a make, and such disagreeing Attributes, is beyond the reach of any of our Faculties: We can as easily conceive how a thought should be united to a Statue, or a Sun-Beam to a piece of Clay: how words should be frozen in the Air, (as some say they are in the remote North) or how Light should be kept in a Box; as we can apprehend the *manner* of this *strange Union*.[1]

The rewriting is not so very different. Glanvill's language still suggests that an empirical point is being made, whereas in fact his difficulty is conceptual. We are made to feel, irrationally, that sunlight is more spiritual than clay, whereas by the strict Cartesian metaphysics which Glanvill is here discussing clay and light are of course equally physical things. But, interestingly, Glanvill has removed the most blatantly physical of his analogies: the hanging of weights on the wind. Perhaps he saw Kennedy Airport in a dream.

Poets and artists have always transposed the abstract into the terms of the concrete, sometimes with a delicious sense of

[1] *Essays on Several Important Subjects*, 1676, p. 4.

unanalysed metaphysical paradox as they do so. I have written elsewhere[1] of the literary history of the universal, treated repeatedly by the poets as if it were a mysterious instance of itself; Beauty as being itself supremely beautiful, and so on. In these matters consciousness of metaphor appears to be the last guarantor of conventional sanity. Schizophrenia, for example, often looks reasonable in everything except its failure to recognise metaphor as metaphor. 'My father sticks needles in my head,' says the schizophrenic; examine his family and, as like as not, you will find this an excellent figurative description of the father's behaviour. But the schizophrenic does not know that it is figurative, and it is this rather than his attitude to his father which can properly be taken as showing him to be insane. Thus R. D. Laing (a talented 'demythologiser' of schizophrenic language) can produce from his gallery of patients, curiously transposed specimens of the great philosophies of the past. For example, he has a Cartesian who feels but does not argue his disjunction from his machine-body,[2] and an existentialist who believes as a matter of blunt fact that everyone is always acting.[3]

The first example is clearer than the second, for the simple reason that Sartre himself is curiously stretched between the metaphysician and the novelist (with an undoubted suspicion of real mental disturbance at times). Laing's subject[4] who *felt* 'persecuted by reality', who 'longed to transcend the world', who felt 'a constant dread of all that is there, of being overwhelmed' is simply, and directly, reminiscent of Sartre. There is, as we have seen, a certain irony in all this. Laing, himself a professed existentialist, clinically diagnoses the mentality of his philosophical master as schizophrenia. At this stage in his career Laing seems both to have believed in Sartrian existentialism and seen its appearance in another as the proper object of *therapy*. As we have seen, in Sartre's case we cannot confidently resolve this difficulty by distinguishing between the metaphysical view and its sub-philosophical equivalent.

But, theoretically, the distinction remains crucial. We can

[1] *Two Concepts of Allegory*, 1967.
[2] 1960, p. 70.
[3] *Ibid.*, pp. 72–5.
[4] *Ibid.*, p. 84.

easily imagine a conversation between a philosophical and a temperamental solipsist which will make this clear:

> *Philosopher:* I do not know that there is anything beyond myself.
>
> *Non-philosopher:* Yes, yes! I know just what you mean. I was walking down a grey street on Thursday, and I suddenly felt that all the houses, the pavement, even the sky—were unreal.
>
> *Philosopher:* Really? I've never felt that.
>
> *Non-philosopher:* But you just said . . .
>
> *Philosopher:* You misunderstood me. My feelings are perfectly ordinary. My doubt is essentially prior to any particular report my feelings may give me; indeed, it is precisely this that I doubt; whether this range of solid, comfortable feelings really refers to anything outside me at all. It is the testimony of the senses which I find doubtful. I mistrust all messengers however clean and neat they may appear. You, on the other hand, clearly place *great* reliance on your feelings, since you are prepared to believe them even when they tell you the most extraordinary things (extraordinary to you, since you have none of the reasons which I have for entertaining solipsism). I think there may be no reality behind *all* our feelings; you have, here and there in the course of your rich sensory life, feelings of unreality.

We have seen that this clarity of distinction is seldom to be found in Sartre. At the same time we have suggested that Hume was a sort of practical specimen of both arms of the distinction since backgammon cured his solipsistic fears. But we can see now that all this was a little too brisk. A truly metaphysical solipsism cannot be affected by natural conviviality, since it operates at a prior level. This, of course, formed the basis of my difference with Kemp Smith in chapter III. It is only the *feeling* of solitude that can be so cured.

Yet we must tread carefully here. The metaphysical assertion is not refutable by feeling, but actually to hold, at a given time, a metaphysical opinion is a psychological condition with psychological consequences. Hence the mere entertainment of a belief originally reached by pure argument can activate *temperamental* feelings of solitude. This seems to be true of Hume himself. Plainly, he is not a *pure* specimen of the distinction before us (in fact Berkeley is far better). In Hume the argument came first, but it swiftly translated itself into feeling. We find occasionally in him, what we found in Glanvill, a logical difficulty in process of changing into an imaginative, almost physical, straining (it is a passage we have quoted before):

> Let us fix our attention out of ourselves as much as possible: Let us chase our imagination to the heavens, or to the utmost limits of the universe; we never really advance a step beyond ourselves, nor can conceive any kind of existence, but those perceptions, which have appeared in that narrow compass. This is the universe of the imagination, nor have we any idea but what is there produced.[1]

Of course Hume raises the question only to reject it. But he thought it needed to be rejected and, moreover, the rare vividness of the writing suggests that he himself has struggled in the way he condemns. Did he not *feel* himself 'inviron'd with the deepest darkness'?[2] And if we set beside the passage from Hume a parallel passage from Berkeley we shall see that it is the Scot who feels his metaphysics as a passion of the mind, and the Irishman who is never even tempted:

> *Hylas:* It is not certain I see things at a distance? Do we not perceive the stars and moon, for example, to be a great way off? Is not this, I say, manifest to the senses?
>
> *Philonous:* Do you not in a dream too perceive those or the like objects?
>
> *Hylas:* I do.
>
> *Philonous:* And have they not then the same appearance of being distant?
>
> *Hylas:* They have.
>
> *Philonous:* But you do not thence conclude the apparitions in a dream to be without the mind?
>
> *Hylas:* By no means.

[1] *Treatise*, I.ii.6, pp. 67–8. [2] *Ibid.*, I.iv.7, p. 269.

> *Philonous:* You ought not therefore to conclude that sensible
> objects are without the mind, from their appearance
> or manner wherein they are perceived.[1]

The *feel* of the mind as it strains at a vacuum is absent.

Again Hume, like Sartre, can make the mistake of supporting
a metaphysical thesis with a striking particular observation,
and as we have seen, the trouble with such star-cases is that
their very appositeness implies the existence of other particular
examples less apposite, and perhaps even contrary. For example,
there are two ways of arguing for the Humian thesis that
belief is reducible to vivacity of impression: first by asking,
what else can you produce as ground for belief? And second
by producing anecdotal examples, like that of the drunkard,
who 'has seen his companion die of a debauch, is struck with
that instance for some time, and dreads a like accident for
himself: But as the memory of it decays away by degrees, his
former security returns. . . .'[2] The trouble with the example is
that it shows, not that all judgment is a function of the vivacity
of impression (what particular example could ever show that?)
but that it shows the possible effect of vivacity of impression
upon judgment or belief—which is almost to demonstrate the
contrary thesis. For why is the story of the drunkard striking?
Because it shows how a man's judgment can be warped by the
nearness of an impression. But if we think of this as an interesting example of distortion we must think that judgment is not
usually thus warped—that is, we must think that judgment
and impression are two different things—*quod non erat demon-
strandum.* The same thing is true of another of Hume's examples
from early in the *Treatise*, the man suspended in an iron cage
who for all his knowledge that the iron is strong trembles with
fear.[3] Clearly a philosopher who can write this way is a man
subject to the common tendency: a man who likes to get his
language *within* the category of experience.

Perhaps, then, we should revise the antithesis with which this
chapter opened. If we ask the fundamental question: 'Did he
know solipsism as an experience?' we must answer 'Yes' for

---

[1] *Three Dialogues*, I, in Luce and Jessop, vol. II. p. 201.

[2] *Treatise*, I.iii.13, p. 144.

[3] *Ibid.*, I.iii.13, p. 148.

both Hume and Wordsworth, and for Berkeley, perhaps 'Hardly at all'.

Wordsworth's experience of unreality reaches us in two versions. The first is the Fenwick note on the *Immortality Ode:*

> . . . it was not so much from [feelings] of animal vivacity that *my* difficulty came as from a sense of the indomitableness of the spirit within me. I used to brood over the stories of Enoch and Elijah, and almost to persuade myself that, what ever might become of others, I should be translated, in something of the same way, to heaven. With a feeling congenial to this, I was often unable to think of external things as having external existence, and I communed with all that I saw as something not apart from, but inherent in, my own immaterial nature. Many times when going to school have I grasped at a wall or tree to recall myself from this abyss of idealism to the reality. At that time I was afraid of such processes. In later periods of life I have deplored, as we have all reason to do, a subjugation of an opposite character, and have rejoiced over the remembrance, as is expressed in the lines –
>
> > 'Obstinate questionings
> > Of sense and outward things,
> > Fallings from us, vanishings, *etc.* . . .'[1]

This whole paragraph is marked by the curious mixture of piety, complacency and anxiety which characterises the ode to which it refers. The sentence beginning 'Many times when going to school have I grasped at a wall . . .' stands out from the surrounding prose with an almost shocking sharpness. The rest is involved in that cosier subjectivism which Wordsworth liked to indulge, for example, when defining the poet:

> What is a Poet? . . . a man pleased with his own passions and volitions, and who rejoices more than other men in the spirit of life that is in him; delighting to contemplate similar volitions and passions as manifested in the goings-on of the Universe, and habitually impelled to create them where he does not find them.

[1] *Poetical Works*, vol. IV, pp. 463–4.

The poet as Narcissus and the world as his looking-glass. The modesty of Shakespeare's metaphor in which the poet holds the mirror up to nature, is strangely reversed.

The other version of Wordsworth's experience reaches us in a letter written by Bonamy Price, quoted in William Knight's edition (1876) of Wordsworth's poetical works. Price merely reports a conversation.

> The venerable old man raised his aged form erect; he was walking in the middle, and passed across me to a five-barred gate in the wall which bounded the road on the side of the lake. He clenched the top bar firmly with his right hand, pushed strongly against it, and then uttered these ever-memorable words: 'There was a time in my life when I had to push against something that resisted, to be sure that there was anything outside me. I was sure of my own mind; everything else fell away, and vanished into thought.'[1]

This is much barer; there is no attempt to preach that because this world is insubstantial the next or previous world must be substantial. Perhaps Wordsworth drew this moral by the five-barred gate, but if he did Bonamy Price did not remember it. Instead we receive a starker picture. Unmoralised, unargued, comfortless, the sense came to him from nowhere.

This remains the primary aesthetic experience for Wordsworth. It, more than any other, pervades his work. Of course he had others, equally pre-theoretical, mere *données* of his peculiar constitution. One in particular perhaps deserves mention, if only because it seems to be the exact opposite of the experience we have been discussing. I mean the place[2] in *The Excursion* where Wordsworth longs, while retaining his 'shrinking sensibility' and 'all the nice regards of flesh and blood', to give up his bodily identity, 'And to the elements surrender it as if it were a spirit!' This is a strange passage because of its double insistence on retention and surrender, yet it is idle to deny that in it union with the environment is seen as deeply desirable. But notice how this experience differs from the first, *as an experience*. First of all, it is a wish and not a

---

[1] *Poetical Works*, vol. IV, p. 467.
[2] IV.510–3, *Poetical Works*, vol. V, p. 125.

passion. Secondly, it is profoundly and confusedly theory-laden, and if we reflect on its theoretic origins we shall see how it is related to the passion of unreality. The theoretic context is the romantic impulse at once to sensitise and to submerge the ego, the tendency we discussed in chapter 3.

Let us focus, then, on the boy Wordsworth, clutching suddenly at the wall. All this really happened on some day, grey or clear, nearly two hundred years ago, at a northern road-side. Perhaps the first thing to notice is that although the experience is philosophically innocent, it has an argumentative structure of its own. Just as the argumentative schemes of Hume are not without temperamental 'affect', so the purest temperamental record we can find is not without a thesis. This boy is clutching at the stones of the wall not just to feel but also to refute. Therefore, before he stretched out his hand, he had encountered not a thing but a proposition; he had sensed that something was the case. There is, moreover, an assumption in the chosen method of refutation which can easily be generalised: *Esse est obstare*, to be is to resist pressure or penetration. Dr Johnson used the same method:

> After we came out of the church, we stood talking for some time together of Bishop Berkeley's ingenious sophistry to prove the non-existence of matter, and that everything in the universe is merely ideal. I observed, that though we are satisfied his doctrine is not true, it is impossible to refute it. I shall never forget the alacrity with which Johnson answered, striking his foot with mighty force against a large stone, till he rebounded from it, 'I refute it thus'.[1]

Here of course the whole atmosphere is different; we have, not solitude but vigorous conversation, humour and energetic confidence. But we should not be too impressed by this difference. The techniques of Wordsworth and Johnson are, after all, almost identical. Their temperaments may have been more akin than we are at first willing to allow. The robustness of Johnson is commonly exaggerated and too often usurps the place in our memories which his Christian fortitude should properly fill.

[1] Boswell's *Life of Johnson*, August 6th, 1763; in the edn. of G. Birkbeck Hill, 1936, vol. I, p. 471.

Johnson was a depressive, and the form his depression most frequently took was fear. Did not Boswell, in the finest psychological metaphor of the eighteenth century, compare Johnson's mind to the Colosseum, with its concentric regularity of architecture, its titanic strength and its latent horror, like the beasts in their cells, intermittently exposed?[1] Those who know the subject do not always smile as they read Boswell's description of Johnson kicking with all his strength at a great stone and rebounding from it. This confidence is perhaps not very far from despair. And in Johnson the essentially argumentative core of the action is manifest, in the shouted word 'refute'.

But, it will be said, the proffered argument fails of its effect, for the reasons already explained. No finding *within* experience can tell us anything about the ontological status of the experience as such. Johnson showed himself that he had the sensation of solidity–which Berkeley of course never denied.

It begins to look as if our two forms of solipsism, the rational and the temperamental, can have no connexion other than by confusion of some sort. They must be left to jog along side by side, and the story of their journey will have been a story of trivial misconceptions.

But in fact the real relation between them is stronger than that; certainly it is much more ironic. The two forms are not mutually corroborative, but they are not mutually irrelevant either; they are incompatible. Wordsworth's and Johnson's sense that the stones you only see (as opposed to the stones you break your skin on) are possibly unreal is essentially contextual. It presupposes that the tangible is different from the more fugitive visible. Thus neither the special quality of the initial fear nor the special force of the rebuttal will be intelligible unless a norm of trustworthy sensation is supplied. But this norm is exactly what the rational solipsist takes from us.

However, the kicking of the stone can *become* a rebuttal of philosophical solipsism, if the kicker once learns to rely not on the mere experience of solidity but rather on the character of the concepts which he has been using all along. If Johnson had kicked his stone in 1950 and not 1763, and if he had done it in Oxford, it might have seemed a pretty piece of wit, to be

---

[1] October 26th, 1769; Boswell's *Life of Johnson*, vol. II, p. 106.

construed as follows: 'I refute Berkeley thus, since I understand that the Bishop says that things aren't really there, and
the only way I can understand "not there" is as meaning that
although they look as if they're there, when you try to grasp
or photograph them, you find out that you were mistaken.
What *else* could "not really there" ever mean? I therefore give
what empirical sense I can to Berkeley's words—and of course
from there on it is the work of a moment to falsify them—ouch!'
Such solemn naiveté was then the mode, and had at least the
merit which is presumably essential to mock-naiveté, namely
sophistication. Note that the force of the argument lies not in
the kicking but in the flag shown, the verificationist challenge;
and though any particular verification will doubtless be
empirical the principle of verification itself is pre-empirical
and utterly metaphysical.

We have been looking so far at the difference between
rational and temperamental solipsism, and have seen that
temperamental solipsism tries to resolve pre-empirical questions
by specifying psychological contents. But now the argument
has yielded a new and piquant antithesis: between the metaphysical thesis that language, if it is to be significant, must
operate within the terms of experience (positivism) and, on the
other hand, the practice of *using* empirical language in a
philosophical context which properly requires a high degree of
abstraction. According to the positivist theory, Johnson's
failure to attain the Berkeleian level of abstraction becomes a
virtue. The very feature of his thought which appeared to unfit
him as the Bishop's philosophical adversary is now the feature
which being present in him confers significance on his language,
and being absent in Berkeley denies significance to *his*.

In the eighteenth century verificationism tended to be
psychologistic. Its imperative was: reduce everything to that
which immediately confronts the mind (note that the imperative
itself could scarcely have sprung spontaneously from the
immediate mental field). In Hume the effort to obey this imperative even when doing philosophy led to various freaks of thought;
and these exhibit—naturally—a certain likeness to those
temperamental transpositions of originally metaphysical
thought which we have been considering. Hence his curious
oscillation between radical philosophy of mind and the synthetic

I

enumeration of psychological facts. He tells us that belief
consists only in the high vivacity of an impression, and supports
the proposition by pointing out (presumably basing the observation on memories of his own feelings when reading) that when
a man believes what he reads a livelier conception (happens to)
arise in his mind.[1] But what was proposed was not a mere
empirical correlation but a latent equivalence—belief was to be
reduced to, not associated with, vivacity of impression. A little
later[2] he says that tragic poets mingle events in which we
believe with fictitious ones, in order that the 'vividness' of
'conception' attaching to the first may flow thence into the
others 'as by so many pipes or canals'. If belief is nothing
but vivid conception, it is presumably legitimate to substitute
terms, and re-word the thesis as follows: 'Tragic poets mingle
vividly conceived events with less vividly conceived events, in
order that the vivacity of the former may raise the general
impact of the piece.' Now this is a very credible (if humdrum)
sentence but it certainly fails to give any idea of what Hume
meant in the sentence he wrote. It is clear that Hume's remarks
on tragic composition actually *depend on* the relation between
truth and vividness being synthetic. Again he argues[3] that the
'mummeries' of the Roman Catholic Church are simply designed
to promote belief. The passage seems almost to be written at
two levels for two different kinds of reader. Reader A sees it
as a gibe at Roman Catholics. Reader B might reply 'But that
is to read Hume as though he were Shaftesbury'[4] and construe
the passage as praise of the Roman Catholic Church since by
this strategy it shows that it, unlike the Church of England,
knows what belief really is.

All this, it might be said, is Hume at his worst, and his least
interesting. Did not Leibniz himself fall into the same error
when he urged[5] an unknown correspondent to scrutinise the

[1] *Treatise*, I.iii.7, p. 98.

[2] *Ibid.*, I.iii.10, p. 122.

[3] *Ibid.*, I.iii.8, p. 100.

[4] Shaftesbury advances a similar thesis about the Roman Catholic
Church, *Miscellaneous Reflections*, II.ii, in his *Characteristics*, vol. 11. pp.
212 f.

[5] See L. Couturat, *La Logique de Leibniz*, Hildesheim, 1961, pp. 578–80,
and A. O. Lovejoy, *The Great Chain of Being*, Cambridge, Mass., 1966,
pp. 144–5. Cf. Leibniz, *New Essays concerning Human Understanding*,
trans. A. G. Langley, New York, 1896, III.vi.12, pp. 332–4.

biological scale for a missing element when his whole argument for the completeness of God's creation had been the purest metaphysics? And does not Hume himself, when his genius is rekindled, transfix such confusion in others, as for example in the *Enquiry*[1] when he points out the philosophic triviality of arguing from the stick which appears to bend under water to the general fallibility of the senses?

The interest of such passages lies not in what they demonstrate but in what they betray. The natural tendency, strong in imaginative writers and, as we have seen, by no means absent in philosophers, to recast philosophical propositions in empirical terms stands in a very odd relation to the philosophic precept: 'Reduce all to what is before the mind.' It should now be obvious: the former satisfies the latter but the latter does not satisfy itself. The sub-philosophic, richly empirical sort of psychological reminiscence about which we have been so disdainful satisfies the precept to stay within experience, but the precept itself does no such thing. Experience can never grade itself in this way. Thus a contradiction is generated which recalls the paradox which I referred to in the chapter on Sartre. It will bear restatement. It is suggested that we divide words into two classes, heterological and homological; a heterological word is a word which does not exemplify its meaning, e.g. 'bottle' (since the word 'bottle' is not itself a bottle); a homological word is a word which does exemplify its meaning—e.g. 'word', since 'word' is a word. 'French' is not homological, but 'français' and 'English' both are; we then ask, 'What about the word "heterological"' itself? Is it heterological or not?'—and return the now familiar answer, 'If it is it isn't, and if it isn't, it is.' So with our present situation: if we accept the thesis that (apart from analytic statements with which we are not here concerned) only empirical language is significant, then the statement 'only empirical language is significant' is itself insignificant; on the other hand, if the thesis is false, and other sorts of statement may be meaningful, then, though false, it can at least be meaningful. This admittedly does not so far equal the paralytic symmetry of Grelling's paradox since it gives us, 'If it's right it's meaningless, and if it's wrong it's

[1] XII.i.117, p. 151.

possibly meaningful.' But, since rightness is conditional on
significance, we revise this, and say, 'If it's right, it's not
right', which is pretty close.

Yet, rough-hew it as we may, this congeries of sentiment and
opinion has formed a continuous body of belief from the late
seventeenth century to the present day. Those abysses from
which logic draws back are lightly crossed by human psychology.
Indeed the strength of this illicit extension of metaphysics
proved wonderful. This book does not explain why, from a few
dry pebbles dropped into the indifferent water, so many
ripples should have spread so far. The stages are all there;
first the scientists with their representative theory of perception; then the representative theory finds its proper predator
in philosophic scepticism, and then the scepticism provokes
the half-hysterical response of a romanticism which ostentatiously prefers its dream to the stony course the scientists
began:

> Natural Objects always did & now do weaken, deaden
> and obliterate Imagination in me.[1]

> The Atoms of Democritus
> And Newton's Particles of light
> Are sands upon the Red sea shore
> Where Israel's tents do shine so bright.[2]

There are even cross-checks in the story; the philosophy of
Hume, as we have seen, prefigured the feeling-reaction of the
romantics. Also, as we have seen, there are some odd reversals.
Hume saw feeling as supplying what reason had failed to give,
and the romantics, by and large, applied the lesson. But what
are we to say when the first and last feeling of the greatest
romantic poet is a feeling *of unreality?* Here feeling confirms
the very disease it was expected to cure. It is a queer story,
but it hangs together.

Yet it seems implausible to name each term in the series as
the sole cause of its successor. After all, in the years that
followed, how many read *The Treatise?* And (with a different

---

[1] Annotations written in 1826 to William Wordsworth, *Poems,* 1825,
p. 44; in *The Poetry and Prose of William Blake,* ed. Geoffrey Keynes, 1956,
p. 821.   [2] 'Mock on, mock on, Voltaire, Rousseau', *ibid.,* p. 107.

emphasis) how *many* read *The Prelude!* An escalation so spectacular implies positive conditions. The receptivity of ordinary culture is here so marked (one is tempted to say, so *active*) as to require an explanation of its own. This I find myself unable to give. But if I confine myself to the central sequence it is not because I mistake it for the whole story.

II

Certainly the mind and heart of literature changed. The image of the house, the enclosed place, assumes an intensity and a significance which would have baffled an Elizabethan (though not, perhaps, the author of *Richard II*). For hundreds of years the place of withdrawal had been green. Pastoral was the genre of the sequestered spirit, the language, as Bruno Snell put it, of the mind;[1] and the choice of possible metaphors is important. The poet discovered himself in an *al fresco* world of sky, water, grass, trees, and animals. C. S. Lewis wrote[2] that Pastoral is a real place and should be visited often; it exists within us. Near as it is, it has seemingly grown more difficult of access with the years. It is as if in the remoter past introspection naturally held the character of a glimpse of freedom. It was the public world that bound and fettered us; but this changed. The place of withdrawal and self-discovery gradually ceased to be rural and became domestic; the enclosing trees insensibly hardened into constricting bricks and mortar, and at last the house began to look uncommonly like a prison: the Captain's granite fort in *The Dance of Death*, the unfurnished room of *Endgame, Huis Clos*. Those who hunt for modern pastoral in novels of rural life are looking in exactly the wrong place, since *modern* pastoral is no longer pastoral. It may be said that in Wordsworth the change has not yet occurred, since his egotism chose the country as its theatre. But landscape in Wordsworth is not a metaphor of his mind, it is the actual object of his perceptions. It is not that pastoral cannot be autobiographical; rather that, if it is autobiographical, it should be so metaphorically. Milton's heart-breaking lines,

---

[1] See Bruno Snell, *The Discovery of the Mind*, trans. T. G. Rosenmeyer (first published 1953), New York, 1960, and Richard Cody, *The Landscape of the Mind*, 1969, *passim*.

[2] *The Allegory of Love*, 1936, p. 352.

> Rough satyrs danced, and Fauns with cloven heel
> From the glad sound would not be absent long,
> And old Damoetas loved to hear our song. *Lycidas* 34–36

are about his time at Cambridge, not about some rural child-hood. To be sure, Wordsworth's Cumberland is infected with mentality, but this is another and less happy state of affairs. The pastoral poet looked into the human heart and found a world. Wordsworth looked at the world and found his own mind. On the rare occasions when he attempts the old way of writing, the image is the one we have learned to predict: 'Shades of the prison-house begin to close . . .'[1] To chronicle so profound a modification of the human spirit it was necessary to change the metaphor.

But we find very little of this language, perhaps because, as a consequence of the change in instinctual epistemology, metaphor itself became suspect. If a man feels the real world slipping from him, he tightens his grip upon it. But a man who will not change a hand-hold is a man who cannot climb. I have argued in the third chapter of this book that the modern hunger for vividness is a symptom of the epistemological malaise. Hume's desperate reliance on 'vivacity' and the modern reader's need to break his skin upon the real are closely related. The pullulating stickinesses of Roquentin's world are only one, extreme example, as the metaphysical sickness of Sartre is extreme. A lower degree of the same desperation can be found in Golding.

In his novel *Free Fall* the 'I' of the narrative addresses the reader as one Cartesian ghost-in-a-machine to another: 'my darkness reaches out and fumbles at a typewriter with its tongs. Your darkness reaches out with your tongs and grasps a book'.[2] It is no accident that the same novel contains much strenuously empirical stuff like this:

> Opposite each house across the brick alley, with the gutter down the middle was a square of brick walls with an entry. The walls were about three feet high. In each square on the left-hand side was a standpipe and beyond it, at the back of the square was a sentry-box closed by a

[1] *Immortality Ode*, 67, *Poetical Works*, vol. IV, p. 281.
[2] *Free Fall*, 1959, p. 8.

wooden door which had a sort of wooden grating. Open the door by lifting the wooden latch and you faced a wooden box running the whole width between the walls and pierced by a round, worn orifice. There would be a scrap of newspaper lying on the box, or a whole sheet crumpled on the damp floor . . .

. . . It must have been a day in April. What other month could give me such blue and white, such sun and wind? The clothing on the line was horizontal and shuddering, the sharp, carved clouds hurried, the sun spattered from the soap suds in the gutter, the worn bricks were bright with a dashing of rain . . . I was playing with a matchbox in the gutter. I was so small that to squat was natural but the wind even in the alley would sometimes give me a sidelong push and I was as much in the soapy water as out. A grating was blocked so that the water sped across the bricks and made a convenient ocean.[1]

The ghost of Wordsworth walks in that 'three feet high' ('I've measured it from side to side . . .'). We are momentarily halted by what might look like coy playfulness in 'sentry-box' (for 'privy') but then we realise that this is not euphemism but the Russian technique of 'making it strange' that we saw in Sartre. Golding wants to duck under the grid of conceptual convention, to make us see with the child's eye. And this remains his nearest approach to full metaphor (the 'ocean' at the end is the child's playfulness, not the writer's). This represents a considerable feat of repression in a verbally brilliant writer, like Golding. Only at one point, perhaps, does the style get out of hand: the 'horizontal' clothes on the line are a little hard to believe. I have never seen a wind which could do that. If I am right to mistrust, then this belongs better with the sort of virtuoso descriptive hyperbole we find very occasionally in seventeenth-century poetry – for example in Donne's 'The Calme':

> And as the Iles which wee
> Seeke, when wee can move, our ships rooted bee.[2]

---

[1] *Ibid.*, pp. 19–20.
[2] Lines 9–10, in John Donne, *The Satires, Epigrams and Verse Letters*, ed. W. Milgate, 1967, pp. 57–8.

To use metaphor requires a certain confidence–to abandon the given for an instant, to substitute another object and trust that it will carry the right significance–all this is for ages more securely grounded than ours. Golding's boldest truancy from the given is hyperbole. To call the brick alley the arena of his hopes, the battle-ground of his peers, is not for him, and not only because these metaphors are hackneyed.

The strands of our argument meet conveniently in Ruskin. The history of pastoral is largely a history of what Ruskin tendentiously described as the pathetic fallacy (who was ever deceived by it?). The epic similes and epithets, in Homer at least, work on us not through a system of echoes, but through the blank acceptance of the absence of such echoes. The dying hero falls and the ground which receives him is 'life-giving'. But in Virgil's tenth eclogue even the laurels, even the tamarisks wept for Gallus. To Ruskin this literary change was obscurely frightening; the whole business of the artist as truth-teller was imperilled by such wanton fictions. Yet something could be saved, if we preserved the 'like' or 'as' of simile, and avoided the mere substitution of metaphor:

> . . . when Dante describes the spirits falling from the banks of Acheron 'as dead leaves flutter from a bough', he gives the most perfect image possible of their utter lightness, feebleness, passiveness and scattering agony of despair, without, however, for an instant losing his own clear perception that these are souls, and that those are leaves; he makes no confusion of one with the other. But when Coleridge speaks of
>
> > The one red leaf, the last of its clan,
> > That dances as often as dance it can,
>
> he has a morbid, that is a so far false idea about the leaf; he fancies a life in it, and will, which there are not; confuses its powerlessness with choice.[1]

Note that for Ruskin because the poet says 'as' he does not lose his 'clear perception'. It is true that he leaves the description of the dead for something else, namely leaves, but because

---

[1] *Modern Painters*, Part IV, Ch. xii ('Of the Pathetic Fallacy'), in *The Complete Works of John Ruskin*, ed. E. T. Cook and A. Wedderburn, vol. V, pp. 206–7.

he says 'as' this is merely a transition from one reality to another (instead of that very different thing, the clouding of a reality with a mendaciously superimposed image). Ruskin, it will be noticed, does not mind movement, and change of immediate subject in a poem, so long as a naive requirement of cognitive fidelity is satisfied. Dante knows the dead and he knows the leaves: the dead are in the river and the leaves are in the cold air; there is no such mingling of identities as we get with metaphor.

I fancy that what worried Ruskin about metaphor was the fact that of its two terms, the image and its significance, it is the significance only which is deemed to be 'real' and yet the image is the only thing mentioned. The poet is thinking of flesh and hair, but he writes:

> . . . there I will behold
> Thy bared snow and thy unbraided gold.[1]

In which case must he not really have been thinking of snow and gold? But, if so, is this devotion? Surely so to stray from the proper matter both of his love and his art is a species of faithlessness. Curiously enough, Johnson had this feeling long before Ruskin, for he wrote of Milton's *Lycidas*:

> . . . passion runs not after remote allusions and obscure opinions. Passion plucks no berries from the myrtle and ivy, nor calls upon Arethuse and Mincius, nor tells of 'rough satyrs and fauns with cloven heel'. 'Where there is leisure for fiction, there is little grief.'
> In this poem there is no nature, for there is no truth . . .[2]

Like Ruskin, Johnson is not worried about the moral aspect only. Certainly he is concerned about the quality of Milton's grief for Edward King, but, as the last sentence shows, behind this concern is another disquiet, this time about Milton's attachment to reality itself.

The lesson of such criticism is this: we must stare at the object and not turn aside, we must close with it, press our faces

---

[1] Thomas Carew, 'A Rapture', 27–8, in *The Poems of Thomas Carew*, ed. W. C. Hazlitt, 1870, p. 63.
[2] Life of Milton, in *Lives of the English Poets*, ed. G. Birkbeck Hill, 1905, vol. I, p. 163.

against its rough recalcitrance, and all may then be well. It is of course a lesson which no-one has ever been able perfectly to apply. Some grey novelists, in whose books endless specificity of reference is never enlivened by metaphor, have perhaps come pretty close. It may be surprising to some (though it should not be) that the subject matter of these books seems so much less substantial than Carew's glittering mistress.

Human knowledge of the world is not a piece-meal passive reception of links and chunks, a mere exposure to the grammar and elements of reality. We know as we learn, by asking, trying, failing, always in a situation, always with a preconception which sometimes succeeds, is sometimes defeated. We saw in the fifth chapter of this book how the murky flame of Sartre's verbal excess occasionally guttered to the near extinction of a mere demonstrative–'*that*'. But 'that' tells almost nothing, and this is as true of inner experience as it is of the art of writing. *Pace* Roquentin, a man who can say (and think) 'tree' will know that moist, branched presence over there far better than the inarticulate person who lacks any such concept (and perhaps better than the person who also lacks the more general concepts of moistness, branched-ness and presence). Our very knowing is an endless throwing out of taxonomic essays, and whether we like it or not we are involved from the first in the web of semantic relations. The first course–to stare in sullen concentration at a single strand, flinching lest the eye should so much as glimpse how this thread joins its neighbour, is not very inviting. Is it not better to rejoice with the old poets, to draw from the web not the first strand but one importantly related to it, thus activating the understanding to comprehend the larger significance of what is given?

When we cast the situation thus in its most radical form it is clear that the admired Dante never really avoided all conceptual truancy. Did he not abandon '*those*' to refer to leaves in general (in order of course to come back to 'those', but then *that* happens in metaphor)? If similes are possible, the function 'as' is acceptable, and if 'as' works, one reference can stand intelligibly for another, and if that is so, then metaphor is possible. It might be said that as long as we preserve the conjunction *as* there is no possibility of the kind of usurpation of the actual which Ruskin feared from metaphor. But then, if a metaphor is read literally (as it must be if the usurpation has occurred) it is no longer a metaphor.

> One ask'd me where the Roses grew?
> I bade him not goe seek;
> But forthwith bade my *Julia* show
> A bud in either cheek.[1]

That, presumably, is metaphor.

> When *Julia* blushes, she do's show
> Cheeks like to Roses, when they blow.[2]

And that, simile. How great is the difference?

But of course the fact that Ruskin's remedy was ill conceived does not mean that no-one was ill. And by listening both to the patients and their ailing physicians it is easy enough to tell what the sickness is. For what are they all crying out for? Reality, truth, life, vividness, 'there-ness'. These are the watchwords of modern criticism. In ancient and Renascence literary theory (except for the special problem of the poet's lies, which is not what is intended in the modern talk of 'truth') they are almost entirely absent.

I suppose the most innocent and commonplace of all the words in the list is 'vividness'. Yet even this appears to have come late into our critical vocabulary. The earliest references for *vivid* in the *Oxford English Dictionary* show the word being used of persons, animals and chemical substances. The first reference for the word in application to a human utterance is to Beresford's *Miseries of Human Life* (1806) and if we read Beresford's words we can see that the example is at best transitional from the older use in physical description – 'Being mounted on a beast who . . . proceeds very coolly to repose himself in the middle of the pond without . . . paying the slightest attention to your vivid remonstrances on the subject . . .' The first instance given of the word as a literary term of praise is from Lockhart's *Life of Scott* (1837) – which adds another mite to our sense of Scott as a focus of innovation. Scott himself, in *Waverley*, is the first in the Dictionary to speak of a *vivid* power of imagination. From there the clue leads

---

[1] 'The Rosarie', *The Poetical Works of Robert Herrick*, ed. L. C. Martin, 1956, p. 18.

[2] 'Upon her blush', *ibid.*, p. 120.

straight back to the philosophers, who appear to have been the first to disengage the word from its physical application and attach it to mental images and ideas. It will be noticed that to speak of a vivid mental image is not the same as to speak of a vivid imagination. The second is nearer to the literary image. The philosopher who performed the first semantic surgery seems, predictably, to have been Locke.

But *vivid* is merely the lowest term of the series. As anxiety grew men opted for the stronger terms, and, as a measure of their anxiety, began to moralise the concepts. In our own day F. R. Leavis is correctly regarded as a moral critic. Yet how puzzling this would be to an eighteenth-century reader, if *per impossibile* he stumbled through *The Great Tradition!* Again and again the moral superiority of a given writer is collected in 'the quality of felt life' he conveys. What has this to do with morals? 'Life', our eighteenth-century reader might say, 'is a term indifferent', or, as we should say, 'morally neutral.' But it is not so in the work of Leavis. All this is easier to chronicle than to explain; behind Leavis stands Lawrence, and behind Lawrence Nietzsche; and it is here that our 'ethical revolution' finds its most powerful expression.[1]

Of course Nietzsche is often not *ethically* revolutionary at all. To argue that Christianity is founded, not on love but on hate, envy and resentment is a surprising historical thesis if you like, but it is ethically the merest orthodoxy, since it presumes that hate is a bad thing and love a good. It will be found that Christians can read these passages of Nietzsche with complete–indeed with penitential–submissiveness. On the other hand there are elsewhere passages where Nietzsche really is ethically

[1] 'Life' is of course a moralised term in the New Testament. The 'life' alluded to by John (e.g. i.4; vi.53, 63) is not only eternal life beyond the grave but is the present possession of those who live according to Christ. The same may be said of Paul (see *Romans*, vi.4; viii.6, 10). Moreover the morality involved is not just a matter of public conduct. I *Corinthians* xiii and xiv suggest that charity does not consist only in virtuous action, and at xiv.7 we are told that moral teaching must have life if it is to be fruitful. It is arguable that certain modern writers (Dostoevsky and D. H. Lawrence who were both deeply versed in the Bible are obvious candidates) were not so much making something as recovering something when they made *life* a key moral term in their thought. But we should not let this argument run away with our historical sense. Paul's *life* (unlike the post-romantic doctrine) is an ascetic paradox; he writes that man, whose life is in Christ, must mortify the deeds of the body if he is to live (*Romans*, viii.11–13).

revolutionary and these are immediately identifiable by their special power to shock and provoke righteous anger.

Let us imagine two nineteenth-century country gentlemen and call them Cox and Dyson. Cox gets up in the morning, yawns, stretches, throws cold water over his head, walks out of his house. There he meets Gray, his surly cringing groom, and, with a fine overflow of animal spirits, beats the fellow into the mire with his riding crop before riding off towards the rising sun. Now imagine Dyson. He also gets up, yawns and so forth (as Cox, above) until he meets his groom, Collins, whereat he experiences a surging impulse to beat the fellow into the mire. At this, however, he pauses and reflects, 'What has this poor fellow ever done to merit such unmannerly treatment from me?' With which thought he climbs slowly on to his horse and rides off. Between these two conventional morality has no difficulty in choosing. Nietzsche has no difficulty either, but he chooses the opposite. For a hundred places in Nietzsche evince his preference for Cox over Dyson. This is real ethical revolution and it may be supposed that we are more or less shocked by it according to the degree to which we have been won over. And the difference between Cox and Dyson can readily be expressed in the terms isolated. The behaviour of Cox shows a quality of unimpeded 'life'.

It is easy to mistake this side of Nietzsche. Thomas Mann in a brilliant essay[1] argued that Nietzsche was essentially an aesthete, and copied out a series of remarks by Oscar Wilde, all of which could have been Nietzsche's. It is a good party trick but little more. Our resentment at the similarity is more instructive than the similarity itself. The whole difference between the two men is that Nietzsche strove to give an ethical status to terms which Wilde was content to leave in the category of the aesthetic. *Beauty, strength, health, life* are moral terms to Nietzsche; he did not merely think the tiger a finer thing than the lamb; he thought it ethically better.

A. W. H. Adkins in his book on Greek ethics[2] gives us an admirable tool for analysing such moments in the history of

---

[1] 'Nietzsche's Philosophy in the Light of Contemporary Events', in *Thomas Mann's Addresses*, delivered at the Library of Congress, 1942–9, Washington, 1963, pp. 67–103. See especially pp. 84 and 98.

[2] *Merit and Responsibility*, 1960.

K

thought, the concept of 'outbidding'. In the following conversation (typical of the Greek heroic age) *brave* outbids *generous*:

> *Galathe:* Hector is a generous man.
> *Podarge:* But he's not brave.
> *Galathe:* I suppose not; no he's not really a good man.

With the rise of the Greek city state and the need for 'co-operative values', a term which sounds thin to our ears, *temperate*, began to outbid even *brave*. Later again, with the rise of Christianity, *loving* began to outbid all the rest and continues to do so down to our own time.

But it is no longer unopposed. In the pages of Lawrence it is easy to imagine the following exchange of bids:

> 'God, that was fine,' said Ottoline. 'I mean, it was really charitable.'
> 'I don't believe anything you say. It may have had a hundred tons of your charity, but there was no life.'
> 'I suppose there wasn't.'

Nietzsche's attack on Christianity was conducted through what was to become the favourite intellectual strategy of the age: that is, to reduce all opposition to the status of epiphenomenon, a mere natural outgrowth from an unacknowledged source, having no objective justification in the surrounding world. 'You are in favour of co-education because your mother took you into her bed when you were three; your "reasons" are mere rationalisations.' Or 'You support the police because you are bourgeois.' We are all familiar with these preliminary moves. Such methods naturally carry the taint of the genetic fallacy, whereby a thing is deemed *really* to be that which it was first: 'Man is really a polymorphous pervert disguised' (do not be confused by the word 'pervert' here—according to this psycho-analytic theory *pervert* is to be defined as 'one who has never, in fact, been properly perverted'). In Nietzsche both elements occur. In *The Genealogy of Morals*, which remains the clearest of his works, the 'scientific project' of treating ethics as a mere cultural phenomenon is qualified by the unscientific assumption that what came first must constitute the fundamental authority of ethics. Value-terms, Nietzsche observes with some acuteness, seem in Hellenic culture to have originated in the self-description of the strong. The form of his subsequent analysis is preordained; evolution is distortion. Aristotle's demonstration of the importance of ends and purposes is not as much refuted as silently reversed. Already we have some of the elements of Nietzsche's 'revolution', when Odysseus raises a bloody weal on the back of the puny Thersites in the *Iliad*[1]. Nietzsche ranges himself with the tall Greeks who laugh delightedly at the sight. Most of us, as we read, will feel the shock which marks the presence of ethically revolutionary material. And we know before we open our mouths to denounce that our opponent has his answer ready: 'Of course you are shocked; the citizens of Athens were genuinely shocked by Socrates's "slavelike" failure to break out and save his life; you are shocked because you are hearing something fundamentally new; your code does not contain it and so your code condemns it.' Yet this is not so formidable. Nietzsche is hardly likely to show us something radically new as long as he is so preoccupied with the very old. The heroic ethics of the *Iliad* are not, of course, beyond our ken. They survive in many a prefect's room or barracks. If we choose to reject them, we do so not from necessary ignorance but from an historical vantage point.

But there remains another component in Nietzsche's new morality. Homer would readily have granted the ethical primacy of beauty and strength. *Health*, on the other hand, might have surprised him somewhat, for it is here that the morning sky begins to cloud over with the anxieties of a later age; and, as for *life*, life to Homer is no more and no less than life.

Here, then, we cannot claim immemorial familiarity with the proposed morality. But we can see what has brought it about. Perhaps it is not Christian values but Nietzschian which are 'merely epiphenomenal'. It is a situation we have seen before. The accuser is the guilty man. For the Nietzschian concepts of energy, life and passion stem quite plainly from romantic tradition. Blake's 'Sooner murder an infant in its cradle than nurse unacted desires'[2] is pure Nietzsche. It might be said that between the tranquil perceptual exaltation of a Wordsworth and the sanguinary ferocity of a Nietzsche no connexion can

[1] II.212–77.
[2] *The Marriage of Heaven and Hell*, in Keynes's edn., p. 185.

exist. But in fact the connexion is not hard to find. The man who has been once touched by the fear of unreality betrays his sickness by his special craving for intensity. Wordsworth, Shelley, Keats, Blake, Nietzsche all carry the mark. As long as we are looking for comfort in the objective realm, we shall be Wordsworthian pursuers of 'the special experience', the marvellous perception. But if we begin to need reassurance in the subjective realm (and we have seen that the loss of a sense of substantial environment is swiftly followed by a loss of ego) we shall be Nietzschians, eagerly conserving, at the cost of all other values, the sense of being alive. The ambiguous word 'experience', which can denote either a public or a mental phenomenon, facilitates the transition. And in any case our original antithesis was partly factitious. Nietzsche often finds food for his spirit in the more vivid aspects of the world around him and, conversely, Wordsworth is not without a Nietzschian anxiety to be sure of his own aliveness. As for Nietzsche's ferocity, we at once concede that it is idiosyncratic. Nietzsche obviously differs from Wordsworth in his exuberant emphasis on the various ways in which his philosophy jettisons traditional values. But we have seen in Wordsworth charity itself discarded in deference to some personal urgency which the poet himself can hardly explain.

But it is not enough to chronicle the historical stages of a concept to prove it epiphenomenal. After all, Nietzsche himself did that fairly well with conventional ethics. What is rather needed is some sort of demonstration that stage one exhaustively accounts for stage two—*nihil in effectu quod non prius in causa*—and in the nature of things this is pretty hard to achieve. Nevertheless some assessment of probabilities seems practicable.

Certain parts of Nietzsche's own reductive analysis are more convincing than others. His thesis that the Christian glorification of suffering is a product of the slave's need to exalt that which he cannot evade is plausible. But that the Christian subordination of Justice to love is wholly derived from the same cause is more questionable. Clearly, judging might be thought of as something done by the ruling class, and despised for that reason. But Christianity does not despise justice. And, more importantly, why is a positive value attached to love? Nietzsche of course can claim that their love was really all hatred, and that follows well enough from the thesis of the slave-ethic, in somewhat the same way as does their predilection for suffering. But now we see the rock beginning to split. Why do they regard love, at the ideal level, as superior to hate? Whence comes this sense of a need to dissimulate their resentment? Whence the content of those ideals which they adopt as a disguise? In the case of suffering, the epiphenomenal explanation is employed to account for an ostensible value of conventional Christianity. But in the case of love, it will readily account only for the betrayal of that value. In any case, the glorification of suffering is, to the most conventional of us, one of the least obviously ethical elements in Christianity. And in the Nietzschian analysis of love, it is precisely the ethical element which is left unaccounted for at the end.

Nietzsche's stratagem fails, then, because it leaves unexplained many elements which most people feel to be essential. This seems to be less true (note that I do not say, 'not true at all') of my own aetiology of 'felt life'. It is one of a class of concepts which has to do with the need for a special sort of reassurance. It is treated as a moral term because it is felt to be important. This analysis differs from Nietzsche's own analysis of *love* in an important respect. Nietzsche sought to account for the introduction of a wholly new concept. But I am concerned with the gradual moralisation of a term already prominent in non-ethical discourse.

But there remains a sense in which my own 'epiphenomenalist' explanation of 'felt life' remains incomplete. After all, I have said that men came to feel a certain need, intensity of experience answered the need, so why should we not grant that such intensity is a good? If the human biological constitution changed so that people needed to eat copper, copper would become a good as bread is now, and copper-providers would be virtuous. Why then should not 'life' be a good, to be weighed against the other goods? I have a two-fold answer: first, the good offered is a false good. The hunger for reality is not satisfied but only exacerbated by increasing doses of 'experience'. Secondly, the 'life ethic' essentially involves the elimination of ordinary moral checks. It does not co-exist harmoniously with charity and mercy. Because it abhors all psychic impediment it becomes the Fascist in the democracy of goods.

III

It will be observed that I, like Nietzsche, refuse to believe that people mean what they say. Just as in his theory Christians prate of love when they are filled with hatred, so in mine writers revel in the substantial reality of things when substantial reality is the very thing they lack. Moreover I have so constructed my theory that the more intense their satisfaction the more confidently do I assert that their fundamental need has been revealed. But this, surely, is the old Freudian method of which the world has grown justly suspicious. Again, we must pause and make the proper distinctions.

My thesis, unlike Nietzsche's or Freud's, turns on the assumption that we do not normally mention that which is obvious. We do not say, 'I crossed the room by moving my legs in order' for the simple reason that there is no other obvious way of crossing a room. No doubt this assumption can produce consequences which some will find surprising. It implies, for example, that when the Elizabethans all began chattering about 'degree' and courtesy, this is not because they were an orderly and well-mannered people, but because they were neither. What sort of reader do you instruct by telling him that he should not blow his nose on his table-napkin?[1] For many centuries no-one troubled to comment on the degree to which objects were '*there*'. I presume that they did not refer to it because it was not a question with them. But then comes an age in which men can write like this: 'I do not think there is anyone who takes quite such a fierce pleasure in things being themselves as I do. The startling wetness of water excites and intoxicates me: the fieriness of fire, the steeliness of steel, and the unutterable muddiness of mud.'[2] Why do we not classify this as a sort of raving tautology? Because it exists in a context which gives it purpose. And now a further difference between my method and that of a psychoanalysis emerges. The psychoanalyst would want to conclude from the intensity of Chesterton's language that Chesterton himself inwardly doubted the reality of his sur-

---

[1] Robert Peterson's translation (1576) of Giovanni della Casa's *Galateo*, ed. and introduced by J. E. Spingarn, Boston, 1914, pp. 23–4.

[2] G. K. Chesterton quoted in Victor Gollancz, *A Year of Grace*, 1950, p. 85.

roundings.[1] My conclusion is more modest: that Chesterton's language makes sense only in a world in which many have felt such a doubt. My argument is in terms of context and significance, Freud's in terms of behaviour and symbolism and psychic development as established by other research. When Chesterton paraphrases Aquinas, the paraphrase as distinguished from the original by the curious experiential strenuousness which is the mark of the modern age. Like Samuel Johnson, Chesterton cannot let the subject go without resorting to blows:

> When a child looks out of the nursery window and sees anything, say the green lawn of the garden, what does he actually know; or does he know anything? . . . A brilliant Victorian scientist delighted in declaring that the child does not see any grass at all; but only a sort of green mist reflected in a tiny mirror of the human eye . . . Men of another school answer that grass is a mere green impression on the mind; and that the child can be sure of nothing but the mind. They declare that he can only be conscious of his own consciousness; which happens to be the one thing that we know the child is not conscious of at all . . . St Thomas Aquinas, suddenly intervening in this nursery quarrel, says emphatically that the child is aware of *Ens* long before he knows that grass is green, or self is self, he knows that something is something. Perhaps it would be best to say very emphatically (*with a blow on the table*)– 'There *is* an is.'[2]

Thus he refuted them. What would Thomas say if he saw himself, thus stripped of his customary argument, and provided instead with so novel a method of demonstration?

Yet from this geniality it is only a step to the arduous if formless philosophising of E. M. Forster's undergraduates on whether the cow was in the field.[3] And here again we may ask an historian's question; how many readers before 1700 could begin to understand why the phrase 'The cow is in the meadow' could

[1] As indeed he did. See Maisie Ward, *Gilbert Keith Chesterton*, 1944, pp. 43–4.
[2] *St Thomas Aquinas*, 1943, p. 133. I have italicised 'with a blow on the table'.
[3] See his *The Longest Journey*, Ch. 1, 1955, p. 7.

be used to express the attainment of psychic and moral health, as it is in that novel?[1]

Thus the boy Wordsworth grasping at the wall may serve as an emblem of modern literature. Whether for personal reasons or for cultural (and in the end that question is not so important) poets and novelists have been grasping at the stonework, held in the harsh pathos of compensatory action. It is part of the mythology of such compensation to regard touch as somehow more fundamental than sight (shut your sceptical eyes and feel with your hands). A journalist wrote in 1967 of a film director that he had 'found a way to take the lens off his camera and allow life itself to touch raw film'.[2] Even Ernest Hemingway was proving more than his virility in his writing. The final pre-occupation of his most magical stories such as 'Big Two-Hearted River', is with the texture of experience, where the golden immediacy of a summer day assumes, as it first did in Wordsworth, a quality of remote longing. Perhaps the proponents of Women's Liberation mistook their victim here; the sexual greed is only one feature of a more general impoverishment. There is after all a special heroism (closely linked with a special absurdity) in fighting for reality as Hemingway fought. In any case, the conventional argument that Hemingway's virile exploits are not heroic, precisely because they are, in the ordinary sub-Freudian sense, compensatory, has never seemed very strong to me. If a young American Indian undergoes ritual torture to prove his manhood, I am content to say that he has proved it. I, who feel no such need to prove myself, am conscious that if I were so tested I should probably fail. Who is the strong man here, the tribesman who feels he must risk life and limb or the sedentary don who, such is his security, feels no such obligation? If Hemingway fought and killed wild beasts to prove his manhood, let us allow that he proved it, only remembering that in saying this we do not concede that the killing of animals is in itself good. It is, after all, a curious requirement that a man should be deemed to have proved something only if he was not trying to do any such thing. No one but the Baconian extends queerly negative restrictions to, say, the physicist. With

[1] See his *The Longest Journey*, 1955, p. 306.
[2] Report on Satyajit Ray in *Time Magazine* (Time-Life International, Amsterdam), August 25th, 1967, p. 25.

the special heroism of *machismo* we can indeed argue thus: though *machismo* may not be worth proving, it has perhaps in certain places been proved. With the larger heroism of proving that the world is there, we find an extra dimension of pathos, which consists in the futility of the methods used. All our writers take arms against a sea of troubles, and their bravery is merely engulfed. The only way to win this war is to begin by assuming your enemy's defeat; to work always in terms of the public situation, to corroborate your confidence in reality by a life-like process of action: trial and error, prediction and consequence. To savour the quality of experience is to explore the mind, since 'experience' is not the name of any public thing. Your enemy will only use your own strength to throw you.

Yet I have to confess that I have written this story, not only from an admiring sympathy but also from a certain impatience. One can have too much of these Underground Men, who are willing to break the hearts of others to prove themselves alive.

But if much of our literature is compensatory in this way, the poetry of T. S. Eliot is not. We must grant that much of his early verse is conventionally burdened, only perhaps, he is more honest than most. The moon in 'Rhapsody on a Windy Night'

> has lost her memory.
> A washed out smallpox cracks her face.[1]

Although the moon is very close to Eliot's own mind, it cannot, for that very reason perhaps, comfort him. The mental usurpation of nature does not end one's isolation. Walter Shandy never felt his separateness from Mrs Shandy so keenly as when he noticed her unremitting agreement with everything he said. But Eliot came last in our brief series not just because of chronology but because in his later poetry a new stratagem was developed. He ceased to press forward and instead leaned back. Instead of saying, 'Feel the roughness of this bark, the wetness of this leaf—how vivid is the world!' he said, 'Come into the secret garden of my mind, listen to the soundless music of my most fugitive thoughts' and, as we read, the marvellous truth begins to dawn, which is that it is all possible reality because it is all intelligible. Without quite knowing how, we sense that the theatre of war has changed, and that we are now fighting over

[1] *Collected Poems*, p. 27.

fresh ground. Indeed Eliot's strategy is more ambitious than
that which we commended just now. Not content with confirm-
ing the public world, his poetry is eager to colonise the private,
to show that in an important sense it is not private at all.

It is a message of profound comfort. The writers who sought
to confirm reality with the rawness of experience but found
themselves confronted with a mental object should not have
faltered since this too is real. And if even this is real, why should
not everything else be? One way of putting the point is to say
that 'subjective', no less than other words, has a meaning and a
range of reference. This has ironic consequences for Bishop
Berkeley's famous experiment with water: Suppose now one
of your hands hot, and the other cold, and that they are
both at once put into the same vessel of water, in an intermediate state; will not the water seem cold to one hand, and
warm to the other?'[1] Philonous is trying to convince Hylas that
our notions of warmth and cold have no objective basis. Yet he
could never have set up such an experiment without an objective measure of temperature. He presupposes the very thing he
seeks to deny. Sterne, with more wit (in both senses of the word)
knew that the waywardness of Tristram's time-sense could not
be forcibly demonstrated without the careful preparation on his
part of a rigid time-scheme. The chronological insanity of
Tristram presupposes the sanity of the rest of us and, in particular, the sanity of Sterne, with whom Tristram is too often
identified. In all this we are availing ourselves of an assumption
which has so far scarcely appeared in this book: the assumption
that if a thing can be intelligibly conveyed in language then it is
part of a system which must at some point involve public
reference. The source of this doctrine is of course Wittgenstein.

IV

Wittgenstein conceived his private language argument in
express reaction against the sense-datum epistemology of
Russell. According to Russell the universe of discourse is
founded on sense-data, each of which is radically private to the
subject. The effect of Wittgenstein's answer is to invert the
edifice, so that part at least of the superstructure forms the
new foundation. A language originating from the naming of

[1] *Three Dialogues*, I, in Luce and Jessop, II, pp. 178–9.

sense-data is a language which no-one could begin to learn. We could not know what was being named, and even if we were told, separately, that there were rules for naming, we could not tell whether or not they had been applied correctly. If a language is to be teachable, there must be a system of checks. If this argument is effective against sense-datum epistemology it is *a fortiori* still more effective against solipsism, which refuses to pass beyond the first stage of sense-datum epistemology. Solipsism is not so much refuted as dispelled, since it cannot even be stated coherently. The general structure of this argument is tolerably clear; its implications less so.

For example, does it imply behaviourism (for the purpose of this discussion I define behaviourism in the terms of its heroic origins as the thesis that our language about mental properties and states can be resolved without remainder into statements about public behaviour: 'The man's writhing on the floor is not a *sign* of his pain; it *is* his pain')? Unfortunately Wittgenstein himself is not much help to us here. The debate as to whether the philosopher himself espoused the doctrines of behaviourism[1] is still in progress.

One difference between Wittgenstein and at any rate the most primitive sort of behaviourist seems to be obvious. The primitive behaviourist simply denies many things which we know to be true, viz. that there are such things as sensations, mental imagery, thoughts, presentiments and the like; but Wittgenstein, on the contrary, is very happy to grant that such things go on, but insists on their fundamental un-mysteriousness and, presumably, on their publicity. At the same time he professes himself eager 'to get rid of the idea of the private object'.[2] How

---

[1] See especially P. F. Strawson's review of the *Philosophical Investigations* in *Mind*, LXIII (1954), pp. 70–99, esp. p. 94 (the review is reprinted in *Wittgenstein, the Philosophical Investigations*, ed. G. Pitcher, New York, 1960, pp. 22–64); P. L. Heath, 'Wittgenstein Investigated', *Philosophical Quarterly*, VI (1956), p. 70; G. Pitcher, *The Philosophy of Wittgenstein*, Englewood Cliffs, New Jersey, 1964; Alan Donagan, 'Wittgenstein on Sensation', *Wittgenstein, the Philosophical Investigations*, pp. 324–51; L. C. Holborrow, 'Wittgenstein's kind of Behaviourism?' *Philosophical Quarterly*, XVII (1967), pp. 345–57; C. W. K. Mundle, *Critique of Linguistic Philosophy*, 1970, esp. pp. 204 f.; Norman Malcolm, 'Wittgenstein on the Nature of the Mind', *Studies in the Theory of Knowledge, American Philosophical Quarterly* Monograph Series, ed. N. Rescher, No. 4, Oxford, 1970.

[2] *Philosophical Investigations*, II, trans. G. E. M. Anscombe, the 1963 reprint of the English text from the 2nd edn. of 1958, p. 207.

is one to get rid of the private object without relapsing into behaviourism?

Two possibilities have presented themselves. The first[1] I do not care for but will try to set out as fairly as I can. Wittgenstein's argument that a language, if it is to be learnable, must deal with what is public does not logically preclude (a) the possibility that utterly private areas may exist and (b) the possibility of referring to them (as opposed to describing them). Alan Donagan writes:

> The existence of the 'Object', of that which accompanies natural pain-behaviour, is not only not irrelevant to the meaning of pain words, it is cardinal. What is irrelevant is not the existence of the object, but what it happens to be. You and I could not have a common word for pain unless our natural pain-behaviour were accompanied by something frightful; but whether that accompaniment is the same for both of us or not, or even whether it changes or not (provided we do not notice it) is irrelevant . . . a sensation is defined by reference to its external circumstances. Yet it is not reducible to those external circumstances; for it is defined as their private and non-dispositional accompaniment. It follows that you and I correctly say that we have the same sensation, say toothache, if we both have something frightful that we would naturally express by holding and rubbing our jaws, by certain kinds of grimace, and the like. Whether the internal character of what is expressed in these ways is the same for you as for me is irrelevant to the meaning of the word 'toothache'.[2]

Wittgenstein himself in a famous passage used the analogy of a beetle in a box:

> Suppose everyone had a box with something in it: we call it a 'beetle'. No-one can look into anyone else's box, and everyone says he knows what a beetle is only by looking at *his* beetle. Here it would be quite possible for everyone to have something different in his box. One might even imagine

---

[1] Versions of this argument can be found in Don Locke's *Myself and Others*, 1968, esp. pp. 104–8, in David Pear's *Wittgenstein*, 1971, p. 152, and Alan Donagan, *op. cit.*

[2] *Op cit.*, pp. 347–8.

such a thing constantly changing. But suppose the word 'beetle' had a use in those people's language? If so it would not be used as the name of a thing. The thing in the box has no place in the language game at all; not even as a *something*: for the box might even be empty. No, one can 'divide through' by the thing in the box; it cancels out, whatever it is.

That is to say: if we construe the grammar of the expression of sensation on the model of 'object and designation' the object drops out of consideration as irrelevant.[1]

Now it is claimed that although I cannot describe the contents of my box I can at least refer to them. They are simply 'whatever I have in my box'.[2] As John Lennon sang,

> 'What do you see when you turn out the light?'
> 'I can't tell you but I know it's mine.'[3]

Evidently this private reservation can play no dominant part in the web of language—it is simply one negligible and useless terminus of reference—but it may *exist*. Thus the private area is saved and our credulity is not strained in the way it is strained by behaviourism.

But have we really gained much? The private area thus saved is not the private area which behaviourism once threatened. The 'heroic age' behaviourists were for 'analysing out' all our talk of inner presentiments, poignant memories, feelings of regret tinged with satisfaction, *etc.* . . . But such stuff is no mere terminal object of reference, no indescribable 'whatever I have in my box'—as is proved by the very verbal facility with which I just began to write about it. Obviously our language for describing inner states, even those which seem destitute of external behavioural manifestation, is healthily vigorous and intelligible.

It would seem better to adopt the second alternative; it differs from the first in that we now refuse to concede that the 'inner' feeling is indescribable. The argument: 'Only that which is public can play a part in language' can be turned round: 'If it plays a part in language, it must be public'. The whole rich

---

1 *Philosophical Investigations*, I.§ 293.
2 C.f. *Myself and Others*, p. 106.
3 'With a Little Help', *Sergeant Pepper*.

texture of our inner lives is, then, in the sense required, public, for it is capable of being conveyed in generally intelligible terms. But although this is manifestly true, it is not easy to see how it is that it is true. *How* do we talk about our inner lives?

What seems clear is that we do not always do it in terms of the associated public situation. Sometimes we do, but in other cases we do not. For example, the simple remark 'I felt surprised' is fairly easy to analyse in terms of observable data: a continuous action suddenly interrupted, a sudden change of behaviour *etc*; but suppose someone says 'my feeling of surprise, though complete, was not untinged with satisfaction'. We may be a little less confident of our external checks. A faint smile might have illuminated the features or it might not. The behavioural situation seems intractably featureless; yet the language is robust and intelligible.

Let us take (for they are simpler) sensations of heat and cold. When a man (say, a sick man) reports a queer 'subjective' sensation—says he feels very cold when placed near a roaring fire—it seems obvious that language works here through a web of normal (but not necessary) conjunctions; that is, 'cold' can be defined as 'the sensation that goes with ice' and 'warmth' as 'the sensation that goes with fire'. So our sick man is in effect saying, 'Although I'm sitting by a fire, I haven't in fact got the fire sensation; I've got the ice sensation.' This is public language (we do not enquire whether *his* ice sensation is different from other people's). But to say that it is public language is quite compatible with saying that the sick man feels what the others do not feel, and do not know about till he tells them. There is no need for any strenuous pleading to the effect that his sensation is accessible to others since when they watch him shiver and blow his fingers they observe his sensations in exactly the same way as he does.

Thus, our sensations of warmth and cold are capable of being reported to others, and are understood by ourselves, in virtue of the fact that there is general, constant but not unbroken correspondence between the sensation and certain public situations. It is obvious that in talking about feelings, we do not confine ourselves to a review of their public correlations, but describe them, so to speak, phenomenally. In the *Philosophical Investigations* Wittgenstein frequently philosophises by conversing with an imaginary interlocutor. At one point this anonymous person says, 'Yes but there is *something* there all the same accompanying my cry of pain. And it is on account of that that I utter it. And this something is what is important—and frightful.'[1] We note that the 'something else' is describable—'frightful'—and, incidentally, that the descriptive adjective was admitted by Donagan despite his theory.[2] As Mrs Andrea McKeown asked C. W. K. Mundle,[3] what do words like 'throbbing', 'dull' and 'stabbing' describe if it is not this frightful something, which any person uninstructed in philosophy would innocently suppose was the sensation itself?

Obviously an expression like 'stabbing' is drawn from the public world in the sense that it was originally applied to such things as knives. But, equally obviously, it is not being applied to a public object here. Nor is it applied on the basis of a normal behavioural manifestation which just happens to be absent in this case. We are left with something like a bare phenomenal similarity. And as for 'throbbing' I am not even sure that that term is drawn from the public world at all (I speak, it will be understood, of present-day linguistic usage, not etymological history). In any case, the public origins of such terms appear to be of small consequence. Words must be got from somewhere. Logic itself had to get its terms from the world of ordinary physical action (think of 'follow' in 'it follows that'). I suppose we may learn the meaning of *throbbing* in either of two ways. We may feel a pulse in a wrist (here it doesn't matter whose wrist) and transpose the term from that to the inner sensation by way of known physical connexions and/or felt similarity. Otherwise, we may learn it as the name of the feeling which goes with running too hard suddenly and stopping, with tying a tight hand round one's arm, and so on—which is to make *throbbing* like *warm*. And this is proper since *warm* is not a term which is felt, in present usage, to be borrowed from the outer sphere (to say 'That metal is hot' is not to provide an outer source for the term since 'hot' there is formally correlative to the sensation: we could substitute 'feels hot' or 'would feel hot' without changing the meaning). Always we find correspondence of outer and inner; comparatively seldom will the correspondence

[1] I.§ 296. [2] 'Wittgenstein on Sensation', p. 347; see above, p. 280.
[3] See Mundle, *Critique of Linguistic Philosophy*, p. 213.

reduce itself to an underlying identity. But our language certainly derives its rich efficacy from the correspondence, and, as we saw, does not attempt the impossible task of differentiating one man's 'warmth' from another's (or one man's 'regret tinged with satisfaction' from another's).

However, the correspondence as we have conceived it, *is* between public objects and private feelings. Wittgenstein, in his paragraph on the beetle in the box, said it would make no difference even if whatever was in the box changed. Donagan accepted this but nervously added the proviso: so long as the change is not noticed. The qualification is in fact crucial. According to our present thesis, if we all always felt *quite* new sensations whenever we sat near fires our sick man could not have made the intelligible report he made, for he would have lacked a norm from which to dissociate himself. Even though we only talk about our feelings *as* they correlate, they are themselves private and the *correlation* is also private. Thus once more we stray onto the ground forbidden us by Wittgenstein. He argued that the notion of a private correlation is empty since it could not be checked by public criteria.

But why should not our memory of past occurrences of the feeling, emotion, sensation or whatever, be a sufficient check? Once memory has established itself as reliable with reference to public criteria, it is irrational to stop our ears to what it can tell us in the private sphere. In a famous passage,[1] Wittgenstein considers the case of a diarist who invents a name, 'S' for a certain sensation, and writes it in his diary whenever the sensation occurs. Wittgenstein affirms that such a person could have no criterion of correctness for the second time he wrote it down. 'Criterion of correctness' is rather grand. Suppose we say 'way of telling whether he is using it accurately', then the answer is plain. How can he tell? Why, he remembers. Pretty clearly, Wittgenstein is here writing in the chains of logical positivism; the Verification Principle,[2] according to which all meaningful statements which are not analytic must be verifiable by the senses, has him in its grip. In the first place, the criterion of meaning is not sense-verifiability but intelligibility, and in the

[1] *Philosophical Investigations*, 1.§ 258.
[2] See Judith Jarvis Thompson, 'Private Languages', *American Philosophical Quarterly*, I (1964) esp. p. 30.

second place verification by the senses will in any case presuppose the validity of memory as a criterion of identity. How
else can you be sure that you are verifying the same utterance?
Norman Malcolm, the holy fool of Verificationism, argued in
his book *Dreaming* (1959) that we cannot really be said to
remember dreams since no external checks are provided. As
Pears observed in his review, '. . . Is Malcolm's account of
remembering too thin and Humian?'[1]

However, although memory may give me some check on my
own inner life, it can scarcely give me a foothold in the mental
life of others. The effect of our reasoning so far has been a tacit
strengthening of traditional scepticism about other minds. The
less we live our mental lives in our behaviour, the more inaccessible we become to others. But not, perhaps, fatally inaccessible.
The right-hand column, so to speak, in our two lists of correspondences remains public. This enables us to report intelligibly
what the others cannot tell unaided. It is objected that we could
never have learned to attribute feelings to others except by a
hopelessly tenuous analogy: I observe feelings in myself corre-
lated with certain public situations and on the basis of this single
example I attribute feelings to the rest of mankind. But it is
very doubtful whether we need to postulate any such analogical
thinking on the part of the learner. C. H. Whiteley writes:

> Let us suppose that A and B are experienced users of a
> language and C is a learner who is in their company and
> hears them speak; and let us suppose that A and B from
> time to time use, say, the word 'drowsy' both with reference
> to one another and with reference to C. Their criteria for
> using it of one another and of C will of course be purely
> behavioural. Now C, in the course of learning the language,
> will observe that A says of B 'B is drowsy' whenever B
> behaves in certain characteristic ways. C will also observe
> that A says of him 'You are drowsy' whenever he, C, has
> certain characteristic feelings. The connection between
> drowsy feelings and drowsy behaviour is established in C's
> mind by the fact that A uses the same word in connection
> with them both. I do not see how else it could be estab-
> lished.[2]

[1] 'Professor Norman Malcolm: Dreaming', *Mind*, n.s., DCC (1961), p. 147.
[2] 'Behaviourism', *Mind*, DCC (1961), p. 167.

When did C analogise? Mundle observes of this passage that it is all right as far as it goes, but it does not go far enough. The child must also learn about occasions when inner and outer do *not* fit. But this is simple enough. Now that language has got under way, he can learn from examples of inhibition or control; the man says, 'I am in pain'; but gives no other sign, or 'He looks angry but he's just pretending' and by being told not to cry.[1]

But, to be sure, all this explains the learning process only. The question: what check has C, when he loses his childish innocence, remains. Consider mental imagery. How does mental imagery tie in with the public world and hence become capable of description? You cannot have my shadow but you can see it. You cannot have my mental imagery but you cannot have any inkling of it either unless I choose to tell you about it. But, note, we talk about our imagery freely, and with rich detail. We certainly cannot explain this as we explained *warm* earlier. Try it: 'The image of a tree is what I normally get when near a tree but here I happen to have the image that goes with fire-extinguishers.' Obviously, it is not like that at all. But try 'Having an image of a tree is something *like* seeing a tree.' This is better. A more fashionable account would run something like this: 'An image of a tree is not *like* a tree; it is a tree. Of course *qua* image it is not, but *qua* content that is what it is; having an image of a tree is simply a special way of relating to a tree.' But this is only the shop-soiled art of losing the private object. Why should we not just say the image (*qua* content, if you insist) is like a tree? Again, ordinary language has conferred its august authority on such a usage ('He's not a bit like my mental image of him!'). We can name the things we imagine because we can recognise them, and no doubt we can recognise them, because we put them there. Normally, when we report our imaginings we simply report the *things* we imagined, but we add the warning note: 'I didn't *see* this; I imagined it.' Once our language for mental imagery has got under way we can of course begin, like Galton's subjects, to specify purely phenomenal characteristics – 'My image of Mr Heath is green and slightly fuzzy round the edges.' The conditions for all this are comparatively simple. All

[1] *Critique of Linguistic Philosophy*, p. 232.

that is needed is a world in which when people *perceive* they all perceive the same thing (supposing that they are all in the same place at the same time) but when people *imagine*, they, at a given time, imagine different things. Thus the phrase 'I imagined' is a signal to our interlocutor not to bother to look for the thing himself.

Once again the language seems to be intelligible basically in terms of public material. To know what is meant by 'I have a mental image of a horse' one needs in practice only to know what a horse is and the purpose of the warning designation, 'I have a mental image of'. The fact that I cannot have your imagery proves not to be troublesome. But the duplicity of inner and outer seems as strong as ever. That *you* have images at all is something *I* can never check.

But the objection is beginning to wear thin. Does anything here contradict our sense of the way the world really is? And, conversely, do not both Cartesianism and behaviourism contradict it fundamentally? Who but a philosopher would ever *want* to check? The meaningfulness of such statements is no longer suspect. The *truth* of particular statements about imagery *is* suspect, but then we all know that it is suspect. But most of us, most of the time, are willing to trust; and this too is reasonable. One person may say he has no mental imagery; another says he has a great deal. One can check the veracity of neither party; yet either statement is intelligible. And, conversely, public behaviour *can* deceive. The man writhing on the floor may be a consummate actor.

Let us treat the whole subject for a moment as a piece of science fiction. Suppose there was a planet inhabited by beings having high-coherency perceptions (e.g. when two are in the same place at the same time they see the same thing) and low-coherency imaginings (i.e. they imagine to a considerable extent the same things as each other–often, in fact, the very things they perceive–but not at the same time as each other). How would such beings talk? They would talk as we talk.

Who but a verificationist would worry in such a situation? The learning process presents no problems. It might be said, 'How do you know what John means when he says, 'I have an image of a star''?' The answer is (we can now give it with greater completeness), 'I know what stars are, I understand the practical function of "have an image of" as a signal, and have images myself.' There are people in Francis Galton's *Inquiries into Human Faculty* who are able to give only the first two parts of this threefold answer;[1] the difference between them and other people is not occult but on the contrary forms the subject of an interesting psychological investigation. In the big city it is the rustic who disbelieves everything he hears. But that does not mean that the Londoners have checked all the information. That is not the way the world works.

Wittgenstein's intermittent efforts to get rid of, conjure away, analyse out the private area are, then, unnecessary. They have a cause (reaction against Russell) but they lack a justification. But does this mean that we can no longer claim that the private language argument is effective against solipsism? In fact, its effectiveness is unimpaired. We have at no point disputed Wittgenstein's contention that a language founded *exclusively* on private data could never really be a language. Our language dealing with material things simply presupposes publicity and our language dealing with feelings, sensations and the like could never have got under way, we grant, without public correlatives. The assertion of anything whatsoever therefore presupposes publicity of some sort, and so the assertion that there is nothing public is nonsense. Wittgenstein's own definition of a private language at I § 243 is thus seriously misleading:

> . . . could we also imagine a language in which a person could write down or give vocal expression to his inner experiences—his feelings, moods and the rest—for his private use?—Well, can't we do so in ordinary language?— But that is not what I mean. The individual words of this language are to refer to what can only be known to the person speaking; to his immediate private sensations. So another person cannot understand the language.

As Mundle has pointed out[2] Wittgenstein seems to take it for granted that if a word is private in its reference it must also be private in the sense of being incommunicable, which is to confound the meaning of a word with that which it refers to

---

[1] The 1953 reprint of the edn. of 1883, p. 58.
[2] *Critique of Linguistic Philosophy*, p. 221 and note.

(*Sinn* with *Bedeutung*). After all, is there not something strange about the way Wittgenstein can so easily specify the practice which cannot, according to his thesis, exist? In spite of that irritated, and irritating 'that is not what I mean', it seems that in the course of his argument he has named that which the argument says cannot be named. It is indeed difficult to see how the argument could otherwise have been stated at all. Thus the implicit incoherence of the solipsist's position is strangely mirrored.

The private language thesis is in good health as long as 'private' means 'incommunicable'. But as soon as it is made to refer to actual contents, which can be unpacked in a list (memories, images, presentiments, *etc.*) we see that it must be wrong. The moral of this is perhaps that we should drop the term 'private' from our argument. Certainly we can get along without it. Take, for example, the following dialogue:

> *A.* All opinions are purely subjective, even the opinion that there is a real world.
>
> *B.* That is your opinion?
>
> *A.* Yes.
>
> *B.* What if there were two men, one of whom held that all opinion was subjective while the other held that *not* all opinion was subjective. Is neither opinion more objectively true than the other?
>
> *A.* Yes, the first.
>
> *B.* Then not *all* opinions are equally subjective?
>
> *A.* I'm sorry, you confused me. Obviously, neither opinion is more objectively true than the other.
>
> *B.* Why do you say that?
>
> *A.* I told you, I believe *all* opinion to be subjective.
>
> *B.* But *that's* no reason—you've just agreed that *that* opinion is no truer than its contrary.
>
> *A.* Hum, yes. I see that I must retract.

A is not of course a fully fledged solipsist. But the solipsist can be described as a person who believes that there is nothing but (his) opinion, and the usefulness of the above dialogue lies in the fact that it shows how 'opinion' in a vacuum is an empty notion. Opinion involves assertion which may be as tentative as you please, but nevertheless assertion. If there were nothing but opinion then all opinion would be pseudo-opinion, a kind of dream which mistook itself for insight of some sort. But in that case the opinion that such pseudo-opinion is all there is must itself be unfounded, a self-deluding and so a self-destroying mechanism. One cannot begin to believe in this cormorant thesis which consumes itself before it can be grasped.

The solipsist might reply, 'It is you who talk about assertion. I naturally *assert* nothing—why should I since I am a solipsist?' to which we answer, 'Either you have just asserted that you are a solipsist (which involves a further, philosophical assertion) in which case you have been refuted, or else you assert nothing, in which case I have no quarrel with you.' And at last there is silence; the corpse lies still.

In the course of this book we have been gradually drawn into using 'empiricist' as a mild term of abuse. But no disparagement of the common man who believes what he sees was intended. Our quarry has rather been that metaphysical empiricism which erects an artificial barrier between the mind and the world. In the writings of such philosophers 'experience' is a curiously elusive concept. It does not, for example, mean, 'the things we experience'. It seems rather to denote a many-coloured gauze curtain suspended between each person and his environment, peculiar to that person and directly known only by him. The stuff of this curtain is mental. It is a tissue of spiritual representatives, and we are told that it is only by making inferences from this complex private datum that we arrive at our knowledge of the real world. We have traced this philosophical view from the 'scientific psychology' of the seventeenth century. We noted at one stage that it is a truth unfortunate for rash theorists that there really is an image on the retina. This situation is duplicated at the psychic level since there really *is* a many-coloured private 'gauze curtain' for us to look at, and it is called imagery. Moreover, there really are sensations. But our language for all of these is logically posterior to our language about the public world. The model of gradually radiating inference from the private area was wrong. A sensation is not a premise; it is a condition of perception.

Both the fears with which this book has dealt, the fear that there is nothing outside ourselves and the fear that there is nothing within, are therefore groundless. You see what I see but you imagine what you alone imagine. Thus our lives are lived in a medium at once sharp and soft—we encounter the hard recalcitrancies of the public world but we bear with us the tenderer cocoon of more personal and arbitrary associations. None of this is radically incommunicable; we can open our hearts when we wish. We do not inhabit glass houses where everyone can look in nor are we shut up, like the boy in the frontispiece, in windowless cells. The degree of our privacy is of our own choosing. We live beneath a common sky.

Index